Check Your Financial Privilege

Check Your Financial Privilege

Inside the Global Bitcoin Revolution

Alex Gladstein

BTC Media, LLC
Nashville, TN.

This content was originally published as a series of articles in *Bitcoin Magazine*.

Proceeds from the sale of this book support the Human Rights Foundation.

ISBN 979-8-9857289-2-7 – (paperback)
ISBN 979-8-9857289-3-4 – (ebook)

Published by BTC Media, LLC
438 Houston St. #257 Nashville, TN 37203
Address all inquiries to contact@btcmedia.org

Printed by Amazon
Cover photo © jacoblund
Formatting by RMK Publications, LLC

The views and conclusions expressed in this manuscript are entirely the author's own and do not necessarily reflect those of BTC Media, LLC or its employees, agents, partners and associates.

Acknowledgments

There are many people who helped make this book possible.

Thor Halvorssen, Garry Kasparov, Céline Assaf, Javier El Hage, and my colleagues at the Human Rights Foundation (HRF), who created an amazing intellectual environment for me to learn about the wider world since joining the team in 2007.

The dissidents and activists whom I met through my work at the HRF who taught me about the value of freedom including Manal al-Sharif, Evan Mawarire, Yeonmi Park, Iyad El-Baghdadi, Srdja Popovic, Marina Nemat, Yang Jianli, Jhanisse Vaca Daza, and Vladimir Kara-Murza.

The personalities and educators in the Bitcoin space who captured my attention in 2017, including Andreas Antonopolous, Matt Odell, Elizabeth Stark, and Jameson Lopp, who helped me understand that Bitcoin is a tool for human rights.

Friends who provided feedback on the essays as they came together throughout 2021, including Nic Carter, Jimmy Song, Allen Farrington, Lyn Alden, Aaron van Wirdum, and Hodl Onward.

The people who lent me their time to be interviewed for these essays, including Ire Aderinokun, Roya Mahboob, Adam Back, Farida Nabourema, Fodé Diop, Isaiah Jackson, Fadi Elsalameen, Erich García Cruz, Alaa Tartir, Mike Peterson, Faisal Saeed al Mutar, Jorge Valenzuela, Boaz Sobrado, Kal Kassa, Ricardo Herrero, Kefah Abukhdeir, Sudan Hodl, Ramon Martinez, and many others.

The team at *Bitcoin Magazine*, including Christian Keroles — who gave me the remarkable opportunity to write a regular column for *Bitcoin Magazine* — as well as Peter Chawaga, who acted as a brilliant editor throughout, and Ellen Sullivan, who led the process of turning my essays into a book.

Finally, and most importantly, my wife Alexandra, who put up with me while I was burning the midnight oil, writing these essays in the early hours or at the crack of dawn, in various places around the world, while juggling our family commitments. Without her, there is no book. So, thank you.

Contents

Preface

Nearly everyone has heard about Bitcoin, but only a tiny few are aware of the deep impact the digital currency is having around the world.

From Sudan to Palestine, from Belarus to Nigeria, and from the Congo to Cuba, tens of millions of people are currently using Bitcoin to escape from broken financial systems and lay the foundation for a brighter future for their families and communities.

But as we enter 2022, it is still apparent that the mainstream media and political discourse does not understand or even acknowledge this phenomenon. Why?

Because they are blinded by their monetary and financial privilege.

Some people are advantaged over others because of the kind of monetary and financial system they are born into.

In social justice parlance, "checking one's privilege" means to accept that not everyone is born equal, and that one must look beyond their own bubble to empathize with the wider world around them.

This book explores what happens when we check our financial privilege: we start to see what lies beneath and beyond, we realize how well we have it compared to others, and we start to understand how the whole system truly works.

So who has financial privilege?

Americans, for starters. As discussed in Chapter III, we make up just 4% of the world population, but have financial privilege over everyone else on earth as we enjoy the benefits of the dollar: the world's most dominant currency, which rules as a central bank reserve, means of trade, and unit of global account.

Beyond the United States of America, anyone who is born into a reserve currency like the euro, yen, or pound also has financial privilege over the 89% of the world population born into weaker systems.

It's all relative. Americans might have financial privilege over South Africans, but South Africans have enormous financial privilege over Zimbabweans. The French (Chapter VI) continue to enjoy financial privilege over their former colonies in Africa. Israelis (Chapter VII) enjoy financial privilege over Palestinians. The Cuban dictatorship (Chapter VIII) enjoys financial privilege over Cuban citizens. Going back decades, the ruling elite in

America (Chapter XI) have enjoyed financial privilege over African Americans and Native Americans.

You, dear reader, likely enjoy financial privilege over your fellow global citizens living in places like Afghanistan (Chapter IX), Sudan (Chapter I), and Iran, which are sanctioned by the powers that be and cut off from the world banking system because of crimes their rulers committed.

Financial privilege is embedded in our world, and has steered the course of history. It has shifted power from the have-nots to the haves. It is getting worse.

But guess what? Bitcoin is going to obliterate financial privilege.

This new currency creates a level playing field where everyone is considered equal in the eyes of the protocol, no matter whether you live in Gaza or Tel Aviv, Havana or Miami, Dakar or Paris, Washington or Caracas. The Bitcoin protocol does not care about your level of wealth, color of your skin, beliefs, family history, religion, or nationality. It is neutral and cannot discriminate.

This book is a collection of essays written throughout 2020 and 2021 as I explored the global impact of Bitcoin, and tried to report on what financial privilege too often obscures. *Bitcoin Magazine* gave me the space to write these essays that aim to contextualize Bitcoin adoption alongside economic and political history.

These pages cover the personal stories of Bitcoin users in Nigeria, Sudan, and Ethiopia; Bitcoin's pre-history and the cypherpunk movement; Bitcoin in comparison to the negative externalities of the dollar system; Bitcoin's Trojan Horse mechanism of adoption; Bitcoin's rising use in El Salvador, Togo, Senegal, Cuba, Palestine, and Afghanistan; Bitcoin as an antidote to monetary colonialism; Bitcoin's humanitarian and environmental impact; Bitcoin as an American ideal; and, finally, Bitcoin as a potential new world reserve currency.

In the process of writing this book, I have learned an enormous amount about the power of money, and how, sadly, it is used as a tool of control and repression around the world. I have also learned that Bitcoin provides hope for a freer future.

Chapter I

Check Your Financial Privilege

In the eyes of most Western elites, investors, journalists, and academics, Bitcoin rates anywhere from an annoyance to a disaster.

In May 2021, American billionaire Charlie Munger described Bitcoin as "disgusting and contrary to the interests of civilization."[1] Warren Buffett, once the world's richest person, sat next to Munger in obvious agreement. He has said Bitcoin is "a delusion" and "rat poison squared," and he has warned that he is sorry about its rise "because people get their hopes up that something like that is gonna change their lives."[2] Bill Gates, who also used to be the world's richest person, has said Bitcoin is a "greater fool theory" investment and that he would short it, if he could.[3]

HBO host Bill Maher skewered Bitcoin in an extended segment on his show, saying that the new currency's promoters are "money-hungry opportunists."[4] A few weeks earlier, *The New York Times* ran a story that said Bitcoin will "ruin the planet."[5] *Financial Times* columnist Martin Wolf has long pegged it as "ideal for criminals, terrorists, and money launderers."[6]

Prominent Ivy League economist Jeffrey Sachs has said that Bitcoin offers "nothing of social value," while former International Monetary Fund (IMF) chief and European Central Bank President Christine Lagarde has called it a tool for "totally reprehensible money laundering activity."[7]

Over the past decade, these financial experts, reporters, and policymakers have continuously pounded the narrative and told the world that Bitcoin is risky, dangerous, bad for humans, and bad for the planet.

They are wrong, and they are blinded mainly by their financial privilege.

How Financial Privilege Blinds Dollar Users to Bitcoin's Importance

The critics cited above are all wealthy citizens of advanced economies, where they benefit from liberal democracy, property rights, free speech, a functioning legal system, and relatively stable reserve currencies like the dollar or pound.

But only 13% of our planet's population is born into the dollar, euro, Japanese yen, British pound, Australian dollar, Canadian dollar, or Swiss Franc.

The other 87% are born into autocracy or considerably less trustworthy currencies. As of December 2021, 4.3 billion people live under authoritarianism and 1.6 billion people live under double- or triple-digit inflation.

Critics in the dollar bubble miss the bigger global picture: Anyone with access to the internet can now participate in Bitcoin, a new money system with equal rules for all participants, running on a network that does not censor or discriminate, used by individuals who do not need to show a passport or an ID, and held by citizens in a way that is hard to confiscate and impossible to debase.

While Western headlines focus on Coinbase going public, Tesla buying billions of dollars' worth of Bitcoin and tech bros getting fabulously rich, there is a quiet revolution happening worldwide. Until now, governments and corporations have controlled the rules of money. That is changing.

To learn more, I spoke to Bitcoin users in Nigeria, Sudan, and Ethiopia, three countries with a combined population of 366 million, well in excess of the number of individuals living in the United States.

The three speak for millions whose lived experience is much closer to that of the average person on this planet. Gates, Munger, and Buffett may not have recently dealt with conflict and violence, black markets, relentless inflation, political repression, and rampant corruption in their daily routine, but most do.

And yet, these Bitcoiners are more hopeful for the future than the doomers listed in the chapter's opening. For them, Bitcoin is a protest, a lifeline, and a way out.

Here are their stories.

Bitcoin in Nigeria

Ire Aderinokun is a Nigerian entrepreneur. She is a front-end developer and user interface designer from Lagos and is the cofounder, COO, and vice president of engineering at Buycoins, a cryptocurrency exchange that went through Y Combinator in 2018 and is now one of the most popular places to buy bitcoin in West Africa. She is a prolific writer, speaker, organizer, and activist and one of the founding members of the Feminist Coalition, a group that champions equality for women in Nigerian society.

Aderinokun talks about Nigeria as a melting pot, like the "United States" of Africa. Three big ethnic groups dominate the country, but the population is split into hundreds of different tribes. This is a strength but also a challenge as it is hard to bring so many different people together. The country is governed through a predominantly Muslim north and a predominantly Christian south, and national leadership rotates between these constituencies. Nigeria boasts the largest economy in Africa, and the largest population with more than 200 million citizens, but much of the wealth is tied to the export of oil.

Like in many rentier states,[8] there is massive corruption and inequality: While the fabulously rich jet set around the world, six Nigerians are impoverished every minute.[9] People who have wealth and power, Aderinokun said, do not let it trickle down and do not invest it back in society. This has resulted in a situation where, in major urban areas such as Abuja and Lagos, there are countless lawyers, for instance, working in restaurants, toiling away in careers that are professionally beneath them, because there are not enough opportunities. Millions head to the big cities for jobs, only to come up empty handed.

As a result, Aderinokun said the country struggles with unemployment, especially among the youth; 62% of the population is under 25 years old. Out of this crisis, however, are upsides. She credits Nigerians with being incredibly entrepreneurial. People do what they need to do to get by and having a side hustle, she said, is natural.

Part of this need to hustle relates to the country's economic situation, where the official inflation rate now stands around 15%, with food inflation even higher. In her personal experience, Aderinokun has seen the naira decline from 100 per dollar to 500 per dollar. People, she said, are quite aware that the elites are stealing from the citizens through currency debasement. It is expected. So much so that when one's family or friend gets a government job, she said, there is an assumption that they will provide for you and a circle of others. The money trickles down through nepotism and the people at the top get fat. This is an example of the *Cantillon effect* in action, where those closest to the point of money creation benefit at the expense of the rest.[10]

Growing up, she saw people try to keep their money in dollars, or send it abroad, or buy real estate. *This* was how Nigerians could protect the fruits of their time and energy, but only a handful had these options. Now, Bitcoin is changing the game, allowing more people to save like never before. Any Nigerian with internet access now has an escape from their unreliable, unequal, exploitative national monetary system.

Aderinokun got her start in Bitcoin with a Coinbase account in 2016. She and her friends initially thought: Could we use this new technology to send money abroad? As it turned out, Bitcoin was easier and faster for sending money from Nigeria to the United States than traditional means. So, she decided to launch Buycoins, a cryptocurrency exchange. Paystack — the Nigerian tech giant — was just a few years old then, and she is grateful that it existed at the time, as it allowed Buycoins to reach customers and create an experience that otherwise would have been impossible.

At first, the payment component of Bitcoin was what really attracted Aderinokun, the idea that it could actually be easy instead of difficult to send money from one place to another, skipping over national borders. This, she thought, is something Bitcoin can fix.

Beyond the exchange itself, Buycoins also released an app called Sendcash to help Nigerians abroad send money home. Perhaps a family member moved to the United States and wanted to send dollars back. The recipient in Lagos would normally need a domiciliary account in dollars, but Aderinokun said those are difficult to open. Even then, the bank wire or using a service like Western Union can be costly and slow, and exchanging from dollars to naira can be difficult. She thought: Could Bitcoin help streamline the process?

With SendCash, users in the United States send bitcoin to the app, and it deposits as naira a few minutes later in any Nigerian bank account: a game changer. Today, the app can also send naira to the United States or Ghana, all using bitcoin as a payment rail.

Aderinokun said that around 45% of the Nigerian population has internet access. So is her mission worth it, if a majority of Nigerians still cannot even access Bitcoin? She said this is a dilemma she often ponders. There are countless internally displaced persons (IDPs) across Nigeria who cannot accept cryptocurrency because they do not have a smartphone. In the end, she said, the work and mission are worth it, because even though there are many who do not have internet access, there are tens of millions who do, and those individuals are sharing access to smart apps with those who do not have them.

As for the Gates and Buffets of the world: Aderinokun said some of Bitcoin's critics may have valid points to debate, around, for example, the environmental impact — but she takes issue with Western elites saying there is no upside, or that it is a Ponzi scheme, or that it is just for fun.

They do not understand, she said, how important Bitcoin is for those who cannot get dollars. For billions, they are trapped in a flawed currency that does not fulfill the purpose of what currency is supposed to do. For many in Nigeria and beyond, Bitcoin is providing another option and solving real problems.

Is it just helping the rich? Aderinokun laughed and said: This is not the case at all. It is providing employment, it is helping people convert their naira to other currencies, it is enabling commerce where it was not previously possible. With the Feminist Coalition, it helped people overcome financial repression and the freezing of activist bank accounts.[11] This is not, she said, just a case of people sitting around watching the price.

Moving forward, Aderinokun thinks more education is essential. Nigerians are still very misinformed about Bitcoin. The main reason they know about it, she said, is because the price keeps going up, and many do not see past that. Scams are a huge obstacle. Although, she said, more people are beginning to understand. They know bitcoin is volatile, but they see that it goes up and to the right over time, instead of down and to the right like the naira.

She also wants to focus on building bridges and ramps between the naira and cryptocurrencies. Buycoins works with a naira stablecoin, the NGNT, which she said can also be helpful to people without traditional bank accounts.

And building on- and off-ramps matters, because the Nigerian government has Buycoins and other exchanges in its crosshairs. In February 2021, the regime pronounced bitcoin as not legal tender and said banks should not hold or treat it as such.[12] They later clarified that individuals could still trade but have pressured regulated financial institutions to stay away. Buycoins has been struggling to hold naira because banks do not want to work with it. But now, Aderinokun said, it has shifted to a peer-to-peer solution. When users need to go in and out of naira, buyers and sellers are matched in a marketplace.

Aderinokun does not actually think it is possible to effectively ban Bitcoin. The most the government can do, perhaps, is what it has already done — forcing institutions to stay away. But it cannot stop individuals from using hardware wallets or conducting peer-to-peer activity in a place like Nigeria. "No one," she said, "can stop me." It is like saying it could ban Facebook, she said. It could shut down the internet but that would have disastrous consequences for the whole nation.

What the government should be doing instead, she said, is trying to understand Bitcoin and working with exchanges to allow Nigerians to connect to the world around them. Aderinokun does not think the government should have an adversarial attitude. In fact, she believes Bitcoin can help it. Maybe it would even be a good thing if the Nigerian government figured out Bitcoin before other nations. But, she said, for the moment it is not even close to understanding how Bitcoin works. When asked if the government is using blockchain surveillance or spying on individual transactions, she laughed. It does not have the abilities or know-how yet, she said.

As for the future, Aderinokun is hopeful, because she has seen Bitcoin's potential. She watched it shine in the context of human rights and activism. In October 2020, in the middle of nationwide protests against SARS — a notorious special police unit that was terrorizing citizens across the country — the Feminist Coalition began accepting donations via Flutterwave, a fintech product. This started off well enough but then the regime started cracking down. Its bank accounts were shuttered.

Bitcoin was the only option left. There was no other way to receive, store, and spend money. For Aderinokun and her cofounders, this was an eye-opening moment. They ended up setting up a BTCPay Server to process gifts from around the world in a way that avoided address reuse and protected donor privacy. Celebrities including Jack Dorsey shared the link, and they raised more than 7 BTC.

It was a great learning experience, she said, as many young people learned about Bitcoin in this moment as a tool for activism. The experience renewed and strengthened her belief in products she is building at Buycoins. People saw that Bitcoin was cool and that the government could not stop it. Because of this, Aderinokun thinks that one day, Bitcoin will be talked about in the same way, with the same importance, as radio, the TV, and the internet.

Asked if she is worried about a world where the government can no longer control the money, she said no, she is hopeful. Just printing more money, she said, has its downsides, taking that option away is not necessarily a bad thing.

Bitcoin in Sudan

Mo, also known by his Twitter handle as Sudan HODL, is a Sudanese doctor. He currently lives abroad in Europe, practicing medicine to support his family back home.

Mo sees his country with brutally clear eyes. He described the capital of Khartoum as a crowded, diverse megacity, filled with pockets of extravagant wealth and surrounded by an enormous belt of poverty. It is a city of contradictions, he said, where palatial residences sit next to utter destitution.

Mo has worked in Darfur, where he described the lack of development as simply stunning. There is no educational or health infrastructure. During his time there, he was one of three or four doctors treating hundreds of thousands of people. There was a total lack of primary care and there were no pediatric hospitals. He was treating women who suffered from fistula.[13] The national ruling class, he said, did not invest in these places. Warlords ultimately filled the power vacuum, with the youth choosing violence instead of school as a way to get ahead.

Mo told a tortured history of his country. Sudan, he said, has been living through a vicious cycle of military coups and authoritarian rule ever since gaining its independence from the British Empire and losing its fragile first democracy.

Islam, Mo said, did not come to Sudan by violence but through traders and Sufis. He said his Muslim ancestors historically had a peaceful interpretation of their religion. But in the 1980s, the rise of Saudi Arabia's oil wealth (see Chapter III) led to the export of the extremist and militant ideology of Wahhabism to many places around the world, including Sudan. Wahhabism was foreign to Sudan's culture but was forced into the country's political structure.

By 1983, military governments had allied themselves with the Muslim Brotherhood and imposed Sharia law, alienating the predominantly Christian and animist south. A democratic revolution in 1985 was short-lived, as Islamists led by Omar al-Bashir staged another coup in 1989, paving the way for three decades of his rule. Society was militarized and the intelligentsia were purged.[14] If one spoke out against the regime, Mo said, they were not just speaking out against government officials: They were speaking against Islam. They were against God himself. This gave Bashir an excuse for his brutality and new jihads against ethnic minorities.

Since colonial times, minorities in South Sudan and Darfur had resisted authority from strongmen in far-away Khartoum. The seeds of this tension were planted in the 1950s when these populations fell under postcolonial Arab rule. Over time, these minority groups rebelled, only to be violently subjugated. The bloodshed peaked in Darfur in the early 2000s, when Bashir committed genocide, using the Janjaweed militias to murder hundreds of thousands and displace millions of people.[15] This triggered the United States and European Union to increase sanctions against Sudan, cutting it off more deeply from the outside world.

Mo thinks it is important to share Sudan's economic history, often overshadowed by the political story. In addition to the extreme inequality on display in Khartoum, there is a bigger picture of low-income workers trying to catch up to high inflation, while those closer to the regime manage to do well. Infrastructure decayed and the average person suffered while Bashir and his cronies loaded up on weapons, real estate, and foreign assets. Modern Sudan is another vivid and tragic example of the Cantillon effect.

It was not always like this. Mo said that under the gold standard, three Sudanese pounds once bought a dollar. There was a middle class, and Khartoum was known as the London of North Africa. But in 1960, the Sudanese central bank took over and devalued the currency, the first instance of what would happen many times over the coming decades.

When Bashir seized power in 1989, he installed a regime of economic terrorism. To instill fear in the population, he chose to make an example of a young man named Majdi Mahjoub, who was a single child living at home, looking after his elderly parents. A Christian minority in a community of traders, Majdi had possession of a few thousand US dollars in his home, the result of many years of family commerce.

Bashir created a new special "economic" division, a sort of secret police, that would go home to home, searching for foreign currency or gold. When the jackbooted thugs came to Majdi's house, they found his savings and arrested him. After a show trial, he was hanged, sending a message to the population: If anyone tries to use anything but the Sudanese currency through our banking system — if anyone tries to own their own money — they will get the death sentence. Even today, according to Mo, many Sudanese are fearful of using dollars or storing money at home.

At the same time, Bashir launched a tribute system to finance his activities. On top of what was taken through traditional taxation and seigniorage, citizens had to pay a portion of their income to help the martyrs of their dictator's wars. The secret monetary police would spy on individuals, freeze bank accounts, confiscate assets, and impose made-up fees on merchants. No reasonable suspicion was required. Mo calls it a system of national extortion.

As far as the currency itself, Mo recalled several times in his life when the system was overhauled. In the late 1980s, his family was living abroad in Saudi Arabia, and when they visited home, a quarter of a Sudanese pound could buy a sandwich or a tasty snack on the street. But after 1992, when Bashir changed the haram and colonial pound for the Islamic dinar, those quarter pounds became worthless. The mid-1990s saw massive inflation, with the "official rate" of the dinar going from around 400 per dollar to more than 2,000. Many years later, in 2007, Bashir decided to ditch the Islamic facade and switch back to the pound. Citizens had a small window to redeem dinars for the new currency, after which they were no longer legal tender, forcing citizens to surrender their savings or watch it disappear.

Today, after a series of devaluations and constant inflation, a Sudanese pound will officially obtain around $0.0025. According to Mo, inflation as of late 2021 is 340%. While the average citizen watched as their wages stagnated and living costs rose, Bashir and his cronies accumulated billions and saved them in foreign currencies, locked away in Swiss bank accounts.[16] Today, the new Sudanese government is struggling to regain all that was looted and lost in the past 30 years.

In the spring of 2019, in a stunning example of people power, the Sudanese population finally pushed out Bashir. A fragile reform government followed, where military leaders of the old regime share power with a technocratic civilian government. People were initially optimistic about the change, Mo said, but the reality did not meet their expectations. At the end of 2021, the military came back into power.

He says the IMF has a deal to help give $5 per month to Sudanese families, and in a country where some only make a dollar a day, this seemed significant. The problem is the families are paid not in dollars but in pounds, so the value disappears after a few months. The sanctions levied on the Bashir regime are now gone, but most fintech products and payment apps are still not available for Sudanese, as corporations shy away due to "risk management."

It is clear that, in some places, a political revolution is not enough. Toppling a tyrant like Bashir is a historical and incredible achievement; but the political situation remains difficult and people are still suffering. So, some, like Mo, are turning to Bitcoin.

In 2015, Mo first heard about this mysterious internet money, as he put it, on YouTube. He spent countless hours watching Andreas Antonopolous videos and read through *The Internet of Money*, which helped him understand the "why" behind the new currency.[17] He started to use it while working abroad, exchanging euros for bitcoin over PayPal on LocalBitcoins.com. He kept things small and mainly to himself. But in 2017, he started talking to family and friends. He told them: This is going to be a part of our future. Many of them are now saving in bitcoin.

As of today, Mo estimates that 13 million of Sudan's 43 million people have internet access, and he thinks that, in a few years, that number will top 20 million. There are more and more people coming online, and there are now smartphones even in remote regions like Darfur and the Nuba Mountains. People are plugging in everywhere.

He said that the Sudanese who do already have smartphones have an extended responsibility to help others with their privilege. In his case, he has a large extended family that he supports. He is their "Uncle Jim": lingo in the Bitcoin world for a knowledgeable friend who helps with Bitcoin matters.[18]

Where there were once financial walls cutting off Sudan from the world, Bitcoin has made bridges. It is now easy for Mo in Europe to send money back to his friends and family. What once took days now takes minutes. And he does not have to trust any third parties or require his family to deal with thieves in government.

Mo is beginning to see just how massive the Lightning Network will be for Sudan because most future users will be in the micropayment space, sending transactions of $5 or $10, and will not be able to afford the increasingly high on-chain fees. Lightning is a second-layer payment network that sits on top of the main Bitcoin system and enables users to send bitcoin instantly for tiny fees anywhere in the world. If international exchanges can choose to service Sudan and enable Lightning withdrawals and deposits, he said that would be an enormous step forward for financial empowerment.

As for the likes of Bill Gates and Warren Buffet, Mo said they might understand the technology behind Bitcoin, but they will never be happy about it because it is coming to seize a place on the global stage that they used to have just for themselves. In direct contradiction to billionaire claims that Bitcoin is worthless and has no social value, Mo knows many Sudanese who rely on it as a lifeline. Maybe, Mo said, the critics just cannot see past their financial privilege.

For Mo personally, Bitcoin has been transformative. He has started a podcast in Arabic for Sudanese youth to talk about Bitcoin, money, freedom, and the future of their country. Fifteen years ago, he could not have imagined being this optimistic.

One of the darkest moments in his life was in 2013 after a peaceful political uprising was completely crushed. Mo left all social media. He could not bear to look at the bloody images and videos streaming from the violence. But now, with twin political and economic transformations, he sees the light at the end of the tunnel. When people say Bitcoin is hope, he says that he agrees.

Bitcoin in Ethiopia

Kal Kassa is an Ethiopian businessman. In a country of close to 120 million people, more than 70% of the population has no access to a bank account. This is a place, he said, where there are still communities that use salt for money.

In the remote northeast Afar region, dotted with volcanoes, rifts, and deserts, the indigenous people mine salt, as they have for generations, and trek for days to barter it in markets for the goods they need. It is their store of value, medium of exchange, and unit of account. The word *amole*, Amharic for salt, is even used today in Ethiopia as the name of a mobile banking app.

According to Kassa, 70% of Ethiopians still live in rural areas. Outside of the capital of Addis Ababa, home to 5 million, very few have bank accounts or smartphones. In total, no more than 25 million Ethiopians are connected. To make matters worse, Ethiopia does not have open capital markets. Individuals cannot freely exchange their national currency — the birr — with dollars and vice versa. Sadly, Kassa said, the country is still under the influence of militant Marxism and economic centralization.

As of mid-2021, the National Bank of Ethiopia enforced a bank rate of 40 birr per dollar, with a black-market rate of 55 birr per dollar. Inflation is officially reported at around 20%. Kassa is not sure what the exact rate is but said that Ethiopians traditionally buy a chicken or sheep or lamb for Easter, and these prices go up steadily every year. When he arrived in Ethiopia in 2013 to start a consulting job, one lamb went for around 1,500 birr. As of late 2021, it can go anywhere from 5,000 to 7,000 birr.

Government wages do grow, Kassa said, but not on par with inflation. He estimated salaries in urban areas have perhaps doubled over the past decade, but goods have gone up by three-to-five times. Since inflation is so high and such a constant phenomenon, the upper classes use the dollar as their unit of account. But outside of the cities, people still account with, and their living standards fall with, the birr. In rural areas, people use cattle or sheep to store value. If they can, they obtain gold, which is rare and still considered very precious. Dollars are officially illegal.

The government is afraid that people will dump the birr for dollars, pushing the price of the birr toward zero. But the government operates a double standard, wanting to retain as many dollars as it can for its own purposes. If, for example, an Ethiopian runs a tourist service, they are allowed to take foreign payments into a dollar account, which they can keep in dollars and use to pay for imported goods for up to around two months. But if they do not use those dollars within that window, the government simply swaps the dollars out for birr at the official rate. Which, of course, means they get the fake price of 40 birr for one dollar and not the real market rate of 55.

Kassa's brother was once arrested and imprisoned once simply because he had a $20 bill in his pocket. In Ethiopia, people are jailed for the crime of using better currency.

Starting in 2018, Ethiopia underwent a series of reforms under a young new leader who was awarded the Nobel Peace Prize for efforts to end hostilities with neighboring Eritrea. The shifts appeared to open up political space and move the country toward liberalism after more than 25 years of a police state. Three years later, however, repression, ethnic tensions, and armed conflict have caused a democratic backslide. Uncertainty and war have caused major capital flight. On top of that, Ethiopia imports more than it exports: Oil, medical goods, and cars, for example, are all brought in from other countries.

In this weak environment, Ethiopians are forced to buy government bonds, which, as Kassa dryly noted, have negative real interest rates. They are, as he put it, donations for the state.

Kassa was born in Ethiopia, but left as a young child, growing up in California. He moved back at the end of 2013, as a senior associate for Grant Thornton, working on privatization on the buy and sell sides. He lived there until the summer of 2020 when the government shut off the internet.

Kassa's phone could still send SMS messages and make calls, but there was no data. The regime justified this as a defense against rebellions, but especially during the pandemic lockdown, this got old very quickly. So, that June, wearing just a backpack, he got on a plane and headed back to the United States.

Kassa first heard about Bitcoin in 2013, when his roommate was mining it at Chapman University, but the idea did not click for him. He spent years thinking bitcoin was just some kind of alternative and speculative investment. He said his penny drop moment actually came when he was at the airport in Addis Ababa in June 2020. As he was boarding the plane, he stood and wondered: If I had my wealth stored in gold or cattle, how could I take it across a border?

Today, Kassa has created Telegram groups where he pays freelancers, graphic designers, and translators based in Ethiopia with bitcoin. In America, he said, most people treat bitcoin as an investment or as a savings account. But he is using it as a medium of exchange and payment, too. It is easier and cheaper, and now a part of his life.

Kassa is focused on the Lightning Network and uses it to pay his contacts in Ethiopia. He helps them set up the open-source, free Blue Wallet and pays them directly with Lightning. He is amazed at how easy it is and how it transmits hard value instantly halfway across the world.

On the other end, his contacts use Blue Wallet as their savings accounts, and they exchange locally into birr when they need to in peer-to-peer markets. This is, he said, hugely preferable to Western Union and birr-denominated accounts, where, for example, on a recent payment, Kassa had to pay $13 to send $100. When Kassa pays his colleagues, he pays them the full amount, rather than paying through the government exchange rate where authorities steal a portion. His contacts are their own banks, and no one can debase or remotely confiscate their funds. This, Kassa said, is a revolution.

Kassa does have concerns and fears about Bitcoin. For example, the Ethiopian government is hyper-concerned about satellite internet. If citizens are caught with satellite equipment, for example, they can go to prison. In this context, he is worried about the safety of people running their own Bitcoin servers. He also thinks that many people may end up using custodial services, since as of right now, many cannot even tell the difference between bitcoin and other cryptocurrencies, and they are far away from understanding the difference between custodial (where you trust a third party to hold your bitcoin) and noncustodial (where you hold the keys to your bitcoin) services. He is cautious about all the new cheap smartphones flooding in from ZTE and Huawei, all from China. He is worried about people installing bitcoin wallets on these phones, as he does not think they are safe. In addition, because the phone networks are not reliable, people still carry cash in cities, even if they have smartphones, as sometimes the service goes out.

Kassa said the biggest obstacle to Bitcoin adoption in Ethiopia might be the false promise of alternative cryptocurrencies. In particular, he has identified Cardano as a threat. In a recent video, the currency's creator spoke about working with the Ethiopian regime to incorporate 5 million students onto the Cardano blockchain and boasts that then they could be tracked with metadata throughout their life and career.

"Our vision and goals," he said, "are directly in line with the goals of the Ethiopian government." In contrast, Kassa is glad that Bitcoin's goals are *not* in line with the aims of the thieves and bureaucrats who run his country. He worried that many may fall prey to schemes like Cardano.

As for Gates and Buffet: Kassa actually did get a chance to go to the Berkshire Hathaway event in Lincoln, Nebraska, a few years ago. It was very powerful, he said, to see 40,000 people coming together as part of a community. But the event was very inward-looking, which explains how Buffet and friends cannot see just how corrupt the world is around them. They do not see the water that they swim in and are seemingly blind to the trillions of dollars of money laundered each year through the banking system.[19] For them to ignore the harms that the dollar system has caused on the developing world, Kassa said, and instead focus on the flaws of *Bitcoin*, is naive and self-serving. He is glad that these investors are dinosaurs. They are not the future.

In contrast, 75% of the population of Ethiopia is under the age of 27. Once they start using Bitcoin, Kassa thinks they will spread the technology quickly to friends and family. Adoption will not take decades but years. When he moved back to Ethiopia in 2013, there were about 5 million people online. Now, there are about 25 million. In the next five years, he expects a majority of the population will be connected and for Bitcoin to follow.

As far as priorities, Kassa thinks spreading education is most important. In 2021, he helped translate *The Little Bitcoin Book* (an intro to the subject) into Amharic.[20] As far as he knows, there is no other Bitcoin content translated as of yet into Ethiopia's three major languages.

When asked if he is worried about the government cracking down on Bitcoin, he said that it will be hard to get in the middle of a hard-working

Ethiopian and a better life. The population is young, agile, creative, and adaptable. It will not be stopped. People, he said, are sick of poverty and earning money only to see it depreciate.

Today, Ethiopians are at war with each other. "We are fighting ourselves," Kassa said. "If we are willing to kill each other to solve our problems, we will definitely be willing to try Bitcoin as an alternative." And that, he thinks, will be a peaceful revolution.

***

After reading the stories of Ire Aderinokun, Mo, and Kal Kassa, and witnessing how Bitcoin is so valuable to people outside of the dollar bubble, then compare this with what Munger, Buffet, Lagarde, Sachs, and others say about Bitcoin: They claim it is something with no social value, that it will just get people's hopes up, only to let them down.

"Disgusting."

"Rat poison."

"I would short it."

"Totally reprehensible."

For most people, it is the government that lets people down. It is the government that is reprehensible. Liberation technologies should be invested in, not shorted.

And for those comfortable in the dollar bubble?

It's time to check your financial privilege.

Chapter II

The Quest for Digital Cash

One summer day in August 2008, long before the citizens of Nigeria, Sudan, and Ethiopia could even dream of a currency beyond government control, Adam Back got an email from Satoshi Nakamoto.

It was the first time Nakamoto had reached out to anyone about a new project that the pseudonymous programmer or group of programmers called *Bitcoin*. The email described a blueprint for what an alliance of digital rights advocates known as the cypherpunks considered the Holy Grail: decentralized electronic cash.

By the mid-2000s, cryptographers had, for decades, tried to create a digital form of paper cash with all of its bearer asset and privacy guarantees. With advances in public-key cryptography in the 1970s and blind signatures in the 1980s, "e-cash" became less of a science fiction dream read about in books like *Snow Crash* or *Cryptonomicon* and more of a possible reality.[21]

Censorship resistance was a key goal of digital cash, which aimed to be money beyond the reach of governments and corporations; but early projects suffered from a seemingly inescapable flaw: centralization. No matter how much cutting-edge math went into these systems, they ultimately still relied on administrators who could block certain payments or inflate the money supply.

More "e-cash" advances occurred in the late 1990s and early 2000s, each one making a critical step forward. But before 2008, a vexing computing riddle prevented the creation of a decentralized money system: the Byzantine Generals Problem.

Imagine that you are a military commander trying to invade Byzantium hundreds of years ago during the Ottoman Empire. Your army has a dozen generals, all posted in different locations. How do you coordinate a surprise attack on the city at a certain time? What if spies break through your ranks and tell some of your generals to attack sooner or to hold off? The entire plan could go awry.

The metaphor translates to computer science: How can individuals who are not physically with each other reach consensus without a central coordinator?

For decades, this was a major obstacle for decentralized digital cash. If two parties could not precisely agree on the state of an economic ledger, users could not know which transactions were valid, and the system could not prevent double-spending. Hence, all e-cash prototypes needed an administrator.

The magic solution came in the form of a mysterious post on an obscure email list on Friday, October 31, 2008, when Nakamoto shared a white paper, or concept note, for Bitcoin.[22] The subject line was "Bitcoin P2P e-cash paper" and the author wrote, "I've been working on a new electronic cash system that's fully peer-to-peer, with no trusted third party."[23]

To solve the Byzantine Generals Problem and issue digital money without a central coordinator, Nakamoto proposed to keep the economic ledger in the hands of thousands of individuals around the world. Each participant would hold an independent, historical, and continually updating copy of all transactions that Nakamoto originally called a timechain.[24] If one participant tried to cheat and "double-spend," everyone else would know and reject that transaction.

After raising eyebrows and objections with the white paper, Nakamoto incorporated some final feedback and, a few months later on January 9, 2009, launched the first version of the Bitcoin software.

As of early 2022, each bitcoin is worth more than $40,000. The currency boasts a daily transaction total greater than most countries' daily GDP and a total market capitalization of close to $1 trillion. Nakamoto's creation is used by more than 100 million people across nearly every country on Earth and has been adopted by Wall Street, Silicon Valley, D.C. politicians, and even nation-states.

But in the beginning, Nakamoto needed help, and the first person they reached out to for assistance was Adam Back.

The Birth of the Cypherpunks

Back was one of the cypherpunks, students of computer science and distributed systems in the 1980s and 1990s who wanted to preserve human rights like the freedom to associate and the freedom to communicate privately in the digital realm. These activists knew that technologies like the internet would eventually give enormous power to governments and believed cryptography could be the individual's best defense.

By the early 1990s, states realized that they were sitting on an ever-growing treasure trove of personal data from their citizens. Information was often collected for innocuous reasons. For example, your internet service provider (ISP) might collect a mailing address and phone number for billing purposes

— but then hand this identifying information along with your web activity to law enforcement without a warrant.

Collection and analysis of this kind of data spawned the era of digital surveillance and eavesdropping, which, two decades later, led to the intricate and highly unconstitutional War on Terror programs that would eventually be leaked to the public by NSA whistleblower Edward Snowden.

In his 1983 book, *The Rise of the Computer State*, *New York Times* journalist David Burnham warned that computerized automation could lead to an unprecedented level of surveillance.[25] He argued that in response, citizens should demand legal protections. The cypherpunks, on the other hand, thought the answer was not to lobby the government to create better policy but instead to invent and use technology that the State could not stop.

The cypherpunks harnessed cryptography to trigger social change. The idea was deceptively simple: Political dissidents from across the world could gather online and work together pseudonymously and freely to challenge state power.[26] Their call to arms was: "Cypherpunks write code."

Once the exclusive domain of militaries and spy agencies, cryptography was brought into the public world in the 1970s through academics like Ralph Merkle, Whitfield Diffie, and Martin Hellman. At Stanford University in May 1975, this trio had a eureka moment. They figured out how two people could trade private electronic messages without needing to trust a third party.

One year later, Diffie and Hellman published "New Directions in Cryptography," a seminal work that laid out a private messaging system that would become key to defeating surveillance.[27] The paper described how citizens could encrypt and send digital messages without fear of snooping governments or corporations figuring out the contents:

> In a public-key cryptosystem enciphering and deciphering are governed by distinct keys, E and D, such that computing D from E is computationally infeasible (e.g., requiring 10100 instructions). The enciphering key E can be disclosed [in a directory] without compromising the deciphering key D. This enables any user of the system to send a message to any other user enciphered in such a way that only the intended recipient is able to decipher it.

In simple terms, Alice can have a public key that she posts online. If Bob wants to send a private message to Alice, he can look up her public key, and use it to encrypt the message. Only she can decrypt the note and read the text inside. If a third party, Carol, does not have the private key (think: password) for the message, she cannot read the contents. This simple innovation changed the entire information power balance of individuals versus governments.

When Diffie and Hellman's paper was published, the US government, through the NSA, tried to prevent the spread of its ideas, even writing a letter to a cryptography conference at the time, warning the participants that their participation might be illegal. But after activists printed hard copies of the paper and distributed them around the country, the Feds backed off.

In 1977, Diffie, Hellman, and Merkle would file US patent number 4200770 for "public-key cryptography," an invention that created the foundation for email and messaging tools like Pretty Good Privacy (PGP) and today's popular Signal mobile app.

It was the end of government control of cryptography and the beginning of the cypherpunk revolution.

The List

The word *cypherpunk* did not appear in the Oxford English Dictionary until 2006, but the community began gathering much earlier.

In 1992, one year after the public release of the world wide web, early Sun Microsystems employee John Gilmore, privacy activist Eric Hughes, and former Intel engineer Timothy May started to meet up in San Francisco to discuss how cryptography could be used to preserve freedom. That same year, they launched the Cypherpunks Mailing List (or "The List" for short), where the ideas behind Bitcoin were developed and eventually published by Nakamoto 16 years later.[28]

On "The List," cypherpunks like May wrote about how monarchies in the late Middle Ages were disrupted by the invention of the printing press, which democratized access to information. They debated how the creation of the open internet and cryptography could democratize privacy technology and disrupt the seemingly inevitable trend toward a global surveillance state.

Like many cypherpunks, Back's college education was in computer science. But serendipitously, he first studied economics between the ages of 16 and 18, afterward adding a PhD in distributed systems. If anyone was adequately trained to one day become a Bitcoin scientist, it was Back.

While he studied computer science in London in the early 1990s, he learned that one of his friends was working on speeding up computers to run faster encryption techniques. Through his friend, Back learned about the public-key encryption invented 15 years earlier by Diffie and Hellman.

Back thought this was a historic shift in the relationship between governments and individuals. Now citizens could communicate electronically in a way that no government could decrypt. He resolved to learn more, and his curiosity eventually led him to The List.

During the mid-1990s, Back was an avid participant on The List, which at its peak, was populated by dozens of new messages every day. By Back's own account, he was the most active contributor at times, addicted to the cutting-edge conversations of the era.

Back was struck by how the cypherpunks wanted to change society by using code to peacefully create systems that could not be stopped. In 1993, Hughes wrote the movement's seminal short essay, "A Cypherpunk's Manifesto":

> Privacy is necessary for an open society in the electronic age. Privacy is not secrecy. A private matter is something one doesn't want the whole world to know, but a secret matter is something one doesn't want anybody to know. Privacy is the power to selectively reveal oneself to the world ...
>
> ... We cannot expect governments, corporations, or other large, faceless organizations to grant us privacy out of their beneficence. We must defend our own privacy if we expect to have any. We must come together and create systems, which allow anonymous transactions to take place. People have been defending their own privacy for centuries with whispers, darkness, envelopes, closed doors, secret handshakes, and couriers. The technologies of the past did not allow for strong privacy, but electronic technologies do.
>
> We the Cypherpunks are dedicated to building anonymous systems. We are defending our privacy with cryptography, with anonymous mail forwarding systems, with digital signatures, and with electronic money.
>
> Cypherpunks write code. We know that someone has to write software to defend privacy, and since we can't get privacy unless we all do, we're going to write it ... Our code is free for all to use, worldwide. We don't much care if you don't approve of the software we write. We know that software can't be destroyed and that a widely dispersed system can't be shut down.[29]

This kind of thinking, Back thought, was what actually changes society. Sure, one could lobby or vote, but then society changes slowly, lagging behind government policy.

The other way, Back's preferred strategy, was bold, permissionless change through inventing new technology. If he wanted change, he just had to make it happen.

The Crypto Wars

The original enemies of the cypherpunks were governments trying to stop citizens from using encryption. Back and friends thought that privacy was a human right. On the other hand, nation-states were terrified that citizens would create code allowing them to escape oversight and control.

Authorities doubled down on old military standards — which classified cryptography alongside fighter jets and aircraft carriers as munitions — and tried to ban export of encryption software to kill its use globally. The aim was to scare people away from using privacy tech. The conflict became known as the "Crypto Wars," and Back was a frontline soldier.

Back knew that the big-picture effects of such a ban would cause many US jobs to move offshore and force vast amounts of sensitive information to remain unencrypted. But President Bill Clinton and his administration were not looking ahead, just at what was directly in front of them. And their biggest target was a computer scientist named Phil Zimmerman, who had, in 1991, released the first consumer-level secret messaging system, called Pretty Good Privacy, or "PGP" for short.[30]

PGP was an easy way for two individuals to communicate privately using PCs and the new world wide web. It promised to democratize encryption to millions of people and end the state's decades-long control over private messaging.

As the face of the project, however, Zimmerman came under attack from corporations and governments. In 1977, three Massachusetts Institute of Technology (MIT) scientists named Ron Rivest, Adi Shamir, and Leonard Adelman, implemented Diffie and Hellman's ideas into an algorithm called RSA. MIT later issued a license for the patent to a businessman named Jim Bidzos and his company, RSA Data Security.

The cypherpunks were uneasy with such a vital toolkit being controlled by one entity, having a single point of failure. All through the 1980s, licensing and fear of being sued had largely prevented them from releasing new programs based on the code.

At first, Zimmerman asked Bidzos for a free license for the software but was denied. In defiance, Zimmerman released PGP as "guerilla freeware," disseminating it through floppy disks and internet message boards. A young cypherpunk by the name of Hal Finney — who would later play a major role in the Bitcoin story — joined Zimmerman, helping to push the project forward. A 1994 *WIRED* feature hailed Zimmerman's brazen release of PGP as a "pre-emptive strike against such an Orwellian future."[31]

Bidzos called Zimmerman a thief and mounted a campaign to halt the spread of PGP. Zimmerman eventually got help from Christopher Allen and his team at Consensus Development to put out a new PGP version, which piggybacked on code that Bidzos had released for free, defusing the corporate threat.

Even still, the federal government ultimately decided to investigate Zimmerman for exporting "munitions" under the Arms Control Export Act. In defense, Zimmerman argued that he was merely enacting his First Amendment rights of free speech by sharing open-source code.

At the time, the Clinton administration argued that Americans had no right to encrypt. They pushed for legislation to force companies to install backdoors ("clipper chips") into their equipment so that the State could have a skeleton key to any message these chips encrypted. Led by White House officials and congressmen like Joe Biden, they argued that cryptography would empower criminals, pedophiles, and terrorists.

The cypherpunks rallied to support Zimmerman, who became a cause célèbre. They argued that anti-encryption laws were incompatible with US traditions of free speech. The activists started to print the PGP source code in books and mail them overseas. Via the publishing of the code in printed form, Zimmerman and others theorized they could legally circumvent anti-munitions restrictions. Recipients would scan the code, reconstitute it, and run it, all to prove the point: You cannot stop us.

Back wrote short pieces of source code that any programmer could turn into a fully-functional privacy toolkit. Some activists tattooed snippets of this code on their bodies. Back famously started selling t-shirts with the code on the front and a piece of the US Bill of Rights with "VOID" stamped over it on the back.[32]

Activists finally sent a book containing the controversial code to the US government's Office of Munitions Control, asking if it could share it abroad. They never got a response. The cypherpunks guessed that the White House would never ban books, and in the end, they were right.

In 1996, the US Department of Justice dropped its charges against Zimmerman. The pressure to force companies to use "clipper chips" subsided. Federal judges argued that encryption was a right protected by the First Amendment. Anti-cryptography standards were overturned, and encrypted messaging became a core part of the open web and e-commerce. PGP became "the most widely used email encryption software in the world."[33]

Today, companies and apps ranging from Amazon to WhatsApp and Facebook rely on encryption to secure payments and messages. Billions of people benefit. Code changed the world.

Back is self-deprecating and said that it is hard to say if his activism in particular made a difference. But certainly, the fight that the cypherpunks mounted was one of the main reasons that the US government lost the Crypto Wars. The authorities tried to stop the code and failed.

This realization would loom large in Back's mind 15 years later, in the summer of 2008, as he worked through that first email from Nakamoto.

From DigiCash to Bit Gold

As the computing historian Steven Levy said in 1993, the ultimate crypto tool would be "anonymous digital money."[34] Indeed, after winning the fight for private communications, the next challenge for the cypherpunks was to create digital cash.

Some cypherpunks were crypto-anarchists — deeply skeptical of the modern democratic state. Others believed it was possible to reform democracies to preserve individual rights. No matter what side they took, many considered digital cash to be the Holy Grail of the cypherpunk movement.

In the 1980s and 1990s, major steps were taken in the right direction, both culturally and technically, toward digital cash. From a cultural perspective, science fiction authors like Neal Stephenson captured the imagination of computer scientists around the world with depictions of future societies — where cash was gone — and different kinds of digital e-bucks were the currency du jour. At a time when credit cards and digital payments were already on the rise, there was a nostalgia for the privacy involved in making a cash payment, where the merchant does not know, store, or sell any information about the customer.

On the technical front, a cryptography scholar at the University of California, Berkeley, named David Chaum took the powerful idea of public-key encryption and started to apply it to money.

In the early 1980s, Chaum invented blind signatures, a key innovation in the evolution of being able to prove ownership of a piece of data without revealing its provenance. In 1985, he published, "Security Without Identification: Transaction Systems to Make Big Brother Obsolete," a prescient paper that explored how the growth of the surveillance state could be slowed through private digital payments.[35]

A few years later in 1989, Chaum and friends moved to Amsterdam, applied theory to practice, and launched DigiCash. The company aimed to allow users to convert European currencies and dollars into digital cash tokens. Bank credits could be turned into "e-cash" and sent to friends outside of the banking system. They could store the new currency on their PC, for instance, or cash them out. The software's strong encryption made it impossible for authorities to trace the money flow.

In a 1994 profile of DigiCash in its heyday, Chaum said that goal was to "catapult our currency system into the 21st century ... in the process, shattering the Orwellian predictions of a Big Brother dystopia, replacing them with a world in which the ease of electronic transactions is combined with the elegant anonymity of paying in cash."[36]

Back said that cypherpunks like him were initially excited about e-cash. It prevented outside observers from knowing who had sent how much to whom, and the tokens resembled cash in as much as they were bearer instruments that users controlled.

Chaum's personal philosophy also resonated with the cypherpunks. In 1992, he wrote that mankind was at a decision point where "in one direction lies unprecedented scrutiny and control of people's lives; in the other, secure parity between individuals and organizations.[37] The shape of society in the next century," he wrote, "may depend on which approach predominates."

DigiCash, however, failed to get the right funding and, later that decade, went bankrupt. For Back and others, this was a big lesson: Digital cash needed to be decentralized, without a single point of failure.

Back had personally gone to great lengths to preserve privacy in society. He once ran a "mixmaster" service to help people keep their communications private. He would accept incoming email and forward it along in a way that was not traceable. To make it hard to figure out that he was running the service, Back rented a server from a friend in Switzerland. To pay him from London, he would mail physical cash. Eventually, the Swiss Federal Police showed up at his friend's office. The next day, Back shut down his mixer. But the dream of digital cash kept burning in his mind.

Centralized digital money could fail operationally, come under regulatory capture, or go bankrupt, à la DigiCash. But its biggest vulnerability is monetary issuance dictated by a trusted third party.

On March 28, 1997, after years of reflection and experimentation, Back invented and announced Hashcash, an anti-spam concept later cited in

Nakamoto's white paper that would prove foundational for bitcoin mining.[38] Hashcash would eventually enable financial "proof of work": a currency that needed the expenditure of energy to produce new monetary units thus making money harder and fairer.

Governments historically have frequently abused their monopolies on the issuance of money. Tragic examples include Ancient Rome, Weimar Germany, Soviet Hungary, the Balkans in the 1990s, Mugabe's Zimbabwe, and the 1.6 billion people today living under double-, triple-, or quadruple-digit inflation everywhere from Sudan to Venezuela.

Against this backdrop, cypherpunk Robert Hettinga wrote in 1998 that properly decentralized digital cash would mean that economics would no longer have to be "the handmaiden of politics."[39] No more making new huge amounts of new cash with the click of a button.

One vulnerability of Hashcash was that if someone tried to design a currency with its anti-spam mechanism, users with faster computers could still cause hyperinflation. A decade later, Nakamoto would solve this issue with a key innovation in Bitcoin called the "difficulty algorithm," where the network would reset the difficulty of minting coins every two weeks based on the total amount of power spent by the users on the network.

In 1998, the computer engineer Wei Dai released his b-money concept.[40] B-money was "an anonymous, distributed electronic cash system," and it proposed a "scheme for a group of untraceable digital pseudonyms to pay each other with money and to enforce contracts amongst themselves without outside help."

Dai was inspired by Back's work with Hashcash, incorporating proof of work into b-money's designs. While the system was limited and turned out to be impractical, Dai left behind a series of writings that echoed Hughes, Back, and others.

In February 1995, Dai sent an email to The List, making a case for technology, not regulation, as the savior of our future digital rights:

> There has never been a government that didn't sooner or later try to reduce the freedom of its subjects and gain more control over them, and there probably never will be one. Therefore, instead of trying to convince our current government not to try, we'll develop the technology... that will make it impossible for the government to succeed.
>
> Efforts to influence the government (e.g., lobbying and propaganda) are important only in so far as to delay its attempted

crackdown long enough for the technology to mature and come into wide use.

But even if you do not believe the above is true, think about it this way: If you have a certain amount of time to spend on advancing the cause of greater personal privacy (or freedom, or cryptoanarchy, or whatever), can you do it better by using the time to learn about cryptography and develop the tools to protect privacy, or by convincing your government not to invade your privacy?[41]

That same year, in 1998, an American cryptographer named Nick Szabo proposed bit gold.[42] Building off of the ideas of other cypherpunks, Szabo proposed a parallel financial structure whose token would have its own value proposition, separate from the dollar or the euro. Having worked at DigiCash and seen the vulnerabilities of a centralized mint, he thought gold was a worthwhile asset to try to replicate in the digital space.[43]

Bit gold was important because it finally linked the ideas of monetary reform and hard money to the cypherpunk movement. It tried to make the "provable costliness" feature of gold digital. A gold necklace, for example, proves that the owner either expended significant time and energy and resources to dig that gold out of the ground and make it into jewelry or paid a lot of money to buy it. Szabo wanted to bring provable costliness online. Bit gold was never implemented, but it continued to inspire the cypherpunks.

The next few years saw the rise of e-commerce, the dot-com bubble, and then the emergence of today's internet mega-corporations. It was a busy and explosive time online, but there was not another major advancement in digital cash for five years. This points to the fact that first, there were not many people working on this idea, and second, making it all work was extraordinarily challenging.

In 2004, former PGP contributor Finney finally announced reusable proof of work, or "RPOW" for short.[44] This was the next major innovation in the path toward Bitcoin.

RPOW took the idea of bit gold and added a network of open-source servers to verify transactions. One could attach some bit gold to an email, for example, and the recipient would acquire a bearer asset with provable costliness.

While Finney launched RPOW in a centralized fashion on his own server, he had plans to eventually decentralize the architecture. These were all key steps toward Bitcoin's foundation, but a few more puzzle pieces still needed to slide into place.

Running Bitcoin

In 1999, Back finished his PhD in distributed systems and began work in Canada for a company called Zero Knowledge Systems. There, he helped build the Freedom Network, a tool that allowed individuals to browse the web privately. Back and his colleagues used what are known as "zero-knowledge proofs" (based on Chaum's blind signatures) to encrypt communications over this network and sold access to the service.

Back, as it turns out, was also ahead of his time on this key innovation. In 2002, computer scientists improved on Zero Knowledge System's model by taking a US government private web browsing project called "onion routing" open source. They called it the Tor Network, and it inspired the age of the virtual-private networks (VPNs). It remains the gold standard for private web browsing today.

In the early and mid-2000s, Back finished his work at Zero Knowledge Systems, was recruited by Microsoft for a short stint as a cybersecurity researcher, and then joined a new startup doing peer-to-peer encrypted collaboration software. All the while, Back kept the idea of digital cash in the back of his mind.

When the email from Nakamoto arrived in August 2008, Back was intrigued. He read it carefully and responded, suggesting that Nakamoto look into a few other digital money systems, including Dai's b-money.

On October 31, 2008, Nakamoto published the Bitcoin white paper on The List.[45] The first sentence promised the dream that so many had chased: "A purely peer-to-peer version of electronic cash would allow online payments to be sent directly from one party to another without going through a financial institution." Back's Hashcash, Dai's b-money, and earlier cryptography research were all cited.

As digital cash historian Aaron van Wirdum wrote, "In Bitcoin, Hashcash killed two birds with one stone. It solved the double-spending problem in a decentralized way, while providing a trick to get new coins into circulation with no centralized issuer."[46] He noted that Back's Hashcash was not the first e-cash system, but a *decentralized* electronic cash system "might have been impossible without it."

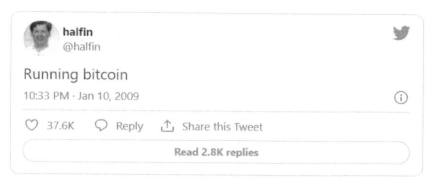

On January 9, 2009, Nakamoto launched the first version of the Bitcoin software. Finney was one of the first to download the program and experiment with it, as he was excited that someone had continued his work from RPOW.

On January 10, Finney posted the famous tweet: "Running bitcoin."[47]

The peaceful revolution had begun.

The Genesis Block

In February 2009, Nakamoto summarized the ideas behind Bitcoin on a peer-to-peer tech community message board:

> Before strong encryption, users had to rely on password protection to keep their information private. Privacy could always be overridden by the admin based on his judgement call weighing the principle of privacy against other concerns, or at the behest of his superiors. Then strong encryption became available to the masses, and trust was no longer required. Data could be secured in a way that was physically impossible for others to access, no matter what reason, no matter how good the excuse, no matter what.
>
> It's time we had the same thing for money. With e-currency based on cryptographic proof, without the need to trust a third-party middleman, money can be secure and transactions effortless. One of the fundamental building blocks for such a system is digital signatures. A digital coin contains the public key of its owner. To transfer it, the owner signs the coin together with the public key of the next owner. Anyone can check the signatures to verify the chain of ownership. It works well to secure ownership, but leaves one big problem unsolved: double-spending. Any owner could try to re-spend an already spent coin by signing it to another owner. The usual solution is for a trusted company with a central database to check for double-spending, but that just gets back to the trust model. In its central position, the company can override the users …

> Bitcoin's solution is to use a peer-to-peer network to check for double-spending ... The result is a distributed system with no single point of failure. Users hold the crypto keys to their own money and transact with each other, with the help of the P2P network to check for double-spending.[48]

Nakamoto had stood on the shoulders of Diffie, Chaum, Back, Dai, Szabo, and Finney and forged decentralized digital cash.

The key, in retrospect, was to combine the ability to make private transactions outside of the banking system with the ability to hold an asset that could not be debased via political interference.

This last feature was not top of the mind for the cypherpunks before the late 1990s. Szabo had certainly aimed for it with bit gold, and others inspired by Austrian economists like Fredrich Hayek and Murray Rothbard had long discussed getting the creation of money out of government hands. Still, generally, cypherpunks had prioritized privacy over monetary policy in early visions of digital cash.

The ambivalence toward monetary policy shown by privacy advocates is still evident today. Many left-leaning civil liberties groups that have protected American digital rights over the past two decades have either ignored or been outright hostile to Bitcoin. The 21-million-coin limit, scarcity, and "hard money" qualities proved foundational to achieving privacy through digital cash. Yet, digital rights advocacy groups have largely not recognized nor celebrated the role that proof of work and an unchanging monetary policy can play in protecting human rights.

To underline the primary importance of scarcity and predictable monetary issuance in the making of digital cash, Nakamoto released Bitcoin not after a government surveillance scandal, but in the wake of the Global Financial Crisis and ensuing money printing experiments of 2007 and 2008.

The first record in Bitcoin's blockchain is known as the "Genesis Block," and it is a political rallying cry. Right there in the code is a message worth pondering:

> The Times / 03 Jan / 2009 Chancellor on brink of second bailout for banks.

The message refers to a headline in *The Times* of London, describing how the British government was in the process of bailing out a failing private sector through increasing both sides of its balance sheet.[49] This was part of a broader global movement where central banks created cash for commercial banks out of thin air and, in return, acquired assets ranging from mortgage-backed securities to corporate and sovereign debt. In the United Kingdom, the Bank of England was printing more money to try to save the economy.

Nakamoto's Genesis Block statement was a challenge to the moral hazard created by the Bank of England, which was functioning as a lender of last resort for British companies that had followed reckless policies and were now in danger of going bankrupt.

The average Londoner would be the one to pay the price during a recession, whereas the Canary Wharf elite would find ways to protect their wealth. No British bankers would go to prison during the Great Financial Crisis, but millions of lower- and middle-class British citizens suffered. Bitcoin was more than just digital cash; it was an alternative to central banking.

Nakamoto did not think highly of the model of bureaucrats increasing debt to save ever-more financialized economies. As they wrote,

> The root problem with conventional currency is all the trust that's required to make it work. The central bank must be trusted not to debase the currency, but the history of fiat currencies is full of breaches of that trust. Banks must be trusted to hold our money and transfer it electronically, but they lend it out in waves of credit bubbles with barely a fraction in reserve.[50]

Nakamoto launched the Bitcoin network as a competitor to central banks, offering the automation of monetary policy and eliminating the smoky back rooms where small handfuls of elites would make decisions about public money for everyone else.

An Engineering Marvel

Initially, Back was impressed by Bitcoin. He read a technical field report that Finney published in early 2009 and realized Nakamoto had solved many of the problems that had previously prevented the creation of an effective digital cash. What perhaps impressed Back most, and made the Bitcoin project stronger than any he had ever seen, was that sometime in early 2011, Nakamoto vanished forever.[51]

In 2009 and 2010, Nakamoto posted updates, discussed tweaks and improvements to Bitcoin, and shared their thoughts on the future of the network, mainly on an online forum called BitcoinTalk. Then, one day, they disappeared and have never been conclusively heard from since.

At the time, Bitcoin was still a nascent project, and Nakamoto was still conceivably a central point of failure. In late 2010, they were still acting as a benevolent dictator. But by removing themselves — and giving up a lifetime of fame, fortune, and awards — they made it impossible for governments to be able to damage the network by arresting or manipulating its creator.

Before leaving, Nakamoto wrote:

> A lot of people automatically dismiss e-currency as a lost cause because of all the companies that failed since the 1990s. I hope it's obvious it was only the centrally controlled nature of those systems that doomed them. I think this is the first time we're trying a decentralized, non-trust-based system.[52]

Back agreed. Beyond being struck by the way Nakamoto revealed Bitcoin and then disappeared, he was especially intrigued by Bitcoin's monetary policy, which was programmed to issue a smaller and smaller number of coins each year until the 2130s, when the last bitcoin would be released and no further bitcoin would be issued. The total number of coins was set in stone at just shy of 21 million.

Every four years, the new bitcoin provided to winning miners as part of the block reward would be cut in half, in an event now celebrated as the "halving."

When Nakamoto was mining bitcoin in early 2009, the subsidy was 50 bitcoin. The subsidy dropped to 25 in 2012, 12.5 in 2016, and 6.25 in April 2020. As of late 2021, nearly 19 million bitcoin have been mined, and by 2035, 99% of all bitcoin will be distributed.[53]

The remainder will be distributed over the following century, as a lingering incentive to miners, who over time must shift to making their profit from transaction fees instead of the ever-shrinking subsidy.

Even in 2009, Nakamoto, Finney, and others speculated that Bitcoin's unique "hard-capped" monetary policy with a limit of 21 million total coins could make the currency extremely valuable if it one day took off.

In addition to the innovative monetary policy, Back thought the so-called "difficulty algorithm" was also a significant scientific breakthrough. This trick addressed a concern Back had originally had for Hashcash, where users with faster computers could overwhelm the system. In Bitcoin, Nakamoto prevented this from happening by programming the network to reset the difficulty required to successfully mine a block every two weeks, based on how long mining the last two weeks took.

If the market crashed, or some catastrophic event happened (for example, when the Chinese Communist Party kicked half the world's Bitcoin miners offline in May 2021), and the total global amount of energy spent mining bitcoin (the "hash rate") went down, it would take longer than normal to mine blocks.

However, with the difficulty algorithm, the network would shortly compensate and make mining easier. Conversely, if the global hash rate went up, perhaps if a more efficient piece of equipment were invented, and miners found blocks too quickly, the difficulty algorithm would shortly compensate. This seemingly simple feature gave Bitcoin resilience and has helped it survive massive seasonal mining turmoil, precipitous price crashes, and regulatory threats. Today, Bitcoin's mining infrastructure is more decentralized than ever.

These innovations made Back think that Bitcoin could potentially succeed where other digital currency attempts had failed. However, one glaring problem remained: Bitcoin was not very private.

Bitcoin's Privacy Problem

For the cypherpunks, privacy was a key goal. Previous iterations of e-cash, like the one produced by DigiCash, had even made the trade-off of achieving privacy by sacrificing decentralization. There could be immense privacy in these systems, but users had to trust the mint and were at risk of censorship and devaluation.

In creating an alternative to the mint, Nakamoto was forced to rely on an open ledger system, where anyone could publicly view all transactions. It was the only way to ensure auditability, but it sacrificed privacy. Back says that he still thinks this was the right engineering decision.

There had been more work done in the area of private digital currencies since DigiCash. In 1999, security researchers published a paper called "Auditable, Anonymous Electronic Cash," around the idea of using zero-knowledge proofs.[54] More than a decade later, the "Zerocoin" paper was published as an optimization of this concept. But to try to achieve perfect privacy, these systems made trade-offs.[55]

The math required for these anonymous transactions was so complicated that it made each transaction very large and each spend very time-consuming. One reason Bitcoin works so well today is that the average transaction is just a couple of hundred bytes. Anyone can cheaply run a server (known as a full node) at home and keep track of Bitcoin's history and incoming transactions, keeping power over the system in the hands of users. The system does not rely on a few supercomputers. Rather, regular computers can store the Bitcoin blockchain and transmit transaction data at low cost because data use is kept to a minimum.

If Nakamoto had used a Zerocoin-type model, each transaction would have been more than 100 kilobytes, the ledger would have grown huge, and only a handful of people with specialized datacenter equipment could have run a full node, introducing the possibility for collusion, censorship, or even a small group of people deciding to increase the monetary supply beyond 21 million. As the Bitcoin community mantra asserts, "Don't trust, verify."

Back said that he is, in retrospect, glad that he did not mention the 1999 paper to Nakamoto in his emails. Creating decentralized digital cash was the most crucial part: Privacy, he thought, could be programmed in later.

By 2013, Back decided Bitcoin had demonstrated enough stability to be the foundation for digital cash. He realized he could take some of his applied cryptography experience and help make it more private. Around this time, Back started spending 12 hours a day reading about Bitcoin. He said that he lost track of time, barely ate, and barely slept. He was obsessed.

That year, Back suggested a few key ideas to the Bitcoin developer community on channels like IRC and BitcoinTalk. One was changing the type of digital signature that Bitcoin uses from the Elliptic Curve Digital Signature Algorithm (ECDSA) to Schnorr. Nakamoto did not use Schnorr in the original design, despite the fact that it offered better flexibility and privacy for users, because it had a patent on it. But that patent had expired.

Today, Back's suggestion is being implemented, as Schnorr signatures were added to the Bitcoin network in November 2021 as part of the Taproot upgrade.[56] Once Taproot is used at scale, most types of wallets and transactions will look the same to observers (including governments), helping to fight the surveillance machine.

Confidential Transactions

Back's biggest vision for Bitcoin was something called Confidential Transactions (CTs). Currently, a user exposes the amount of bitcoin they send with each transaction. This enables auditability of the system — everyone at home running the Bitcoin software can ensure that there are only a certain number of coins — but it also enables surveillance to happen on the blockchain.

If a government can pair a Bitcoin address with a real-world identity, they can follow the funds. CTs would hide the transaction amount, making surveillance much more difficult or perhaps even impossible when used in conjunction with CoinJoin techniques.

In 2013, Back talked to a handful of core developers — the "Bitcoin Wizards," as he calls them — and realized it would be extremely difficult to implement CTs, as the community understandably prioritized security and audibility over privacy.

Back also realized that Bitcoin was not very modular — meaning one could not experiment with CTs inside the system — so he helped come up with the idea of a new kind of experimental testbed for Bitcoin technology, so that he could test out ideas like CTs without harming the network.

Back quickly realized that this would be a lot of work. He would have to build software libraries, integrate wallets, get compatibility with exchanges, and create a user-friendly interface. Back raised a $21 million seed round in Silicon Valley to try to build a company to make it all happen.

With seed funding in hand, Back teamed up with noted Bitcoin Core developer Greg Maxwell and investor Austin Hill and launched Blockstream, which is today a unicorn and one of the world's biggest Bitcoin companies. Back remains CEO and pursues projects like Blockstream Satellite, which enables Bitcoin users around the world to use the network without needing internet access.

In 2015, Back and Maxwell released a version of the Bitcoin "testnet" they had envisioned and called it Elements. They proceeded to enable CTs on this sidechain — now called Liquid — where, today, hundreds of millions of dollars are settled privately.

Bitcoin users fought what is known as the "Blocksize War" against big miners and corporations between 2015 and 2017 to keep the block size reasonably limited (it did increase to a new theoretical maximum of 4 megabytes) and keep power in the hands of individuals, so any plan to significantly increase the size of blocks in the future could be met with stiff resistance.[57]

Back still thinks it is possible to optimize the code and get CTs small enough to implement in Bitcoin. It is still several years away, at best, from being added, but Back continues on his quest.

For now, Bitcoin users can improve their privacy through techniques like CoinJoin, CoinSwap, and by using second-layer technology like the Lightning Network or sidechains like Mercury or Liquid.

In particular, Lightning — another area where Back's team at Blockstream invests heavily through work on c-lightning — helps users spend bitcoin more cheaply, quickly, and privately. Through innovations like this, Bitcoin serves as censorship-resistant and debasement-proof savings tech for tens of millions of people around the world and is becoming more friendly for daily transactions.

In the near future, Bitcoin could very well fulfill the cypherpunk vision of teleportable digital cash, with all of the privacy aspects of cash and all of the store-of-value ability of gold. This could prove one of the most important missions of the coming century, as governments experiment with and begin to introduce central bank digital currencies (CBDCs).

CBDCs aim to replace paper money with electronic credits that can be easily surveilled, confiscated, auto-taxed, and debased via negative interest rates. They pave the way for social engineering, pinpoint censorship and de-platforming, and expiration dates on money.

But if the vision for Bitcoin's digital cash can be fully achieved, then in Nakamoto's words, "We can win a major battle in the arms race and gain a new territory of freedom for several years."[58]

This is the cypherpunk dream, and Adam Back is focused on making it happen.

Chapter III

The Hidden Costs of the Petrodollar System

In its growth from conceptual white paper to trillion-dollar asset and global tool for human rights, Bitcoin has attracted an enormous amount of criticism. Detractors focus on its perceived negative externalities: energy consumption, carbon footprint, lack of centralized control, and inability to be regulated. Regardless of the validity of these arguments, few critics stop to think comparatively about the negative externalities of the world's current financial system of dollar hegemony.

This is, in part, because many critics see Bitcoin as a Visa-like payment platform, and they analyze its performance and costs by "transactions per second." But bitcoin is not a fintech company competing with Visa. It is a decentralized asset competing to be the new global reserve currency, aiming to inherit the role gold once had and the role the dollar holds today.

The world relies on the US dollar and US treasuries, giving America unparalleled and outsized economic dominance. As of 2021, nearly 90% of international currency transactions are in dollars, 60% of foreign exchange reserves are held in dollars, and almost 40% of the world's debt is issued in dollars, even though the United States only accounts for around 20% of global GDP.[59] This special status that the dollar enjoys was born in the 1970s through a military pact between America and Saudi Arabia, leading the world to price oil in dollars and stockpile US debt. As we emerge from the 2020 pandemic and financial crisis, American elites continue to enjoy the exorbitant privilege of issuing the ultimate monetary good and numéraire for energy and finance.

The past few decades have seen a vast global rise in economic activity, population, democratic progress, technological advancement, and living standards, but there are many flaws in this system that are rarely spoken about and that weigh heavily on billions of people across the globe.

What *would* the world look like with an open, neutral, predictable base money instead of one controlled and manipulated by one government representing only 4% of the planet's population? This chapter explores the seldom discussed and staggering downsides of the current system in the hope that we can replace it with something more fair, free, and decentralized.

These pages will cover the rarely discussed creation of the petrodollar and lay out how America has supported brutal dictators, compromised its national security, harmed its industrial base, propped up and protected the fossil fuel industry, and even waged conflict abroad, all to bolster the dollar's status as global reserve currency. While this strategy worked for US leaders for many decades, today the world is inexorably moving to a more multipolar financial structure, and possibly, toward a bitcoin standard.

Birth of the Petrodollar

The British Empire was the unquestioned economic hegemon of the 19th century but began to lose steam early in the 20th century, especially after World War I. The United States emerged much healthier than war-torn Europe and as the country with by far the most gold. By the outbreak of World War II, the dollar had unquestionably eclipsed the pound as the world's most influential national currency.

Governments still relied on gold as the underlying global reserve currency, but US and UK policymakers were determined to create a more "flexible" system. In the waning months of World War II, leaders from 44 countries gathered in a hotel in Bretton Woods, New Hampshire, to choose a new financial bedrock. British economist John Maynard Keynes pushed the idea of the *bancor*, a global unit of account that many nations would manage. But the United States preferred the idea of the dollar at the center, pegged to gold at $35 per ounce. Since international trade deficits still had to be settled in gold, America's substantial control of the world's gold supply and favorable balance-of-payments position provided the leverage to get its way.

Over the coming decades, the world shifted to the Bretton Woods standard, with national currencies pegged to adjustable dollar amounts, where the United States was trusted to custody and hold enough gold to prop up the whole system. Up until the early 1960s, it did a reasonably good job. Dollars replaced gold in central bank vaults across the world. becoming the dominant medium of exchange for international settlement, backed by a promise to pay in gold. America became the largest creditor nation and an economic powerhouse. However, beginning with Cold War expenditures and amplifying after the assassination of President John F. Kennedy, the US government chose a path of huge social and military spending. With President Lyndon B. Johnson's "great society" social programs and the invasion of Vietnam, US debt skyrocketed. Unlike World War II or the Korean War, Vietnam was the first American war waged almost entirely on credit.[60]

As Niall Ferguson wrote in *The Ascent of Money*, "In the late 1960s, U.S. public sector deficits were negligible by today's standards, but large enough to prompt complaints from France that Washington was exploiting its reserve currency status to collect seigniorage from America's foreign creditors by printing dollars, much as medieval monarchs had exploited their monopoly on minting to debase the currency."

French economist Jacques Rueff called this the "monetary sin of the West," and the French government coined the term "exorbitant privilege."[61] Poor British fiscal policy forced a devaluation of the pound in 1967, and the French, fearing that unsustainable American spending would result in similar negative results, wanted their gold back before a dollar devaluation.

By 1971, US debt had simply grown too high. Just $11 billion in gold backed $24 billion in dollars.[62] That August, French President Pompidou sent a battleship to New York City to collect his nation's gold holdings from the Federal Reserve, and the British asked the United States to prepare $3 billion worth of gold held in Fort Knox for withdrawal.[63] In a televised speech on August 15, 1971, President Richard Nixon told the American people that the United States would no longer redeem dollars for gold as part of a plan that included wage and price freezes and an import surcharge in an attempt to save the economy.[64] Nixon said closing the gold window was temporary, but few things are as permanent as temporary measures.[65] As a result, the dollar was devalued by more than 10%, and the Bretton Woods system ceased to exist. The world entered a major financial crisis. When asked about the impact that the "Nixon Shock" would have on foreign nations, Nixon made his position clear: "I don't give a shit about the lira."[66]

As David Graeber wrote in *Debt: The First 5,000 Years*, "Nixon floated the dollar in order to pay for the cost of a war in which he ordered more than four million tons of explosives and incendiaries dropped on cities and villages across Indochina … the debt crisis was a direct result of the need to pay for the bombs, or, to be more precise, the vast military infrastructure needed to deliver them. This was what was causing such an enormous strain on U.S. gold reserves."

Post-1971, for the first time in history, the world was in a pure fiat standard. The dollars held by central banks across the globe lost their backing, and there was a geopolitical moment where US dominance was called into question and where a multipolar financial world was a distinct possibility. Adding even more pressure, in 1973 the Arab petroleum exporters of the Organization of the Petroleum Exporting Countries (OPEC) decided to quadruple the price of world oil and embargo the United States in response to its support for Israel during the Yom Kippur War. In just a few years, a barrel of oil rose from less than $2 to nearly $12. Faced with double-digit inflation and declining global faith in the dollar, Nixon and his Secretary of State and National Security Advisor Henry Kissinger came up with an idea that would allow them to keep "guns and butter" going in the post–gold standard era and alter the fate of the world.

In 1974, they sent new Treasury Secretary William Simon to Saudi Arabia "to find a way to persuade a hostile kingdom to finance America's widening deficit with its newfound petrodollar wealth." Simply put, a petrodollar is a US dollar paid to a petroleum exporter in exchange for oil. As a *Bloomberg* report says, the basic framework was "strikingly simple."[67] The United States would "buy oil from Saudi Arabia and provide the kingdom military aid and equipment. In return, the Saudis would plow billions of their petrodollar revenue back into Treasuries and finance America's spending." This was the moment that the US dollar was officially married to oil.

On June 8, 1974, in Washington, Kissinger and Crown Prince Fahd signed agreements establishing Saudi investment in the United States and American support for the Saudi military. Nixon flew to Jeddah a few days later to continue working out details.[68] Declassified documents later revealed that the US government confidentially enabled the Saudis to purchase treasuries "outside regular auctions and at preferential rates."[69] In early 1975, they purchased $2.5 billion of treasuries, beginning a spree that would later become hundreds of billions of petrodollars invested in US debt. Decades later, Gerry Parsky, who was deputy to Treasury Secretary Simon at the time, said that this "secret arrangement with the Saudis should have been dismantled years ago" and that he was "surprised the Treasury kept it in place for so long."[70] But even so, he said he "has no regrets" since "doing the deal was a positive for America."

By 1975, other OPEC nations followed Saudi Arabia's lead. If you wanted to buy oil from them and their store of nearly 80% of world petroleum reserves, you had to pay in dollars.[71] This created new demand for America's currency at a time of global uncertainty and even at a time of continued inflation. Industrializing nations needed oil, and to get it, they now had to either export goods to the United States or buy dollars in foreign exchange markets, increasing the dollar's global network effect. In 1974, 20% of global oil was still transacted in the British pound, but that number fell to 6% by 1976. By 1975, Saudi imports of US military equipment had risen from $300 million to more than $5 billion.[72] Oil prices, boosted by the premium that came with being able to be sold for dollars, would remain sky high until 1985.[73]

Impact of the Petrodollar

In his research on the petrodollar, political economist David Spiro argues that historic OPEC dollar profits were "recycled" into US treasuries to subsidize the "debt-happy policies of the U.S. government as well as the debt-happy consumption of its citizenry."[74] Petrodollar recycling — which later transformed into recycling by countries like Japan and China — over time pushed down interest rates and allowed the United States to issue debt very cheaply. This system was created and held in place not by pure economics but by politics through the pact with Saudi Arabia. As Alan Greenspan said in 1977, reflecting on his experience as chairman of the Council of Economic Advisers during President Gerald Ford administration, the Saudis were "non-market decision-makers."[75]

Graeber points to petrodollar recycling as an example of how US treasuries replaced gold as the world's reserve currency and ultimate store of value. The kicker, he explains, was that "over time, the combined effect of low interest payments and inflation is that these bonds actually depreciate in value ... economists prefer to call it 'seigniorage.'"

Since its creation in 1974, the petrodollar system has changed the world in many significant ways, including,

The creation of a tight alliance between the United States and the Saudi Arabian dictatorship, as well as other tyrannies in the Gulf region.

The steep rise of the "eurodollar" shadow global economy as petrodollars (created outside the control of the Federal Reserve) flooded banks in London and North America and were then recycled into US treasuries or loaned back out to emerging markets.[76]

The financialization of the American economy as the artificially strong dollar made exports uncompetitive, hollowed out the middle class and shifted focus from manufacturing to finance, technology, defense, and services, all while increasing the leverage in the system.

Additional stress on the Soviet Union, which was now faced with an increasingly dollarized world market, where the United States could print money to buy oil, but it had to dig oil out of the ground.[77]

Painful issues for emerging market economies, which became mired in dollar-denominated debt that was difficult to pay back and stuck in a system that prioritized dollar accumulation over domestic investment, harming income and triggering debt crises everywhere, from Mexico to East Asia to Russia to Argentina.[78]

Steady growth of the oil and fossil fuels industries at the expense of nuclear power and regional energy independence.

And, of course, the continuation of the United States as a military-financial hegemon and the ability of the United States to run humongous deficits to finance wars and social programs, all in part paid for by other countries.

There are petrodollar theory critics who say the phenomenon is largely a myth. They say the dollar has been dominant simply because there has been no competition. Dean Baker from the Center for Economic and Policy Research has said that "while it is true that oil is priced in dollars and that most oil is traded in dollars, these facts make relatively little difference for the status of the dollar as an international currency for the economic well-being of the United States."[79]

Meanwhile, modern monetary theorists like Warren Mosler and Stephanie Kelton downplay the importance of the petrodollar, saying "it doesn't matter" or "it's irrelevant" as it does not limit what the United States can do domestically and that, internationally, it does not matter what oil is priced in because countries can just swap currencies before purchase. Critics point to the fact that the dollar was already the world reserve currency before 1973, that the pricing of commodities in dollars is "just a convention," and that "there would be no real difference if the euro, the yen, or even bushels of wheat were selected as the unit of account for the oil market."[80] They also say the dollars involved in the oil trade are "trivial" compared with other sources of demand.

But the decision of Saudi Arabia and OPEC to price their oil exports in dollars and invest the profits in US debt was not a strict market decision, and not one of fortune or happenstance. It was a political one, done in exchange for protection and weapons, and one that sparked countless additional network effects that over time solidified the dollar as the world's reserve currency. When countries are forced to exchange their own currencies for dollars to buy oil, this strengthens that trading pair for that country, extending US influence beyond energy markets. In *Debt*, Graeber does mention the debate over whether or not oil sales denominated in dollars give any seigniorage to the United States but says that, regardless, what ultimately matters is "that U.S. policymakers seem to feel the fact that they are symbolically important and resist any attempt to alter this."

American Foreign Policy and the Petrodollar

In October 2000, Saddam Hussein did attempt to alter the petrodollar system when he announced that Iraq would sell oil in euros, not dollars.[81] By February 2003, he had sold 3.3 billion barrels of oil for 26 billion euros.[82] With his French and German trading partners, the "petroeuro" was born which, if expanded, would help a euro market develop against lots of other currencies, boosting the euro's strength and eroding the dollar's exorbitant privilege.[83] But one month later, the United States, aided by the United Kingdom, invaded Iraq and overthrew Saddam. By June, Iraq was back to selling oil in dollars again.[84]

Did America go to war to defend the petrodollar? This possibility is almost never discussed in retrospective analyses of the war, which tend to fixate on questions of Iraq's alleged weapons of mass destruction stockpile, human rights abuses, or terror links. But at the time, the euro was actually seen by many as a realistic challenger to the dollar.[85] Given that the ouster of Hussein, in retrospect, helped deter change and give the petrodollar system many more years of dominance, it seems like one of the more reasonable explanations for the most mysterious war in modern American history.

In 2021, the journalist Robert Draper appeared on Ezra Klein's show to discuss his new book, *To Start a War: How the Bush Administration Took America into Iraq*.[86] With a decade of hindsight, they covered many of the possible motives for the invasion but ultimately called it a "war in search for a reason." To this day, there is no consensus for why exactly the United States invaded Iraq, and the official reasons have proven to be completely contrived.

According to former Treasury Secretary Paul O'Neill, by February 2001, President George W. Bush's administration was already talking internally about the logistics of invading Iraq.[87] "Not the why," he said, "but the how and how quickly." Blueprints were already being made. On 9/11, just a few hours after the attacks, Deputy Secretary of Defense Paul Wolfowitz ordered a comprehensive study of Saddam Hussein's ties to terrorist organizations.

Over the next 18 months, the Bush administration sold the war effort, and by March 2003 had achieved wide support, especially with the help of Secretary of State Colin Powell who spent his credibility on a PR campaign at the United Nations and on news television. Both houses of Congress supported the removal of Hussein, including Senators Hillary Clinton, John Kerry, Harry Reid, and Joe Biden. In the media, outlets ranging from "Fox News" to *The New York Times* supported the invasion, as did 72% of the American people in polling in the weeks leading up to the invasion.[88] The public rationale was clear: Saddam Hussein was dangerous, was believed to have weapons of mass destruction (WMDs), could slip them to Al Qaeda, and needed to be stopped. At the time, Vice President Dick Cheney said, "There can be no doubt that Saddam has WMDs."[89] The war was also marketed as a humanitarian effort and was given the name Operation Iraqi Freedom. But in retrospect, America did not invade Iraq to promote human rights. There was no connection to Al Qaeda or 9/11. And, despite Cheney's promises, no WMDs were ever found.

Other motives were and continue to be discussed, including countering Iran, which makes little sense given most Iraqis are Shia and their political structure ended up tilting more toward Iran during the occupation, and given that the United States had *supported* Hussein in previous decades for this very purpose.[90] The flimsy nature of the official reasons for war led many to believe that oil was the root cause. This would not be unusual. Over the past 150 years, natural resources have been at the root of many wars, invasions, and occupations that have shaped our world, including the Scramble for Africa, the Great Game in Central Asia, the Sykes–Picot Agreement, the overthrows of Mossadegh and Lumumba, and the first Gulf War.

George W. Bush, Colin Powell, Secretary of Defense Donald Rumsfeld, Coalition Provisional Authority Paul Bremer, and British Foreign Secretary Jack Straw all publicly denied that the war was about oil. But former Federal Reserve Chairman Alan Greenspan wrote in his memoir that "I am saddened that it is politically inconvenient to acknowledge what everyone knows: the Iraq war is largely about oil" and told the media that removing Hussein was "essential" to secure world oil supplies.[91] Former head of US operations in Iraq General John Abizaid said, "Of course it's about oil; we can't really deny that."[92] And former Defense Secretary Chuck Hagel admitted in 2007 that "people say we're not fighting for oil. Of course we are."[93]

It is true that America, even at the time, did not consume a large portion of its oil from the Middle East.[94] In 2003, the United States received most of its oil from domestic production plus sources in Canada, Mexico, and Venezuela. In this light, invading Iraq simply to "control" oil seems like a weak reason. And most could easily predict that a hot war would damage Iraq's oil infrastructure, creating long delays before production could get back up to speed. But perhaps the war was not waged for oil in a general sense, but specifically, to defend the petrodollar system.

In post-invasion May 2003, weeks before Iraq switched back to selling oil in dollars, Howard Fineman wrote in *Newsweek* that the Europeans were debating the United Nations over whether or not to continue searching for the WMDs that they could not find.[95] He reported that the real dispute was not "about WMDs at all. It's about something else entirely: who gets to sell — and buy — Iraqi oil, and *what form of currency will be used to denominate the value of the sales.*"

As Graeber asks:

> How much did Hussein's decision to buck the dollar really weigh into the U.S. decision to depose him? It's impossible to say.

His decision to stop using 'the enemy's currency,' as he put it, was one in a back-and-forth series of hostile gestures that likely would have led to war in any event; what's important here is that there were widespread rumors that this was one of the major contributing factors, and therefore, no policymaker in a position to make a similar switch can completely ignore the possibility. Much though their beneficiaries do not like to admit it, all imperial arrangements do, ultimately, rest on terror.

With hindsight, the early 2000s were an era when, presented with the challenge of the euro, it made sense for the United States to take action. And so, whether or not the defense of the petrodollar was the main aim of the invasion of Iraq, the outcome was the same: Other countries saw what was done to Hussein and were, for many years, careful about pushing their own "petro" currency. And the oil? Iraq's production more than doubled from 2001 to 2019, eventually climbing to 5 million barrels of oil per day. The financial world has become multipolar over the past few years, but as of 2019, more than 99% of crude oil trade payments were still in dollars.[96]

Dictators, Inequality, and Fossil Fuels

Beyond the Iraq War, there are several other key and much more obvious negative externalities of the petrodollar system. American support for the Saudi dictatorship is one. Even though 15 of the 19 hijackers on 9/11, plus Osama Bin Laden himself, were Saudi, the US government has forcibly resisted any attempt to investigate the Saudi regime for involvement in the attack and instead invaded and bombed other countries in retaliation. The petrodollar is one of the primary reasons why the murderous House of Saud is still in power.

In 2002, former US Ambassador to Saudi Arabia Chas Freeman told Congress: "One of the major things the Saudis have historically done, in part out of friendship with the United States, is to insist that oil continues to be priced in dollars. Therefore, the U.S. Treasury can print money and buy oil, which is an advantage no other country has."[97] In 2007, the Saudis warned the United States that it would drop the petrodollar system if they pursued the "NOPEC" Congressional bill that would enable the US Justice Department to pursue OPEC governments under antitrust laws for manipulating oil prices. The bill was never enacted.

According to a 2016 *New York Times* story, Saudi Arabia "told the Obama administration and members of Congress that it will sell off hundreds of billions of dollars' worth of American assets held by the kingdom if Congress passes a bill that would allow the Saudi government to be held responsible in American courts for any role in the Sept. 11, 2001, attacks."[98]

In 2020, then-Attorney General William Barr prevented the name of a Saudi diplomat linked to 9/11 from entering the public domain because such a disclosure risked "significant harm to the national security."[99] In the wake of the murder of *Washington Post* columnist Jamal Khashoggi, President Donald Trump would not push for action against Mohamed bin Salman (MBS). On *NBC News*, he said, "I'm not like a fool that says, 'we don't want to do business with them.'"[100] President Joe Biden has also refused to penalize MBS directly, even though he has been presented with evidence from his own intelligence agencies showing that he ordered Khashoggi's murder, saying it would be too costly for America.[101]

These are just a few examples of how — despite the Saudi regime's bloody war in Yemen, its torture of female political prisoners, and its assassination of Khashoggi — America's relationship with the kingdom remains steadfast and protected at the highest levels. According to research from the Stockholm International Peace Research Institute, "Between 2015 and 2019, the six Gulf states bought more than one-fifth of arms sold globally, with Saudi Arabia, the United Arab Emirates (UAE), and Qatar ranking as the world's first, eighth, and tenth largest arms importers. Saudi Arabia alone purchased one-quarter of total US arms exports during that period, up from 7.4% in 2010–2014." The oil pricing pact first made in 1974 remains strong in 2021, despite very different times.

Domestically, certain factions of America have prospered because of the petrodollar, but the impact on the median American has been negative. As was recently written in *Foreign Affairs*, "the benefits of dollar primacy accrue mainly to financial institutions and big businesses, but the costs are generally borne by workers. For this reason, continued dollar hegemony threatens to deepen inequality as well as political polarization in the United States."[102] Corporations and asset owners have benefited most in the system's low-interest rate environment. As Yakov Feygin and Dominik Leusder argue in "The Class Politics of the Dollar System," "Dollar primacy feeds a growing American trade deficit that shifts the country's economy toward the accumulation of rents rather than the growth of productivity. This has contributed to a falling labor and capital share of income, and to the ballooning cost of services such as education, medical care, and rental housing."[103]

As the petrodollar system kept international demand for the dollar artificially strong throughout the decades, America's manufacturing base became weak and uncompetitive and lost jobs overseas. Normally, a currency that is too strong ends up creating a deficit issue and is forced to devalue to sell exports. But, as investor and analyst Lyn Alden points out in "The Fraying of the US Global Currency Reserve System," that has never happened with the United States due to the continual payment of its deficit by foreign nations.[104] In 1960, the economist Robert Triffin identified this phenomenon, now known as the Triffin dilemma: To remain the world's reserve currency, the United States must provide global liquidity by running increasingly large deficits, which one day must undermine faith in the dollar.

The US financial sector has ballooned, now accounting for 20% of GDP, compared with 10% in 1947.[105] This financialization has enriched the asset-holding elite on the coasts while ruining Rust Belt workers who deal with stagnant wages. This has sparked populism and extreme inequality, where the US average wealth is still relatively high among advanced nations, but its median wealth is relatively low. In this way, Alden and other macroeconomic thinkers like Luke Gromen argue that dollar hegemony actually hurts the United States in its competition with nations like China, which are able to continually borrow dollars to stockpile hard assets, and consolidate control over important global supply chains.

And then, of course, we have the petrodollar itself and its impact on the environment. As *Reuters* reported, "If dollar-denominated oil usage declines in favour of home-produced wind, solar or hydro energy sources, then the swelling pool of global petrodollars recycled and invested by the world's big oil producers since the end of the gold standard in the 1970s may drain with it."[106] Simply put, a global shift to renewables would put a big dent in the demand for fossil fuels, which could deal a knockout blow to the petrodollar system and the ability for the United States to run up massive deficits without consequences. Oil interests have aggressively resisted attempts to develop nuclear energy and renewables over the past few decades.[107] The US military continues to be the single largest consumer of petro resources.

When the global reserve currency is literally reliant on the sale of oil, the world has a massive carbon emissions problem. Not to mention the fact that, as discussed, the petrodollar is defended by the US military's global presence, which has a carbon output the size of a mid-sized nation, is exaggerated in size by America's need to protect the dollar, and is boosted by the oil price-spiking wars it fights on various continents.[108] It is truly impossible for the petrodollar system to be green when it is based on black gold.

Bitcoin and a Multipolar World

US foreign policy has kept the petrodollar dominant for many decades, but its power is inarguably beginning to wane. Many Americans, including this author, have been incredibly privileged by this system, but it will not last forever.

Gromen calls the petrodollar system a "company town," where the United States has enforced control over oil pricing with threats and violence.[109] After the fall of the Soviet Union, he says, America could have restructured the system and held another Bretton Woods, but it held on to the unipolar moment. Beyond protecting the system against disruptions like the petroeuro, Gromen says that America extended the life of the system by launching NAFTA and helping China join the World Trade Organization in 2001. These steps allowed the United States to continue exporting manufacturing and treasuries abroad in exchange for goods and services. He notes that in 2001, China's treasury holdings were $60 billion, but rose to $1.3 trillion a decade later. From 2002 to 2014, America's biggest export was treasuries, where foreign central banks bought 53% of the issuance, using it as a new form of gold. But since then, China and other governments have been divesting treasuries and pushing us toward a new system, in expectation of that "gold" losing value. According to Gromen, they realized if dollars were still priced in oil as the United States continued to run higher debt-to-GDP ratios (up from 35% in the 1970s to more than 100% today), the price of oil would eventually skyrocket.[110] Europe was not able to disrupt the petrodollar system in the early 2000s, but over time the United States' hegemony and ability to stop other nations from pricing oil in their own currencies has eroded.

More and more countries are denominating oil trade in other currencies, like euros, yuan, and rubles, partly because they fear reliance on a weakening system and partly because the US government continues to use the dollar as a weapon.[111] The American sanction system is incredibly powerful, as it can cut enemies off from the SWIFT payment network or from the World Bank or International Monetary Fund (IMF).[112] As the *Financial Times* reported, "By using American banks as a cudgel against Russia, Joe Biden has shown a willingness to weaponize the U.S. financial system against foes, continuing a tactic honed during the Obama years and dramatically ramped up under Donald Trump."[113]

In early 2021, President Biden publicly denounced the Nord Stream 2 Pipeline project, which would build on the momentum Russian President Vladimir Putin already has with Rosneft, pricing more than 5% of the world's oil in euros by connecting Europe and Russia.[114] Team Biden reportedly wanted to "kill" the project, and its officials have commented that dollar primacy remains "hugely important" to the administration and that "it's in our national interest because of the funding cost advantage it provides, [because] it allows us to absorb shocks ... and gives us enormous geopolitical leverage."[115] This is a striking indication of just how important the petrodollar system remains politically to the United States, 50 years after its creation, despite critics who say the world uses dollars for pure market reasons.

Many countries want to escape from US financial control, and this desire is accelerating global de-dollarization. For example, China and Russia are, as of 2020, transacting in dollars just 33% of the time, versus just 98% seven years ago.[116] China is expanding oil trading denominated in yuan, and many worry about the Chinese Communist Party's new "DC/EP," or digital yuan project, being a ploy for increased international use of the yuan. Meanwhile, former European Commission President Jean-Claude Juncker has said, "It is absurd that Europe pays for 80 percent of its energy import bill — worth 300 billion euros a year — in U.S. dollars when only roughly 2 percent of our energy imports come from the United States."[117] While the dollar is still dominant, trends point to other major currencies gaining traction in the coming years.

Beyond a shift to a multipolar currency world, another threat to the petrodollar could be the SDR, or "Special Drawing Right," employed by the IMF, which is based on the dollar, euro, pound, yen, and yuan. Inspired by Keynes and his failed *bancor* idea from Bretton Woods, the SDR has achieved more traction in the past few years, with more than 200 billion units in circulation and another 650 billion possibly being created.[118] But few governments in a position of economic power would willingly hand their monetary control over to an unelected alphabet soup organization.

As for gold, the world is not going back. As Jacques Rueff wrote in the 1960s, "Money managers in a democracy will always choose inflation; only a gold standard deprives them of the option."[119] The left-wing historian Michael Hudson explains that in the 1970s, he tried to make an apolitical case for the US government to revert to the gold standard, teaming up with the right-wing scholar Herman Khan: "He and I went down and gave a presentation to the U.S. Treasury, saying, 'gold is a peaceful metal because it's a constraint on the balance of payments. If countries had to pay their balance-of-payments deficit in gold, they would not be able to afford the balance-of-payments costs of going to war.'[120] That was pretty much accepted and that was why the United States basically responded, 'That's why we're not going back to gold. We want to be able to go to war and we want the only alternative to hold central bank reserves to be the United States Dollar.'" Gold is, by the account of most economists today, simply too restrictive.

A 2020 study in the *Journal of Institutional Economics* posited four potential future monetary outcomes for the world: continued dollar hegemony, competing monetary blocs (where the European Union and China act as counterweights to the United States), an international monetary federation (where at the top of the international hierarchy stands no longer a state, but the Bank for International Settlements and the SDR), and international monetary anarchy, where the world shrinks into less connected islands.[121] The authors, however, miss a fifth possibility: A bitcoin standard where the digital currency becomes the global reserve asset.

Since its creation in 2009 by Satoshi Nakamoto, bitcoin has grown in value from less than a penny to more than $40,000, spreading to every major urban area on Earth as a store of value and, in some places, a medium of exchange. In the past year, Fortune 500 companies like Tesla, sovereign wealth funds like Singapore's Temasek, and even the government of El Salvador have started to accumulate bitcoin or invest in Bitcoin companies. Many call it digital gold.[122]

We are very possibly witnessing the birth of not just a new ultimate store of value but also a new global base money, neutral and decentralized like gold, but unlike gold in that it is programmable, teleportable, easily verifiable, absolutely scarce, and resistant to centralized capture. Any citizen or any government can receive, store, or send any amount of bitcoin simply with internet access, and no alliance or empire can debase that currency. It is, as some say, the currency of enemies: Adversarial parties can use the system and benefit equally without detracting from each other.

As bitcoin's value goes up against fiat currencies, more and more corporations and individuals could begin to accumulate. Eventually, more governments might, too. At first, they might add it as a small part of their portfolio alongside other reserve currencies, but eventually, they might try to buy, mine, tax, or confiscate as much as they can.

Born at a time when the previous world reserve currency had reached its apex, Bitcoin could introduce a new model, with more possibilities but also more restraint. Anyone with an internet connection will be able to protect their wages and savings, but governments, unable to so easily create money on a whim, will not be able to wage forever wars and build massive surveillance states that contradict the wishes of their citizens. There could be a closer alignment between the rulers and the ruled.

The big fear, of course, is that America will not be able to finance its exorbitant social programs and military spending if there is less global demand for the dollar. If people prefer the euro or yuan or bonds from other countries, the United States in its current form would be in big trouble. Nixon and Kissinger designed the petrodollar so that the United States could benefit from global demand for dollars tied to oil. The question is, why can't there be a global demand for dollars tied to bitcoin?

No matter the base money, there could still be fiat currency and government debt, priced according to the economic power and bitcoin position of those countries. In the emerging Bitcoin world, America is leading in many categories, whether it is infrastructure, software development, actual holdings by the population, and, increasingly given current trends, mining. America is also built on liberty, equality of opportunity, free speech, private property, open capital markets, and other values and institutions that Bitcoin reinforces and reverberates. If Bitcoin did eventually become the global base money, then America is in a position to capitalize on that transformation.

This means no more reliance on dictators and secret pacts in the Middle East, no more need to threaten or invade other countries to preserve dollar primacy, and no more opposing nuclear or renewable energy technology to protect the fossil fuel industry. Unlike the petrodollar system, Bitcoin could very well accelerate the global energy transition to renewables, with miners always choosing the cheapest sources of electricity, and trends pointing to cheaper renewables in the future.[123]

Under the bitcoin standard, everyone would play by the same rules. No government or alliance of governments can manipulate the monetary policy. But any individual can opt into a nondiscretionary, rules-based currency and control a savings instrument that has historically appreciated versus goods and services. This would be a dramatic net benefit for most people on Earth, especially when considering that billions today live under high inflation, financial repression, or economic isolation.

This transition may not be so pleasant for authoritarian regimes, which are more closed, tyrannical, violently redistributionist, and isolated than liberal democracies. But in this author's view, that would be a good thing, and one that could force reforms where activism alone has failed.

The world's multipolar drift is inevitable. No one country can, in the near future, gain as much power as America had at the end of the 20th century. The United States will still be a powerhouse for a long time to come, but so will China, the European Union, Russia, India, and other nations. And they may compete in a new monetary system that moves away from the petrodollar and all of its costly externalities: A neutral bitcoin standard that plays to the strengths of open societies, does not depend on dictators or fossil fuels, and is ultimately run by citizens, not the entrenched elite.

Chapter IV

Bitcoin Is a Trojan Horse for Freedom

From Ulysses to Satoshi

If Bitcoin does eventually spread throughout the global financial system, how exactly would it accomplish this unlikely feat?

In Book II of the "The Aeneid," Virgil foreshadows a potential mechanism of Bitcoin adoption. In one of the most iconic plotlines of classical mythology, he explains how trickery and subterfuge can be more persuasive than traditional weapons and violence. [124]

The Greek forces, having failed to capture the City of Troy after a decade-long siege, attempt an ultimate attack on their enemy not by strength, but by guile, through a clever plan hatched by Ulysses.

In the fields outside of Troy's impregnable walls, the Greek army departs but leaves behind a massive wooden horse. A lone remaining soldier leads the Trojans to believe that the horse is a tribute to Minerva, the goddess of war and strategy, and is an apology for the blood that the Greeks spilled. The Trojans think their rival has sailed off in surrender, and — despite warnings from Cassandra and Laocoön, who gives us the famous saying, "Beware of Greeks bearing gifts" — they bring the horse into the city as a trophy of victory. Blinded by zeal, they think it will make them invincible.

Little do they know, the horse is packed with armed soldiers, who, under cover of night, slip out and open the gates for their comrades waiting outside, who had hidden their fleet behind an island in the nearby sea. The Greeks sack the city, and Troy falls, defeated from the inside by its new treasure.

Thousands of years later, the "Trojan Horse" has been popularized in computer science as a malicious program disguised as a helpful update. But it is also an effective metaphor for how Bitcoin stealthily co-opts actors who do not care about or do not like freedom to promote it anyway.

The meme begins with wealthy individuals, corporations, and, now, even governments, which see bitcoin as glittering digital gold. Out of self-preservation and greed, they are incentivized to buy, mine, or one day tax this new prize to accumulate the soundest money and gain an advantage over their rivals. Bitcoin does, after all, on its exterior, look very appealing: It is the best-performing financial asset in the world over the past 13 years.

Bitcoin's trillion-dollar success is attracting interest from the rich and powerful everywhere from Wall Street to Beijing to Silicon Valley. In the last year, Bitcoin FOMO has seeped into the minds of professional investors, corporate treasury managers, and even sovereign wealth funds and presidents (see Chapter V) who do not want to get left behind.[125]

As a 2020 *Bloomberg* headline announced, "Bitcoin Is Displacing Gold as an Inflation Hedge."[126] The article shows how value is demonstrably flowing out of gold and into bitcoin. Companies like Tesla and Square star among a growing group of dozens adding the new currency to their balance sheets.[127] NYDIG is introducing the multi-trillion-dollar insurance industry to bitcoin as a hedge against declining yields.[128]

As MicroStrategy CEO Michael Saylor says, Bitcoin is the hardest money and acts, over time, like a one-way street. Just as no Argentine wants to "cash out" their US dollars back into pesos, ultimately, few will want to "cash out" their bitcoin back into dollars. It is early days now, but it is hard to overstate the eventual impact that bitcoin will have not just on the $10 trillion gold market but the $20 trillion art and collectible market, the $100 trillion stock market, the $225 trillion real estate market, and the $250 trillion bond market over the coming decades.[129]

Number Go Up and Freedom Go Up

But Bitcoin is not just "number go up" (NGU) technology. Hidden behind the eye-popping gains is a powerful "freedom go up" (FGU) technology that its new adopters are, knowingly or not, pushing forward. NGU and FGU are inextricable.

Bitcoin's decentralized digital cash did not emerge from Y Combinator, but rather it was the holy grail of the cypherpunks, the group of civil liberties advocates (the stars of Chapter II) concerned about how personal freedoms could survive the great electronic transformation of society. Their goals were to separate money from governments and corporations, check the growth of the global surveillance state, and preserve human rights in an increasingly digital age. Satoshi Nakamoto's greatest trick was to animate these aspirations into something that looks like and functions as digital gold.

So, while, yes, Bitcoin gives anyone — regardless of their nationality, status, wealth, gender, race, or beliefs — access to the best savings technology on the planet, it *also* gives them unstoppable, programmable money that cannot be debased or censored and that fights surveillance and confiscation. Dissidents, democracy protestors, opposition leaders and independent journalists worldwide are beginning to realize this, from Minsk to Lagos to Los Angeles to Buenos Aires.[130]

World leaders speak pretty words about human rights, but when they get down to brass tacks, the platitudes are swept aside. As a reminder of this cold reality, refer to the dictators on the United Nations "Human Rights" Council or the Financial Action Task Force (FATF); the list of household corporate names sponsoring the 2022 genocide Olympics; or the roster of Wall Street icons who attend Saudi Arabia's "Davos in the Desert" events.[131]

As human rights activists know well, it can be hard to effectively promote freedom in a society that willingly sells morals out for profit. Bitcoin sneaks in and rewires the system from the inside, aligning profit seeking with permissionless financial liberation.

A Stealthy Revolution

But who conjured this horse and dragged it to the city gates?

This time, it was not a plotting army camped outside Wall Street. Nakamoto's creation spreads not by force but by voluntary choice. The financial establishment is simply beginning to like the way it looks. It promises great riches and that is no mirage: It will continue to deliver. But most of the elites do not realize what they are bringing into the inner sanctum.

In a world of increasingly centralized control and social engineering, Bitcoin provides a check by empowering the individual at the expense of the authority. Yes, billionaires and dictators can buy a lot of bitcoin, but they cannot control the system as they can with fiat money. Unlike with the dollar, euro, or yuan model, they cannot tweak issuance, censor transactions, make special rules or bailouts for the aristocracy, or perform mass remote confiscation or debasement.

Of course, governments and corporations will try to hijack Bitcoin for their own ends. Some already have. *The Blocksize War* is a book that chronicles the attempts of Chinese billionaires and Silicon Valley titans to forcibly transform Bitcoin from a freedom tool into a retail payments mechanism. These attempts failed because the network lacks a single point of control.[132]

And Bitcoin is more clever than any Trojan Horse that Virgil or Homer could have imagined. In this plotline, each individual can custody their bitcoin by moving it to an address they control with a set of digital keys. Unlike in 1933, when the US government was able to seize the gold of citizens with Executive Order 6102 by attacking points of custody, that does not work if hundreds of thousands or even millions of Americans are holding their keys.

The adoption process is creating millions of new fortresses in cyberspace, all more secure than Troy.

The ancient Greeks and Romans would appreciate the irony of mega-corps and governments willingly and even enthusiastically letting the one thing that can erode their growing power into their city gates. NGU is one hell of a drug.

In some ways, Bitcoin has succeeded so far by hiding behind its strangeness. Just as the Trojans were baffled by the monstrous horse standing outside their city gates, the establishment has balked at Bitcoin. It has gone from $0 to $40,000 with most people on Earth not batting an eye. Less than 2% of humans have adopted it but more than that, it seems, have mocked it. Even in early 2022, virtually all top economists, political scientists, diplomats, and central bankers still dismiss Bitcoin as something that will not work or is not worth their time. This dismissal has allowed Bitcoin to grow largely unfettered. And now the horse has been rolled inside the city.

Transforming Self-Interest into Greater Freedom

What the Davos establishment thought was just NGU tech was also FGU tech. This alignment of incentives is sorely needed in a world that depends too often on altruism and empathy. Take the global struggle for human rights. The international business community mostly overlooks the Chinese Communist Party's Uyghur gulags, subjugation of Hong Kong, staggering surveillance state, and colonization of Tibet. In this scenario, self-interest and freedom are in conflict: To save profits, companies, celebrities, athletes, and heads of state sacrifice morals and either cave to Beijing's demands or keep silent about its brutality. Even philanthropists are failing on freedom. The "Effective Altruism" movement, for example, completely ignores civil liberties.[133]

With Bitcoin, self-interest and freedom are aligned. Even if one has zero altruism, as one buys or mines bitcoin, they drive up the network's security model and make a more robust freedom tool for everyone else. Refreshingly, Bitcoin does not care about one's intentions. It enables greater liberty and empowerment not by some ambitious humanitarianism but by each participant's honest self-preservation.

And this dynamic continues to expand. For instance, bitcoin exchanges today are adopting the Lightning Network not for privacy reasons — they are adopting it to reduce fees — but they are spreading the freedom tech anyway as they popularize a way to transact off-chain on an onion-routed, surveillance-busting second layer.

On the horizon, a Bitcoin upgrade called Cross Input Signature Aggregation (or SigAgg for short) could eventually incentivize exchanges to engage in collaborative spends which would further fluster the surveillance state.[134] Again, corporations will not push this privacy improvement for moral reasons but to improve their bottom line. This is Bitcoin's game theory: transforming greed into freedom.

Tesla stacking bitcoin does not just help Tesla. It increases Bitcoin's global network effect, driving up the interest and price, attracting more developers and improving UX, increasing the number of miners and strengthening network security, and multiplying new HODLers in a giant positive feedback loop.

To recap: Bitcoin will continue to gain worldwide adoption because of its effectiveness as digital gold, but hidden within the prized Trojan Horse is a remarkable freedom technology. At this point, the reader may think Bitcoin proponents must be saying, "Quiet in the back! Keep the noise down. We just need to last a few more hours until midnight, and then we can pop ourselves out of this horse and let the rest of our army into Troy."

But it is already too late. There is nothing the Trojans can do.

Authoritarian regimes will inevitably want to "stack sats" (as bitcoin saving is commonly called). Some already have found Bitcoin a helpful tool to escape sanctions, including Venezuela, Iran, and North Korea. But over time, the officials tasked with storing and spending the bitcoin will learn what it is — money the government cannot control — and they will share that knowledge with others, trickling it down through society. Just like "Trojan Horse" computer viruses, Bitcoin will infect authoritarian regimes, appearing helpful at first but proving debilitating over time.

Some miss this and misinterpret the Trojan Horse allegory. A small but influential chorus of American critics say Bitcoin is an enemy of a free society like the United States, and that it is unpatriotic and even treasonous.[135] In reality, Bitcoin will be a lot more difficult for authoritarian, closed societies like China to deal with than open ones like America. We already have property rights, checks and balances, and free speech — all values that Bitcoin reinforces (see Chapter XI). But these three things are diametrically opposed to what the Chinese Communist Party is trying to achieve. Bitcoin will, over time, erode the control that tyrannies like the CCP have over their citizens. And given that Bitcoin checks arbitrary power and the surveillance state, it may help steer open societies in a better direction, too.

Today, tens of millions of people already own bitcoin. They are happy about the value it gives and the value it will continue to provide. They own a piece of digital real estate on a board that cannot be expanded.

But most do not read the fine print. They did not see the newspaper headline buried in the Genesis Block, or notice details like Satoshi Nakamoto's chosen birth date of April 5 (the same date FDR passed Executive Order 6102 to make holding gold illegal in America), or study the history of the cypherpunks (see Chapter II).

At its core, Bitcoin was built to break us free from the existing system. It is the red pill. And all adopters are going to play a part in the revolution, whether they want to or not.

Many authoritarians, central bankers, and establishmentarians may already realize what is concealed in Bitcoin's Trojan Horse. There are plenty of modern Laocoöns and Cassandras saying, "We need to stop this thing!" But, just like in the kingdoms of lore, these words will fall on deaf ears.

The prize glitters too bright.

Chapter V

The Village and the Strongman

As Fast as Lightning

It was late August 2021, and I was standing in a small coffee shop just off an unpaved street, in a Central American village with no traffic lights, an hour's drive west on curvy jungle roads from the nearest major city.

I had walked there from my hotel, passing a half dozen restaurants with sheet metal and tarp roofs, trekking carefully down a steep and muddy ravine that locals use as a path to get from the main road to the beach. It was hot and humid in El Zonte, El Salvador, and the nearby ocean was rough and tinted brown from the sediment rushing into the sea from the summer rains.

There was no supermarket in town, and most of the residents I passed on the street had no bank accounts. Despite the lack of infrastructure and it being low season, the town was buzzing with activity. There was an excitement and feeling of hope and opportunity that had not been felt before. Something special was happening.

The coffee shop's barista, Karla, had just finished making a perfect cappuccino and was preparing my bill on a tablet on the counter in front of me. She spun it around in my direction and presented a digital QR code. I took out my iPhone, opened my bitcoin wallet, scanned the pixelated image, and pressed send. Less than two seconds later, Karla's tablet flashed green. The transaction was settled.

I had paid for my coffee instantly, without using the banking system. I bought the drink, in effect, with digital cash.

Just as if I had paid with a $5 bill, Karla did not learn anything about me in the transaction. There were no third parties to vacuum up my identity, no social engineering programs learning about my preferences, no ability for corporations or governments to know my last purchase or predict my next one. In fact, better than a $5 bill, we did not have to deal with change.

I did not need to tell any bank or any financial company about my trip to El Salvador. I was not worried about my credit card not working. In El Zonte, one today can glimpse the potential of a peer-to-peer global financial system. I was impressed by how many merchants accept bitcoin, how easy it was to pay, and how familiar most people were with the technology.

I wanted to tip Karla, so she took out her personal phone and flashed a QR from her own bitcoin wallet. I scanned it and sent her $10 worth of BTC, which traveled instantly to her wallet over the appropriately named Lightning Network. I told her that if she saved these 25,000 satoshis for 10 years, she could probably buy a car with them in 2031.

Karla had only been using Bitcoin for a few months, but seemed to understand that I was not joking. Like most Salvadorans — even the ones already in the Bitcoin economy — she's still not sure about the new currency and is still taking her salary in dollars. But she told me that she was saving her tips in bitcoin, and that all things considered, it was "worth the risk."

Five days after my chat with Karla, a new national law came into effect in El Salvador, making Bitcoin legal tender alongside the US dollar. First announced on June 5, 2021, by President Nayib Bukele, the move stunned the world and made headlines across the biggest media outlets.

Many Bitcoin enthusiasts had predicted that, one day, governments would start adopting Bitcoin. But most thought the state would convert fiat to BTC to hold as a store-of-value reserve asset on a central bank balance sheet. Virtually no one foresaw that the first government to officially adopt Bitcoin would use it as a payments network and as a medium of exchange.

With bitcoin now legal tender, Salvadorans do not have to pay capital gains taxes if their BTC rises in value against the dollar, and they can use it to settle debts with the banking system. If the government rollout proceeds as promised, they will soon be able to use Satoshi Nakamoto's invention to buy goods or services anywhere in the country.

However, on the morning of the law's implementation on September 7, 2021, skepticism filled the air. Would the state-run "Chivo" app work? Would Lightning be a part of the system? No one knew, as the administration, led by the young populist Bukele, had kept citizens in the dark about the rollout's details.

Just a few days before the law came into effect, I was one of many who doubted it would go smoothly. I certainly did not think that Chivo wallet functionality — which was kept a mystery to even project insiders until the last second — would integrate Lightning. So, on the morning of launch day, I was shocked to receive a message from a Salvadoran friend, telling me that they had somehow pulled it off.

He gave me his Lightning address and I sent him $5 of BTC. The funds settled from California to El Salvador instantly, with fees so small that my wallet said they were $0.00. Moments later, my friend used the Chivo wallet to send the $5 back to me, again, with virtually no fees.

Compare this to the typical experience of a Salvadoran trying to receive a remittance from the United States through Western Union, where one might have to get on a bus, spend an hour waiting in line, go through an intensive KYC process, only to receive $92 out of a $100 payment due to extortionate fees.

The humanitarian implications that Lightning apps could have for Salvadorans are massive. The nation's GDP is 23% dependent on remittances, and the population is more than 2.5 times as reliant on these flows as is the rest of Central America.[136] The funds mainly originate in the United States where more than two million Salvadorans live and regularly send money back to their families.

Later that morning, *Bitcoin Magazine* journalist Aaron van Wirdum walked into a McDonald's in San Salvador expecting that it would not be ready to take bitcoin.[137] To his enormous surprise, when he asked to pay in bitcoin, the cashier presented him with a QR code that directed him to a webpage with a Lightning invoice. He paid it instantly and went to enjoy his *desayuno típico*, astonished. The magic internet money that van Wirdum had written about for close to a decade was now usable as an easy and fast means of payment not just at McDonald's, but at Starbucks, Pizza Hut, and Wendy's.

Van Wirdum conducted another demo a few days later, going to a Chivo cashpoint to try and withdraw $20.[138] When the QR code popped up on the ATM screen, he took a photo of it and sent it to a friend abroad who then paid the invoice with *their* bitcoin wallet, thousands of miles away. Without any fuss, the machine spit out a crisp $20. The only ID check van Wirdum encountered during the transaction was a simple text verification, which he passed with a phone number whose SIM card he had bought with cash from a merchant in El Salvador. This possibility would have blown the mind of any mid-1990s cypherpunk.

Launch day was a mixed bag. The government had to take Chivo offline early in the morning to iron out last-minute issues, and it was only released onto app stores gradually throughout the day. Some users reported problems with signing up and analysts spotted a variety of design issues. Concerns over bugs, surveillance, and rug pulls abounded.

Bitcoin itself crashed 17% intraday against the dollar, leading Bukele to joke that he was "buying the dip" as he announced that the state had bought 550 bitcoin with public funds. The amount, roughly $21 million at time of purchase, was possibly done with respect to Bitcoin's "21 million" monetary policy. The global media largely mocked the purchase, along with the rest of the rollout, which was derided everywhere from *WIRED* to *The Wall Street Journal*.

But at the end of the day, the Chivo app worked. Some of the more glaring bugs were fixed, even with a sense of humor. And debate over the logistics of the rollout obscured the bigger picture: A government had officially begun connecting its population to an open monetary network, a remarkable event in geopolitical history. Just as England once pioneered central banking and government money as notes, here was El Salvador, marking the start of perhaps a new era with a decentralized digital currency as legal tender. Bukele could have pursued a central bank digital currency, or a monetary partnership with China, but instead chose free and open-source monetary software.

Two of the most visible outcomes of the Bitcoin law's implementation are the state-run Chivo app — which any Salvadoran can download then use their national ID number to claim $30 of bitcoin gifted by the government — and the Chivo ATMs, which will apparently number close to 200, dotting El Salvador and locations inside the United States with physical places for citizens to convert Chivo balances to US dollars, for free.

Bitcoin supporters and critics alike were surprised when the Bukele administration revealed that the rollout would begin just three months after it first announced the law. Politically, Bukele's New Ideas party has a supermajority in parliament and was able to pass the law quickly despite protests from the opposition. But technologically, no country had ever done this before.

Details have surfaced that in July and August 2021, a collection of companies — ranging from Athena to OpenNode to BitGo to IBEX Mercado — helped the Bukele administration create, market, and activate the Chivo wallets, Chivo cash points, and merchant relationships across the country. The government claims to have allocated approximately $223 million to finance the Bitcoin rollout, all taken from funds loaned by the Central American Development Bank.

Over the summer, the Bukele administration operated in an opaque manner. Until the last second, no one knew which companies were hired to build the apps, ATMs, and backend. No one knows what the government is going to do with the bitcoin it bought. No one knows exactly how the $150 million trust — established to provide liquidity for citizens who wish to trade their bitcoin for dollars — is going to work. Instead of sharing these details in a traditional manner, Bukele leaks them live, on occasion, through his Twitter account, personifying digital populism.

At the same time that the Bitcoin bill came into effect, Bukele's government also announced that it would be purging more than 100 judges. The Supreme Court (which Bukele had stacked with his own supporters earlier this year) also ruled that he would be able to run for another presidential term in 2024, violating the constitution. The Human Rights Foundation, where I am employed, has been one of many international organizations to strongly criticize Bukele's anti-democratic actions.

The contradiction is striking. On the one hand, there is a government rolling out a new currency to its people that cannot be debased, censored, or remotely confiscated. On the other hand, the same government is following the blueprint Hugo Chávez used in the 2000s in Venezuela to consolidate power, only much faster.[139]

The situation is filled with contradictions: A grassroots, peaceful, village-based movement started in El Zonte inspired a national, forced, top-down law. A money beyond government control was pushed by a government that wants to control more and more of Salvadoran society. A populist leader forced into law a bill that would not have stood a chance in a country like the United States, where the financial system exerts such a high degree of control over elected politicians. These paradoxes make quick analysis difficult. It is not a black-and-white picture.

In 10 years, will the world look back at the Bitcoin law as a failed experiment or as a visionary decision? Only time will tell. Meanwhile, debates over Bitcoin adoption will rage on between promoters and naysayers.

Zooming out, it seems borderline impossible that El Salvador of all places would be the first country to roll out a next-generation financial technology like Bitcoin. But in history books, the claim will not be held by Japan, the United States, Germany, or even Brazil. Instead, students decades from now might read about El Salvador, or, as the country's name reads when translated from Spanish, "The Savior."

An Unlikely Place for a Financial Revolution

Sandwiched between Guatemala and Honduras, El Salvador — the smallest and most densely populated country in Central America, with an average GDP per capita of around $3,500 — is a most unlikely ground zero for a financial revolution.

And yet, baristas, *pupusa* sellers and surf instructors in the village of El Zonte are more familiar with the concept and use of Bitcoin than most titans on Wall Street and in Silicon Valley; and they have a far deeper understanding of *what it is* than most central bankers or Fortune 500 CEOs.

How a country where the average monthly income is less than $300 ended up beating all of the world's industrial powers in being first to adopt the

Lightning Network as a national payments system seems the stuff of a Hollywood film. But, as they say, the truth is stranger than fiction.

Historically, El Salvador has suffered a fate similar to many Global South nations, where despite rich agricultural resources, the country must import food. Large-scale commercial operations have dominated El Salvador over the past century, harnessing the best agrarian pockets for export to global consumers, at the expense of locals. The fight over land ownership culminated in 1932 with *La Matanza*, the country's most deadly massacre, where the army killed more than 30,000 peasants.[140]

Most of the country's land consolidation historically revolved around coffee, which was known as *el grano de oro*, or the grain of gold. By the 1920s, the crop constituted 90% of the country's exports.[141] By the late 1970s, coffee accounted for half of El Salvador's GDP, making the country the world's third-largest producer.[142] Roughly 10% of the country's territory is still covered in coffee plantations.[143] The phrase "Banana Republic" is a cruel one, but in some ways accurately describes the fate of many Salvadorans, as they have often fallen subservient to the interests of multinational corporations and foreign powers.

In 1979, a brutal civil war broke out, rising up from the decades-old conflict over land and external control, pitting a right-wing regime against leftist guerillas. Salvadorans were victims of a Cold War–proxy conflict between the United States and USSR. The United States backed the Salvadoran regime with weapons and cash to fight off revolutionaries who vowed to claim back land from alien corporations.

The official American narrative was that these guerillas were part of a communist plot backed by the USSR, Cuba, and East Germany.[144] And for many years, the Soviets had indeed supported the radical left-wing FLMN with arms and training. At the end of President Jimmy Carter's administration, the United States responded by backing the "largest counterinsurgency campaign since the Vietnam War."[145]

The Salvadoran regime was sensationally brutal but gained constant support from the United States in its war against Marxist terror. In 1980, Archbishop Oscar Arnulfo Romero, who had used his platform to criticize the junta — calling for them to "stop the repression" — was assassinated while giving a private mass.[146] The shooting was orchestrated by Roberto D'Aubuisson (also known as "Blowtorch Bob" after one of his favorite methods of torture), who had graduated from the School of Americas, an infamous military training center at Fort Benning, Georgia. After the murder, national violence metastasized.[147]

The United States ended up giving $5 billion to the Salvadoran regime during the 1980s to keep communism at bay.[148] The flow of funds was frozen briefly in 1980 by an outgoing Jimmy Carter, after regime forces raped and murdered three American nuns and a US missionary, but were activated again shortly before Ronald Reagan took office.[149] When the decision to renew support was publicly questioned, President Reagan's policy advisor Jeanne Kirkpatrick defended the move, saying that the nuns "were not just nuns ... [they] were also political activists."[150]

In the early 1980s, more US aid dollars and military support flowed to El Salvador than to any other country, save Israel or Egypt. The US embassy staff in San Salvador was the size of its staff in New Delhi, despite serving a country that was 200 times smaller. El Salvador was, in Washington's eyes, a critical line of defense against Soviet influence.[151]

The 12-year civil war destroyed the country's infrastructure, setting manufacturing, commerce, agricultural production, and living standards back decades. By 1998, for example, the purchasing power of urban Salvadorans was only one-third of what it was in 1980. For a war that was in part a conflict over wealth and land distribution, the tragedy was that inequality and real wages were worse off after the war than before.[152]

More than one million people were displaced and more than 75,000 were killed, often in barbaric fashion as a warning to the rest of the population.[153] According to a UN truth commission, some 85% of victims were murdered by US-backed paramilitaries and death squads.[154]

Historians are still digging up the remains of those killed by US-backed forces in the early 1980s, including at the site of one horrific incident in El Mozote. In this mountainous area of small villages in December 1981, more than 900 people were massacred by the Atlacatl Battalion, a special armed unit that had been trained on American soil.[155] Two hundred and forty-eight of the dead were children less than six years old. It is considered the largest massacre in modern Latin American history and a "central parable" of the Cold War.[156]

First-hand accounts from El Mozote are painful to read. The unspeakable cruelty of the rampaging soldiers is vividly captured in a *New York Times* report, written by a journalist who visited the area a few weeks after the atrocity.[157] And yet, a few months later, Reagan certified to the US Congress that "although serious problems remain, we conclude that the Government of El Salvador is making a concerted and significant effort to comply with internationally recognized human rights."[158]

Defenders of US involvement during El Salvador's civil war justify the bloodshed by saying that if Americans had not intervened, the country would have fallen the way of communist Cuba. But 75,000 lives and 15 years of lost economic activity is a heavy price to pay. Over the past 25 years, El Salvador has been healing and recovering, but it remains without strong rule of law and is still marked by an extraordinary amount of violence.

More than 500,000 Salvadorans fled during the 1980s, establishing a strong flow of migrants to the United States. But after the civil war ended in 1992, President Bill Clinton allowed special rules for Salvadoran migrants to expire.[159] Tens of thousands were sent back home empty-handed. Many of these young men formed and joined gangs, for example, MS-13, which was founded in Los Angeles and only pushed to El Salvador by Clinton's decision.[160]

Between 2000 and 2017, approximately 2.5 million people were murdered in Latin America, Central America, and the Caribbean compared to 900,000 killed in wars in Syria, Iraq, and Afghanistan over that same time.[161] El Salvador lies at the center of this violence, mostly as a result of gang warfare. In 2015, it was considered the most dangerous country in the world not at war.[162]

According to a 2015 report,

> Fear permeated daily life, particularly in poor communities where the gangs stake out most of their territories. Residents who cross the invisible line between them — usually an innocuous-looking bridge, road or park — risk beatings or even death. Taxi drivers dread wrong turns that can lead to robbery or kidnap. Shopping trips, lovers' trysts and football matches are all circumscribed by safety concerns. Even staying at home is no guarantee of safety...
>
> Shopkeepers, hairdressers and restaurant owners are frequently assailed by extortionists, who typically threaten arson attacks or to cut off the ears or fingers of spouses or children. Parents watch with rising alarm as their sons and daughters approach pubescence — and the inevitable pressures that follow to join the local gang. There is often no one to turn to for support: teachers are intimidated by students and police are afraid to enter many communities.[163]

Regardless of one's views on Bitcoin, it is stunning that a place that was spoken about like a war zone not so long ago is now being discussed worldwide as a pioneer of a new financial technology.

The Trauma of Dollarization

A national economic struggle has accompanied El Salvador's post-war violence. Today, coffee, cattle, lumber, and fishing make up a commodity export base that cannot meet the needs of the growing population. The country has seen progress since the end of the war, but it has also been unable to settle its external debt and remains reliant on foreign aid, borrowing, and remittances. Economic growth has also been set back by catastrophic natural disasters, with destruction from Hurricane Mitch in 1998 causing $400 million in damage and a 7.6 magnitude earthquake in 2001 causing $2.8 billion in damage.[164]

As the Salvadoran saying goes, "Our greatest export is our people."[165] Research points to remittances as one of the major reasons for El Salvador's decline in poverty over the past 25 years.[166] The flows — making up roughly a quarter of GDP — are vital, but all of that time and effort expended by Salvadorans in Los Angeles, Washington, or New York goes toward building things and providing services to Americans, not Salvadorans at home.

In 2001, the Salvadoran government implemented the US dollar as legal tender, in a move that quickly replaced the traditional colón as the national currency. President Francisco Flores announced the transition in November 2000, and implementation occurred on January 1, 2001, just 39 days later. The country was 98% dollarized in only 18 months.[167] The sudden shift gave no space for public discussion and raised suspicion that the move was made to benefit elites, not the majority of the population.

Unlike in Ecuador, which was dealing with severe inflation, dollarization in El Salvador was not brought in to fix an emergency. Inflation was 4.3% in the year 2000.[168] Rather, dollarization was a macroeconomic prescription. Advocates said it would help preserve the purchasing power of workers and protect them from government monetary abuse. It was billed as something that would make commerce easier, prevent debt monetization, attract foreign investment, and lower interest rates. Banks especially could benefit, as lower interest rates meant they could borrow more cheaply from abroad and lend out inside the country for profit.

However, according to Silvia Borzutzky, a professor of political science at Carnegie Mellon University who studied El Salvador's dollarization, the policy "had extremely negative effects on the lowest-income groups without doing much to help the overall economy."

A 2002 survey conducted by the Instituto Universitario de Opinion Publica showed that only 2% of Salvadorans considered dollarization an achievement, while 62.2% thought it had been damaging to the nation. Another 2002 survey by the University of Central America found that 61% of Salvadoran respondents said that dollarization had a "negative effect on their personal economic situation." According to a University of Central America paper, "The most benefited sector from the dollarization process has been the financial system, which no longer faces the risk that its payments will be increased from possible devaluation decided by the political circle."

At the time of dollarization, 21% of El Salvador's population could not read and an even larger percentage had trouble pricing things in the dollar economy, where everything was divided by the 8.75 colón-to-dollar exchange rate. According to a contemporary study,

> Businesses were not permitted to increase prices in dollars over what they cost in colónes. Thus, in the formal market, prices are rounded up to the next cent, and inflation from rounding up is minimal. In the informal market, where the poor operate, the situation is entirely different ... there is almost no regulation, so vendors have often set prices in dollars much higher than what they were charging in colónes. One participant observed, 'some people take advantage of the change, and for what used to be seven colónes they now charge a dollar.' From seven colónes to a dollar is 25 percent inflation.[169]

Even more loss of purchasing power came as a result of the difference in spending habits among poorer classes, who buy things several times per day as opposed to once a week or month like the middle or upper classes do, resulting in a more constant exposure to rising prices. The major stated benefit of dollarization — lower interest rates — even escaped lower-income populations, as the poor do not typically get loans from banks but rather from the extortionate informal sector. According to data from 2002, 70% of the credit in El Salvador was lent at the time by four banks, with loans to 400 clients constituting 60% of the total borrowing.

Other frustration from dollarization came from a feeling that the policy was pulled over the population quickly and without consultation, and that the native currency was replaced by an imperial one, from a foreign power that had helped a brutal regime destroy the country during the civil war.

Negative attitudes about dollarization persisted for many years. In a 2007 *Los Angeles Times* report, a potato seller named Janette was interviewed, saying that she used to sell 100 pounds every day but now was "lucky to move that much in a week." She was quoted as saying, "Life is harder now. The dollar is a curse."

In the mid-2000s, average Salvadoran wages rose just 4%, while food and drink prices rose 14%. Farmers and agricultural vendors faced the struggle of not just higher commodity prices but less demand for their products. Another character in the *Los Angeles Times* story is a chicken farmer who was forced to cull her flock and abandon her business as a result of dollarization, resulting in an outcome where she could no longer even afford to eat chicken herself.[170]

In a fate shared by other countries that use a more powerful economy's currency — like, for example, the CFA countries of West and Central Africa (see Chapter VI) — dollarization meant that the Salvadoran government could not tweak the currency to keep goods and services competitive, and that wages remained expensive compared to those of other countries.[171] Five years after dollarization, El Salvador's imports had grown "nearly three times faster than exports," which were harmed by the rise of China, which devalued its currency to stay competitive.[172]

Even today, 20 years later, when the macro effects of dollarization seem to have been positive on El Salvador as a whole, there are negative trends that do not show up in the official data. For example, when the US government monetizes debt in order to pacify financial crises and artificially boost the value of American stocks and real estate, US citizens are provided stimulus checks, and US corporations receive bailouts. But these lifelines are not extended to the average Salvadoran, who feels the cost of rising prices, without the benefits.

Dollarization is a painful memory for many Salvadorans, and the idea of a new top-down currency change is scary. The sudden announcement and implementation of the Bitcoin law in summer 2021 brings back old fears.

Usually, when a government changes the currency, it is not good for the people.

Will this time be different?

The Village

One could say that the unlikely story of Bitcoin adoption in El Salvador all started about 15 years ago, before anyone had ever heard of Satoshi Nakamoto, when Jorge Valenzuela and Ramon "Chimbera" Martinez got lucky.

Growing up in El Zonte, a seaside village of no more than 3,000 people, they told me that there were precious few opportunities for young men like them to do something different. Their families had lived in the area for generations, taking care of property for wealthy landowners from the capital or fishing off the coast.

"My father is a fisherman, Jorge's father is a fisherman," Martinez said. "We live in a natural paradise, with warm weather, good food … and friendly people, but our families never had real economic opportunities."

Their lives might have continued along that path had it not been for a social worker, who came to El Zonte and planted a seed of inspiration in them, taught them about hope, and tried to set them on a new path. "We grew a dream to change our reality," Martinez said.

The social worker's investment paid off. Valenzuela and Martinez found careers in building restaurants, managing properties, and teaching people how to surf. Bit by bit, they helped build El Zonte into what it is today.

"We learned that to change our community, we had to change other people first," Martinez said. "If you just change on your own, it's not enough."

But the road was tough. Martinez said that while he and Valenzuela had benefited from mentorship, most people around them did not.

"We lost friends, we lost family, we started to see kids that didn't dream anymore," said Martinez. The economic depression and gang violence was bad but that was not the main problem. It was the missed opportunities that really hit hardest.

In 2006, Martinez and Valenzuela, along with their friend Hirvin Palma, created a program that they call a "point of light in the darkness," which aimed at creating families for kids without them.

"A lot of kids don't have a father," Martinez said. "So, we created a social fabric to tackle that, to create change through children."

They would mentor kids who lost their way and give them a new support network. Over the years, some of the hundreds of students they have worked with have made it to university, instead of into gangs. They called the program "Fill Up the Tank of Love."

"We all have a tank," Martinez said, "but it needs to be full."

The problem was, Martinez and Valenzuela's programs started to lose steam a few years ago, as cash flows began to dry up. One day, Martinez said, an American came to them with an idea.

After the civil war, surfers and backpackers started to come to the area around El Zonte. One of those tourists was a Californian named Mike Peterson.

"When we first met Mike," Martinez said, "he was one of the few that actually started spending time with us locals, who started to believe in this community."

Around 2013, the three started working together in earnest, providing scholarships, mentorships, and jobs for youth in the area.

In 2019, an anonymous donor came to Peterson and promised a large gift to the community, under the condition that it would be sent in bitcoin and was spent in El Zonte in a circular fashion.

"We didn't know anything about Bitcoin," Martinez said, "but we are dreamers, and we believed in Mike."

The first vendor to accept bitcoin was Valenzuela's mother, who goes by Mama Rosa. In 2019, she started selling pupusas for bitcoin to kids who had earned sats (community lingo for satoshis, the smallest denomination of bitcoin, with 100 million in 1 BTC) through Martinez and Valenzuela's programs for doing community work.

One evening, I walked down the street in El Zonte with a group of friends to Mama Rosa's pupuseria. It is a modest road-side operation, a few feet away from the local highway, but serves as a popular gathering point for locals and is a place with special history in the El Zonte story.

We ordered a variety of pupusas and paid in bitcoin. At the end of our meal, I sat down with Mama Rosa and asked her: What was it like when her son said she should start taking payments in a magic internet money? Did she think he was crazy?

She laughed. "I didn't think he was crazy, but I was hesitant about the currency," she told me.

The last time the government made a big currency change, she had suffered. When I brought up dollarization, Mama Rosa grimaced, as if in physical pain.

"We didn't want the dollar; we wanted to keep the colón," she said. After the transition began, she encountered significant price inflation. "It was very difficult," she said.

So, at first, with this in mind, she was not sure about Valenzuela's plan. But she believed in him and started accepting the new currency, and more notably, started saving some of it on her phone wallet.

Today, she keeps all of her earnings in bitcoin. She knows it is volatile but has accepted that feature. She proudly pointed behind her to an impressive truck that was sitting next to the restaurant and told me that she was able to buy it recently as the result of the growth of her bitcoin savings. When I asked her if she was surprised at the rise of bitcoin's value, she laughed.

"Of course, I'm surprised," she said. "I'm making bank!"

She told me that she is incredibly proud of her son, not only because he made smart and wise decisions, but because he is improving the lives of so many people.

I asked her what advice she would give her fellow countrymen and women who are afraid of the Bitcoin law.

"There is a lot of mistrust of anything new," she said. "On top of that, scammers have been here calling people, trying to defraud them out of their bitcoin by asking them to send it to them for a good or service and then disappearing. To get the full benefits, we need education and knowledge."

"But in the end," she said, "there's nothing to fear. It's just another currency."

Bitcoin Beach

Valenzuela told me that the initial idea behind Bitcoin Beach had little to do with remittances. The goal was to create a circular economy. A key part of the effort was the construction of Hope House, a modern multistory building in El Zonte where education around Bitcoin could happen.

But a big challenge remained. Merchants said: "If I can't touch it, I won't use it."

So, at first, Bitcoin Beach leadership gave paper claims to students and others who were part of the program. If bitcoin dipped, Hope House would make them whole. At first, the students all wanted to trade their claims for dollars. But eventually, they started keeping more and more of their claims, and eventually learned how to be their own bank and hold actual bitcoin in their own wallets.

Valenzuela told me that when they finally convinced the first small merchants in town to accept bitcoin, it was the first time most of them transacted digitally, and the first time they started to think seriously about savings.

"Remember," Valenzuela said, "people here don't have bank accounts."

"In our communities, we have no financial literacy courses, and no one provides advice to the youth," Valenzuela said. "But Bitcoin is a great teacher."

Families started saving up for assets for the first time in their lives.

"People here don't have access to stocks or real estate," said Valenzuela.

Bitcoin helped bring inclusion to the financial system. Valenzuela said that you could feel the community starting to save for the future, and that it was a big psychological shift.

Bitcoin Beach educated a group of community leaders to help people navigate the waters of how to use the new currency. Valenzuela called them a "tribe for financial inclusion." Thanks to them, he said, "the outcome is that kids are not as interested in going to the dark side. They are more interested in the future."

This is why they named Bitcoin Beach's flagship new building — nicely built and well-equipped by any standard — Hope House. Martinez said it is part of a dream about a future where people would have the freedom to choose their destiny.

Thanks to the new paradigm, Martinez said, people worldwide are now talking about El Salvador in a different way. It is not just about gangs and money laundering. People are talking about a rhetoric and narrative that is optimistic.

"People talk about the food, the pupusas, the surfing, the weather, the investment options — it's becoming a land of opportunity," Martinez said.

"When we first brought an ATM machine in," Martinez said, "People laughed. They aren't laughing now."

"We're finally first in something besides murder rate. All of this innovation happened not in Europe or the United States or even Silicon Valley," Martinez said, "but right here in El Zonte. Other towns and cities are now calling us, asking us for our secret. There is no secret. Only hard work and community building."

Today, Bitcoin Beach is sharing its philosophy with other communities in the region, one by one. Valenzuela and Martinez go to new towns every week, help people set up wallets, and give them a bit of bitcoin. If the government did this, they said, people would be skeptical. But because they are villagers like them, they are open.

"It's beautiful that the entire country can now have access to the financial system. This is what we hoped for 15 years ago," Martinez said, with a big smile. "The beginning of the dream has been achieved. Our hometown is not a scary spot on a map anymore, but an exciting place to go. So now we are celebrating."

"But the Bitcoin law is just the beginning. It's not going to make our work any easier," Martinez said. "It took us two and a half years to build a community around this idea with just 3,000 people. A country of six million? That will take time."

The Gift

When I sat down with Peterson on his porch at his home in El Zonte, he told me that he originally came to El Salvador in 2004. Things seemed like they were on the upswing. It had been a decade since the civil war, and people were hopeful.

His family bought a home in the small surf town and started spending several months a year there, volunteering and helping with community efforts connected to church groups that were running orphanages, helping with ex-gang member rehabilitation, and working with victims of sex trafficking.

But the Great Financial Crisis, spawned by Wall Street, hit El Zonte and El Salvador hard. The gangs were already a problem, he said, but got much worse in 2008 and 2009. The violence rose to a crescendo in 2016.

Today, a skate park sits across the street from Peterson's house, right on the beach. But a few years ago, a small home was located on the property.

On the night that Donald Trump was elected US president in the 2016 election, Peterson was watching the results come in at home. He heard a series of bangs and went outside to look. He could not see anything so went back inside. But in the morning when he went out on the street, he saw the police pulling a body out of the house across the way.

His neighbor was murdered with 40 bullets, just a stone's throw from where I was sitting, interviewing Peterson five years later. That was the third person murdered in three weeks on Peterson's block in El Zonte, he said. People during that time did not go out at night, he said. Some even fled the country, going to Nicaragua or Guatemala. Local business owners were paying protection money to gangs.

"If you didn't pay," he said, "they would kill you."

Peterson said this was a cycle that impacted the lower classes the most: The impoverished feel like the wealthy are keeping them down, so they respond with violence, but in the end mostly the lower class get hurt, as only the wealthy can afford to hire private security.

In the middle of all this, Peterson was in his third year of working with Valenzuela and Martinez on community projects in El Zonte. He said there were 10 to 15 leaders active in the community, pushing everything forward, but called Valenzuela the "quarterback of the operation." They kept their heads down and kept working throughout 2017 and 2018. Thankfully, national and local crime dropped steeply during that time. But they still faced funding issues.

In the spring of 2019, one of Peterson's friends asked if he wanted a connection to a donor who was interested in Bitcoin philanthropy. He said sure, he'd be happy to talk. He had been a fan of Bitcoin but had never thought of implementing it into his work until that point.

The donor was anonymous, so Peterson met with his liaisons. The requirement was that a gift could be made toward community work in El Zonte, but it would be made in bitcoin, and bitcoin needed to be baked into the local programs. The donor did not want the bitcoin to be sold into dollars, they wanted it to circulate, to become part of the local philosophy and not just a "hoop to jump through."

Peterson was open to the idea because the local banking system was extortionate, bureaucratic, and broken. It was "so hard" to get money in from the United States, with hour-long bus rides, long waits, high fees, and inexplicable delays a common occurrence.

In his own personal experience, about 10 years ago, Peterson tried to buy a car, but had trouble getting the money out from his American account through an ATM to make the purchase. The wire took weeks, and by the time he finally got the cash, the car owner had sold it to someone else. He noted that when foreigners try to buy property and develop the area, there's a one- to two-week lag time between sending and clearing, where both parties are taking risk, and deals often fall through.

But these are just minor inconveniences compared to the high fees that the impoverished deal with.

"They always pay the highest price," said Peterson.

So, Peterson came up with a pitch for the donor, including hand-drawn diagrams of how bitcoin would circulate in town, and a three-year plan for adoption. By the end of the summer, the gift was approved, and Bitcoin Beach started running official programs to pay individuals in bitcoin for cleaning up the community, doing road repair, and starting construction projects.

Peterson also made contact with the Chicago-based company Athena, which helped sneak a Bitcoin ATM into town. This, Peterson said, made a big psychological difference, as residents appreciated how they could easily cash out bitcoin into dollars on demand. By the fall, Peterson said middle-class people from the capital were driving down to El Zonte on the weekends to buy bitcoin at the ATM. Momentum was starting to build.

In November 2019, Peterson traveled to a Bitcoin conference in Uruguay, where he met the British podcaster Peter McCormack. He told McCormack that he should visit El Zonte. Peterson was shocked when McCormack said, "That sounds great, I'll come this week."

After his visit, McCormack recorded an interview with Peterson, which made the rounds on his popular show, *What Bitcoin Did*.[173] This ended up being important, Peterson said, as it was how many people in the Bitcoin community first heard about El Zonte.

In July 2020, an article in *Forbes* came out, profiling Bitcoin Beach.[174] It was, according to Peterson, the "first time El Salvador had ever been featured in a positive light" in a world-class financial magazine.

Between the *Forbes* article and McCormack's podcast, future key contributors to El Zonte including Galoy founder Nicolas Burtey, Strike founder Jack Mallers, and Square product lead Miles Suter, would find out about the community, inspiring future visits in the fall and following spring.

As a result of the pandemic, tourism ground to a halt in El Zonte in 2020. Most hotels closed. Bitcoin Beach responded with a UBI-type program, where $40 worth of bitcoin was distributed on regular occasions to families in need. If one of these payments had been saved until January 2022, it would be worth more than $300.

By the end of 2020, Peterson, Valenzuela, and Martinez thought that not just El Zonte but the whole country could potentially grow to have bitcoin as a currency. But they never envisioned the kind of aggressive rollout that would come the following year.

In early 2021, Peterson said that he drove to the capital with Suter, Martinez, and Valenzuela for a meeting with the minister of tourism, Morena Valdez. They spoke for two hours about the idea of El Salvador adopting a Bitcoin strategy. Peterson said that they pitched it as a cheap and easy idea to help change the national narrative from gangs to opportunity. They argued it was like a "life hack" for international recognition. Peterson said that she seemed to get it but only a little bit.

By May, though, Peterson could feel that something was happening. Instead of making overtures to the government, officials were coming down to El Zonte and looking at the operations of Hope House closely. In April and May of 2021, the vice minister of education and the minister of tourism visited personally.

Peterson said that the transition had not "been all roses" since the Bitcoin law announcement in June. Salvadorans are suspicious of a scheme from a central government with a long history of corruption.

When it comes to the strong national opposition to the Bitcoin law, Peterson said that in general, people do not understand Bitcoin and feel in the dark, ignored, and believe the new program will be used to steal from the public — a fair concern given that the last three Salvadoran presidents all looted the country.

Peterson said that people are also skeptical of the story of El Zonte. It is rare — or even unheard of — for anonymous people to make big gifts in El Salvador, so there is a lot of suspicion around the founding gift made to Bitcoin Beach. Peterson's response is that "if someone had wanted to create a scheme, would they have started it with two Salvadorans who didn't go to high school and a computer illiterate foreigner in a small village? No, you'd start in the capital."

Despite broad national skepticism, Peterson sees Bitcoin adoption going well over the next few years.

"It's typical for a technology to 'leapfrog' in the developing world and be embraced faster: skipping over landlines straight to cell phones, for example," he said. "Especially because Bitcoin doesn't require a lot of capital investment or need a huge new infrastructure beyond the ATMs. Everything is software; the leapfrog can happen because people already have phones."

Peterson thinks that long term, the Bitcoin law will have four big impacts:

First, it creates a culture of savings. Today, he said, if you drive around San Salvador there's a ton of fast-food restaurants and the price of those meals does not compare favorably with daily wages. Many people, he said, spend their remittance on fast food and, in general, the money is not put to productive use because there is no hope for tomorrow. Bitcoin allows them to break this cycle.

Second, it provides business opportunities. He said that between hotel development, tech sector back-office support for payments, and consulting for other countries and businesses around the world that want to add bitcoin payments, the job creation could be significant.

Third, the efficiencies that will be gained as a result of saving fees and time on remittances are massive. It is hard for Americans to understand, Peterson said, but people spend hours of their week dealing with remittances, wait in huge lines, and pay high fees.

Fourth, the sense of pride that you see in people knowing that they are leading the way instead of following from behind. The difference, he said, between subsisting in poverty and breaking out. In a country with such a tragic history and cycles of violence, going from a dark spot on the map to an exciting destination is priceless.

So, what's next for Bitcoin Beach?

"We've had to wrestle through this," Peterson said. "Do we focus on El Zonte, or do we go national?"

He said that they ultimately decided to return to their roots and work on promoting Bitcoin as a tool for the local youth. Others can handle the national work.

"Our goal is for young people to be successful and build a better future, not to do Bitcoin adoption," Peterson said. "But we believe the latter will bring more benefits."

Peterson said that communities like Bitcoin Beach are replicable, but only if the objective is deeper than just promotion of the technology. The mission has to be to improve a community.

If bitcoin had crashed last year, he said, they would still be doing what they are doing with dollars. But he said that Bitcoin had all kinds of benefits he did not predict: helping people with financial literacy, thinking about the future, and delaying gratification.

"Bitcoiners have hope," Peterson said. "And that feeling is spreading here. We think the future will be better than today."

The Strongman

A political chameleon and opportunist, 40-year-old Bukele has evolved in his career from a member of the leftist FMLN to creating his own party, New Ideas, which is broadly characterized as right-wing. His approval rating rests around 90%, making him the most popular politician in the hemisphere and possibly in the world.

Bukele's popularity comes in large part from a perception that he has helped clean up crime and build new infrastructure to make the country safer and more attractive. El Salvador's murder rate had already dropped from more than 100 homicides per 100,000 people in 2015 to around 40 by the time he came into office — declining into the 20s during his administration — but he gets a lot of credit for the overall shift.[175] Independent newspapers like *El Faro* allege that Bukele has reduced violence by making deals with big gangs, but few would complain about the decline.

The big problem is that Bukele has abused his popularity to dismantle democratic institutions. The world saw a glimpse of this behavior in early 2020, when Bukele pushed a spending bill through the National Assembly by encircling the building with snipers and bringing armed troops into the chamber. In February 2021, his party won a legislative supermajority, and in the following few months, he commandeered the judiciary. Five Supreme Court judges were sacked in May and replaced with his supporters. At the same time, Bukele fired the attorney general, who was investigating corruption in his government. Sparking concerns about transparency, he also told the National Assembly to keep pandemic-related government expenditures secret.

On August 31, 2021, the legislature passed a bill that purges all judges with more than 30 years of service or over the age of 60 — amounting to about a third of the body — and allows Bukele to replace them. Some of these judges were investigating war crimes committed in the 1980s by the government against civilians, including the atrocities at El Mozote.[176] If the cases are closed, it is possible that no one will be held accountable for what happened there. Also in August, Bukele officials pushed forward a proposal to rework the constitution that, among other changes, removes a clause that forbids one-party rule.[177]

On September 3, the Supreme Court, now sympathetic to Bukele, ruled that presidents could run for a second consecutive turn, paving the way for him to run for re-election in 2024. The decision clearly goes against the constitution.[178]

The US ambassador to El Salvador recently compared Bukele to Hugo Chávez. But as Human Rights Watch has pointed out, it took Chávez five years to get control over Venezuela's Supreme Court, seven years to conduct a mass judicial purge, and 10 years to bypass electoral limits.[179] It took Bukele just two years to do the same.

It is likely no coincidence that the Bitcoin implementation took place at the same time as the Supreme Court ruling. Bukele has a world-class Twitter game and has been using it masterfully lately — even poking fun at the International Monetary Fund (IMF), and telling the United States to mind its own business — but has not said anything about the Supreme Court. Similarly, the day before Bukele announced his plan in June to make bitcoin legal tender in El Salvador in a video at the Bitcoin 2021 conference in Miami, his government broke an anti-corruption agreement with the Organization of American States.[180]

In the blueprint for dictators — used by Putin, Erdogan, Chávez, and so many others worldwide — once a leader consolidates political control, he typically goes after the media, and then any powerful business people who might get in their way. This summer, Salvadoran officials made a move in this direction by expelling the *El Faro* journalist Daniel Lizárraga.[181]

As *El Faro* wrote, "In previous administrations, journalistic investigations revealed the improper use of public funds and systemic corruption. Among other outcomes, these investigations led to the prosecution of corruption cases at the highest levels of government, as well as the discrediting of the two main political parties covering up those acts. Those investigations paved the way for Bukele and his party."

The newspaper argues that he is trying to disable the very institutions that made it possible for him to get where he is today.

When I spoke to *El Faro* editor Carlos Dada by phone, he told me that a country like Switzerland or Germany should have experimented with Bitcoin, "not El Salvador, where the people have no way of seeing what the government is doing, and where no one knows what Bitcoin is. With dollarization, at least we knew what the dollar was."

He later summed up his position on social media: "Bitcoin has been imposed on an impoverished population by an opaque, authoritarian and corrupt government."[182]

Dada has received death threats for his work. He told *The New Yorker* that he was looking up from his desk one day earlier in 2021 and saw a drone floating outside the window.[183] He gave it "the opportunity to biometrically examine my middle finger."

Privacy advocates like Matt Odell and Anita Posch have voiced concerns that the Chivo app could grow to replace cash transactions, which have, by default, excellent privacy. Moving these payments into a digital system where the government has full knowledge over all aspects of transactions could push the country in the direction of a surveillance state.

In the end, why did Bukele push the bill? Was it to distract the world from his brazen consolidation of power? To — as his critics most often allege — launder money through a network that's harder to monitor than the banking system? Or to try and get citizens into his Chivo system, where he can better surveil and control them? Was it to make a backup plan, in case international lenders cut him off? Perhaps — as his supporters say — to strike first in a digital arms race, modernize the country, and attract investment and talent? Or was it simply to put El Salvador, and his own persona, on the international map?

Any mix of these reasons is possible, but one thing is for sure: Bukele is a lot more internationally famous today than he was in 2020 and is now the most recognizable leader in Central America.

Geopolitically, there is a $1 billion IMF loan to El Salvador pending, and the United States and other international entities may try to pressure Bukele to make concessions before the money gets cleared. They prefer he stays on the Washington consensus and not start a Nakamoto consensus trend. Whether these concessions would be targeted with regard to his erosion of democracy, or his promotion of Bitcoin, is not yet clear. Shortly after the Bitcoin law was passed, the Biden administration sanctioned 11 Salvadorans close to Bukele for corruption. And on September 5, 2021, the US State Department published a press release accusing Bukele of undermining democracy.[184]

Critics say that Bukele will use Bitcoin as a tool to fight back against US sanctions. But as *The Economist* pointed out, it is unlikely that the United States will pressure Bukele too strongly: Biden is facing an immigration crisis, and instability in El Salvador could increase the flows of migrants into the United States, causing political problems for the White House.[185] On August 27, 2021, the US government made a military gift to the Salvadoran army, including eight helicopters.

On June 8, as the Bitcoin law was being passed by the Salvadoran legislature, Bukele joined a Twitter Spaces organized by the investor and entrepreneur Nic Carter and answered questions from an audience that numbered more than 20,000. I had the opportunity to ask him two questions: One, would Salvadorans be able to use any wallet they want, or would they be forced to use the Chivo wallet (he said the choice would be theirs, a promise which has held up). And also, I asked if the state had planned to do any bitcoin mining with its natural resources. On the latter, he initially said no, but then quickly began describing the idea of using volcanoes to mine bitcoin with El Salvador's stranded geothermal energy.

The next day, Bukele posted a video taken at a geothermal site, saying the state was preparing to mine bitcoin using 95 megawatts (MW) of 100% clean energy.[186] He later posted sketches of a futuristic bitcoin mining facility. As of January 2022, these have evolved into working operations to mine bitcoin using heat from dormant volcanoes, and a plan to sell "volcano bonds" backed by renewable energy reserves. If his administration is able to effectively set up these operations, it could provide a non-IMF revenue stream and a way to finance development that other emerging market countries could emulate.

Despite its upside for empowering individuals, improving remittances, and putting El Salvador on the map, the Bitcoin law is perhaps the most unpopular action Bukele has taken since becoming president. According to a summer 2021 poll administered by the Universidad Centroamericana José Simeón Cañas, around 95% of Salvadorans do not think adoption should be mandatory, and a majority do not think the government should use public funds on bitcoin, with seven out of 10 saying the law should be overturned.[187] The survey also revealed how little Salvadorans know about Bitcoin, with 43% saying that they thought it was a physical currency, and 20% saying that 1 BTC was worth a dollar or less.

When I attended an anti-Bitcoin law protest on September 1, 2021, in downtown San Salvador, I encountered this lack of knowledge first hand and was also reminded of Bukele's authoritarian behavior. That morning, police arrested Mario Gomez, a computer scientist who has been very critical of the Bitcoin law on social media. He was later released, but the action was a clear move of intimidation.

At the protest, I met the leader of the Salvadoran union for judicial employees. She told me that people were afraid of losing their freedom and are still scarred by dollarization. She said lots of families still cannot connect to the internet and that — despite the iPhone in her shirt pocket — even some people in the capital have trouble getting online.

Out in the rural areas, she said, there are even fewer connections. The opposition keeps repeating this talking point, though it is worth mentioning that El Salvador as a whole has around one and a half cell phones per person, that virtually everyone in El Zonte had a phone, and that two-thirds of the country uses social media.[188] Regardless, she said, "The law will favor the 1%."

The protestors claimed they were against the law, not the technology, and admitted or revealed through their statements that they knew very little about Bitcoin. If one does not understand the empowering potential of Bitcoin, then of course, one would think that the $200 million spent on the project is a waste of money that should be going elsewhere to help the people.

The protestors' qualms about Bukele's lack of transparency and lack of consultation with the people around the Bitcoin rollout are legitimate and important. The fact is, very few Salvadorans had heard of Bitcoin until recently, and most do not know the first thing about it. So, people are afraid and think it's a tool for money laundering.

"The law opens the door for more evil people to benefit," the union leader told me.

I asked her if she would like to learn more about Bitcoin.

"I'm not interested," she said.

Being Your Own Bank

Enzo Rubio is a Salvadoran entrepreneur, the founder of Point Break Café where Karla works, and the owner of a larger location in the nearby town of El Tunco. He told me that he grew up in San Salvador and moved down to the El Zonte area in 2016, mainly to surf.

Loving the area, Rubio opened his coffee shop in El Tunco in 2017.

"I love coffee, and there was no good coffee around," he said.

He said it went well, feeding off a new wave of tourists coming as the violence started to decline. El Tunco is much larger than El Zonte, with many more shops, restaurants, hotels and foot traffic in general.

One of his most loyal customers was the owner of the Garten Hotel in El Zonte. In 2018, he convinced Rubio to establish a second location there, which finally opened in November 2020 after several years of construction.

Rubio immediately noticed how tight the community was in El Zonte. He also knew that there was something going on there with Bitcoin.

"I didn't know what," he told me, "but I had heard the buzz."

One of his first customers was Burtey, the developer of the popular Bitcoin Beach wallet, who was visiting El Zonte with his wife and kids. They came in during one of the first days the cafe was open, and asked for a couple of cappuccinos. When it came time to pay, Burtey asked: "Do you accept bitcoin?"

Rubio said no, but he would like to.

"In less than two minutes, Nicolas had set me up with a wallet, and had paid me $8.50 worth of BTC. It was my first transaction," Rubio said. "Now it's worth around $25."

Burtey's family helped Rubio put up a sign indicating that he accepted bitcoin. In the first few months, Rubio said, it actually accounted for 10% to 15% of his sales. He told me that he was fortunate that business at both locations was doing well, so he did not need to sell the bitcoin. He watched it grow in dollar terms over time.

Maybe, in a different year, the price would have gone the other direction, and he would have been panicking.

"Right place, right time," Rubio said.

By the start of 2021, Rubio had saved more than $500 in bitcoin, both from tourists but also from locals who earned sats doing community work through Hope House.

He had some early concerns about liquidity, but once he realized Hope House would cash BTC out for dollars for him anytime, he stopped worrying. The fact that it was liquid made all the difference, as did the Lightning Network. Waiting 10 or 20 minutes for a transaction to settle is impractical. But Lightning is a game changer.

Rubio recalled when Mallers visited.

"One day my friend called me, and he was very excited," he recalled. "He said, Jack Mallers is here! He told me to go look for the guy in the hoody."

Mallers, Rubio said, would come to the cafe three or four times a day, paying in bitcoin, and it helped him and his staff become comfortable with frequent orders. It was "good exercise," said Rubio. When I visited Point Break Café in August 2021, the process was smooth, as if Karla had used Bitcoin her whole life.

In the beginning, Rubio said, Karla needed to call him whenever someone wanted to pay in bitcoin, and he would send her a QR code. But now, with the Strike account on a tablet, things are easy.

Rubio calls Karla's story a "clear case of financial inclusion."

I posted a video of me buying coffee from Karla using Lightning on Twitter, and it went viral, attracting more than 650,000 views.[189] I included Karla's Strike and Bitcoin Beach tip pages, and she was inundated with tips of all sizes from dozens of countries around the world.

"It was amazing to watch," Rubio said, telling me that, at one point, tips were coming in a steady stream for hours. "When something goes viral, when you see millions of people watching your TikTok video, that's great, but this was way better, because it wasn't likes, it was satoshis."

"Now, like so many others around here, she's creating a savings strategy," he said. "It's the same for me. I've had several other businesses, but never set aside money for emergencies. Bitcoin gives you a bigger motivation to save instead of spend. We know that dollar inflation is maybe 3% to 4% per year officially, but down here things get more expensive, even by the week. I know that the more I wait to spend the BTC, the more my purchasing power will be."

The whole region is really picking up economically, Rubio said. El Tunco does three times the business that his location in El Zonte does, but the latter now does the volume that the former used to do.

"Point Break Café is now the place to go," Rubio told me. He said he's been interviewed by *Bloomberg* and *The Wall Street Journal*.

Indeed, I visited El Zonte during a typically dead time in low season, when the humidity and heat peaks, and when it rains almost every day. And yet, even mid-week, the hotels were packed. There was a hum of energy every night.

When I asked Rubio about Bukele, though, his tone changed. Rubio finds it contradictory that Bukele is forcing Bitcoin on the population.

"Bitcoin is so anti-government," he said. "So, it's surprising that any government wants to bring Bitcoin to the people."

Earlier this year, Rubio thought a legal tender law would be impossible. He had seen Bukele tweet about Bitcoin a few times in 2017, so knew that it was in his mind for a long time. But why would the government give the people the ability to transact outside the banking system?

"There are so many AML laws," he said. "Opening the economy up to Bitcoin is the other way around."

Two months before it announced the Bitcoin law, Rubio said, there were rumors even that the government would switch the country back to colónes. His mother was warning him, saying they need to take their money out of the banks, worried about a haircut in the event of a currency conversion.

The law stunned Rubio.

"There is one discussion about Bitcoin," Rubio said, "and another discussion about how the government is implementing its adoption."

"Bitcoin is about challenging the government," he said. "It's about taking away the power of the government to fiddle with our economy and our money and savings, not about government intervention."

He called the act of making it compulsory to receive bitcoin "a big mistake."

He is also critical of the Chivo wallet, which he says is "not even a government wallet, it's a private company that was created in just a few short weeks just for this purpose."

Rubio is worried that it is a scheme to spend the taxpayers' money to build something, but where the private company gets the rewards.

"It's not regulated by any public agency," he said.

Rubio tries to do his part to boycott the government wallet. He has not downloaded it yet, and he does what he can to help people use other wallets.

"The revolution is about being your own bank," he said. "You can't do that if you're using Bukele's wallet."

Si No Tienes Las Llaves, No Es Tu Dinero

Was it good when King John signed the Magna Carta? When the Chinese Communist Party permitted private enterprise? When the Cuban dictatorship introduced the internet?

In all cases, yes. These political shifts helped improve lives for billions of people. But the authoritarian rulers who made these sweeping changes do not necessarily deserve praise. If Bitcoin is successful, it will continue to co-opt many leaders. But Bitcoin exists to separate money from state, and even as we liberate the former, we should remain cautious of the latter.

Today, Bukele is moving fast. In the span of writing this chapter, in the summer of 2021, the topic of his running for another term went from speculation, to maybe something he would do in a future year, to something that his new Supreme Court made an actual ruling on, paving the way for his re-election. He seems aware of the international criticism, in September 2021 tweeting, "¿Y la dictadura?" to his 2.9 million followers, and satirically changing his profile to say "dictator."

His supporters, of course, say he needs more time to clean house, end corruption, and implement his reforms. But anyone who has studied populism and dictatorship will know that that is what the fans of strongmen always say. I visited El Zonte with citizens from neighboring countries like Nicaragua and Venezuela. They had seen this movie before and were alarmed at the political red flags popping up in El Salvador.

A Bukele dictatorship is not inevitable, but it looks more likely every day, unless the president changes his behavior. In the meantime, the peaceful protest and empowerment tool of Bitcoin has been associated with Bukele and his regime in many people's minds. That association will be difficult, if not impossible in some cases, to break.

What can human rights activists do? Beyond traditional tactics of supporting the independent media and keeping a spotlight on government behavior, a worthy effort would be to encourage Salvadorans to use noncustodial bitcoin wallets and to avoid the government wallet. After all, any funds in Chivo are not real bitcoin, just confiscatable promises to pay.

"*Si no tienes las llaves, no es tu dinero*" — not your keys, not your coins — could become a rallying cry.

If Bitcoin is going to make a positive long-term impact on El Salvador, then education seems like one of the most important things to focus on right now. Just as Karla and Mama Rosa said, onboarding was hard at first. People are hesitant about Bitcoin and only see its value later, over time. Today, there are more than six million Salvadorans in this skeptical mindset, virtually all of whom have not used Bitcoin and do not know what it is.

Without a sustained and localized effort to spread knowledge about how to use Bitcoin in a noncustodial way, where it can check the power of the government and protect individual freedom, the people may not benefit.

What is clear from visiting El Zonte and talking to the community leaders is that Bitcoin is not something you can sprinkle on a town and make it come to life. Alone, it is not a sufficient tool to empower a population.

Yes, it is true that Bitcoin helped a small village change the world. But without Valenzuela, without Martinez, without Peterson, without Mama Rosa, and without entrepreneurs willing to take risks like Rubio and Karla, no change would have happened.

It would be wise to remember that a village started El Salvador's Bitcoin movement, not a strongman.

Chapter VI

Fighting Monetary Colonialism with Open-Source Code

In the fall of 1993, Fodé Diop's family was saving up for his future. A brilliant 18-year-old living in Senegal, Fodé had a bright path in front of him as a basketball player and an engineer. His father, a school teacher, had helped him find inspiration in computers and in connecting with the world around him. His athletic talents had won him offers to study in Europe and in the United States.

But when he woke up on the morning of January 12, 1994, everything had changed. Overnight, his family lost half their savings. Not due to theft, bank robbery, or company bankruptcy — but a currency devaluation, imposed by a foreign power based 5,000 kilometers away.

The previous evening, French officials met with their African counterparts in Dakar to discuss the fate of the "franc de la Communauté Financière Africaine" (or Franc of the Financial Community of Africa), known widely as the CFA franc or "seefa" for short. For Fodé's entire life, his CFA franc had been pegged to the French franc at a rate of 1 to 50, but when the late-night meeting concluded, a midnight announcement set the new value at 1 to 100.

The cruel irony was that the economic fate of millions of Senegalese was completely out of their own hands. No amount of protest could overthrow their economic masters. For decades, new presidents came and went, but the underlying financial arrangement never changed. Unlike a typical fiat currency, the system was far more insidious. It was monetary colonialism.

The Mechanics of the CFA System

In their eye-opening book, *Africa's Last Colonial Currency: The CFA Franc Story*, economic scholars Fanny Pigeaud and Ndongo Samba Sylla tell the tragic and, at times shocking, history of the CFA franc.[190]

France, like other European powers, colonized many nations around the world in its imperial heyday, often brutally. After its occupation by Nazi Germany in World War II, the "Empire colonial français" began to disintegrate. The French fought to keep their colonies, inflicting a massive human toll in the process. Despite waging a costly series of global wars, Indochina was lost, then

Syria and Lebanon, and, eventually, French territory in North Africa, including the cherished oil- and gas-rich settler colony in Algeria. But France was determined not to lose its territories in West and Central Africa. These had provided military manpower during both World Wars and offered a cornucopia of natural resources — including uranium, cocoa, timber, and bauxite — which had enriched and sustained the metropole.[191]

As 1960 approached, decolonization seemed inevitable. Europe was united in disengaging from Africa after decades of depredations and state-sponsored looting. But the French authorities realized they could have their cake and eat it, too, by ceding political control while retaining monetary control.

This legacy still stands today in 15 countries that speak French and use a currency controlled by Paris: Senegal, Mali, Ivory Coast, Guinea-Bissau, Togo, Benin, Burkina Faso, Niger, Cameroon, Chad, the Central African Republic, Gabon, Equatorial Guinea, the Republic of Congo, and the Comoros. As of January 2022, the French still exert monetary control over more than 2.5 million square kilometers of African territory, an area 80% the size of India.

France began formal decolonization in 1956 with "La Loi-cadre Defferre," a piece of legislation giving colonies more autonomy and creating democratic institutions and universal suffrage. In 1958, the French constitution was modified to establish La Communauté (The Community): a group of autonomous, democratically-administered overseas territories.[192] President Charles de Gaulle toured colonies across West and Central Africa to offer autonomy without independence through La Communauté or immediate total independence. He made it clear there would be perks and stability with the former, and great risks and even chaos with the latter.

In 1960, France actually had a larger population — around 40 million people — than the 30 million inhabitants of what are now the 15 CFA nations. But today, 67 million people live in France and 183 million in the CFA zone. According to UN projections, by the year 2100, France will have 74 million, and the CFA nations more than 800 million. Given that France still holds their financial destiny in its hands, the situation is increasingly resembling economic apartheid.

When the CFA franc was originally introduced in 1945, it was worth 1.7 French francs. In 1948, it was strengthened to 2 French francs.[193] But by the time the CFA franc was pegged to the euro at the end of the 1990s, it was worth 0.01 French francs. That is a total devaluation of 99.5%. Every time France devalued the CFA franc, it increased its purchasing power against its former colonies and made it more expensive for them to import vital goods. In 1992, the French people were able to vote on whether or not to adopt the euro through a national referendum. The CFA nationals were denied any such right and were excluded from the negotiations that would peg their money to a new currency.

The exact mechanism of the CFA system has evolved since its creation, but the core functionality and methods of exploitation are unchanged. They are described by what Pigeaud and Sylla call "dependency theory," where the resources of peripheral developing nations are "continually drained to the benefit of core wealthy nations ... the rich nations do not invest in income-poor nations to make them richer ... [this] exploitation evolved over time from brutal slavery regimes to the more sophisticated and less obvious means of maintaining political and economic servitude."

Three central banks service the 15 CFA nations today: the Banque Centrale des États de l'Afrique de l'Ouest (BCEAO) for West African nations, the Banque des États de l'Afrique Centrale (BEAC) for Central African nations, and the Banque Centrale des Comores (BCC) for the Comoros. The central banks hold the foreign exchange reserves (i.e., national savings) for the individual nations in their region, which must keep an astonishing 50% with the French Treasury at all times. This number, high as it is, is a result of historical negotiations. Originally, the former colonies had to keep 100% of their reserves in France, only in the 1970s did they earn the right to control some and cede "just" 65% to Paris. Today, there are partial reforms ongoing in some CFA nations to further reduce the reserve requirement, but critics have called these measures window dressing on the problem of foreign control. The CFA nations have no discretion whatsoever with regard to their reserves stored abroad. In fact, they do not know how this money is spent. Meanwhile, Paris knows exactly how each CFA nation's money is spent, as it runs "operation accounts" for each country at the three central banks.

As an example of how this works, when an Ivorian coffee company sells $1 million worth of goods to a Chinese buyer, the yuan from the purchaser gets exchanged into euros in a French currency market. Then the French treasury assumes the euros and credits the amount in CFA francs to the Ivorian account at the BCEAO, which then credits the coffee maker's account domestically. Everything runs through Paris. According to Pigeaud and Sylla, France still manufactures all of the notes and coins used in the CFA region — charging 45 million euros per year for the service — and still holds 90% of the CFA gold reserves, around 36.5 tons.

The CFA system confers five major benefits to the French government: bonus reserves to use at its discretion; big markets for expensive exports and cheap imports; the ability to purchase strategic minerals in its domestic currency without running down its reserves; favorable loans when CFA nations are in credit, and favorable interest rates when they are in debt (for stretches of history the French inflation rate has even exceeded the loan interest rate, meaning, in effect, France was forcing CFA nations to pay a fee to store their reserves abroad); and, finally, a "double loan," in which a CFA nation will borrow money from France, and, in looking to deploy the capital, have little choice given the perverse macroeconomic circumstances but to contract with French companies. This means the loan principal immediately returns to France but the African nation is still saddled with both principal and interest.

This leads to a kind of "petrodollar recycling" phenomenon (similar to how Saudi Arabia would take dollars earned through oil sales and invest them into US treasuries as detailed in Chapter III), as CFA exporters historically would sell raw materials to France, with part of the proceeds being collected by the regional central bank and "reinvested" back into the metropole's debt through French or, today, European government debt. And then there is the selective convertibility of the CFA franc. Businesses can easily sell their CFA francs for Euros today (previously French francs), but citizens carrying CFA francs outside of their central bank zone cannot exchange them formally anywhere. They are about as useless as postcards. If an Ivorian is leaving their country, they must exchange the notes for euros first, where the French Treasury and the European Central Bank (ECB) extract seigniorage through the exchange rate.

The monetary repression at play is that France forces the CFA nations to keep a huge amount of reserves in Parisian coffers, preventing the Africans from creating domestic credit. The regional central banks end up loaning out very little at very high rates, instead of loaning out more at low rates. And the CFA nations end up, against their wishes, buying French or, today, European, debt with their strategic reserves.

The most surprising part, perhaps, is the special privilege of first right of refusal on imports and exports. If you are a Malian cotton producer, you must first offer your goods to France, before you go to the international markets. Or if you are in Benin and want to build a new infrastructure project, you must consider French bids before others. This has historically meant that France has been able to access cheaper-than-market goods from its former colonies and sell its own goods and services for higher-than-market prices.

Pigeaud and Sylla call this the continuation of the "colonial pact," which was centered around four fundamental tenets: "The colonies were forbidden from industrializing, and had to content themselves with supplying raw materials to the metropole which transformed them into finished products which were then resold to the colonies; the metropole enjoyed the monopoly of colonial exports and imports; it also held a monopoly in the shipping of colonial products abroad; finally, the metropole granted commercial preferences to the products of the colonies."

The result is a situation in which "the central banks have ample foreign exchange reserves remunerated at low or even negative rates in real terms, in which commercial banks hold excess liquidity, where access to household and corporate credit is rationed and in which the states are increasingly obliged, in order to finance their development projects, to contract foreign currency loans at unsustainable interest rates, which further encourages capital flight."

Today, the CFA system has been "Africanized," meaning the notes now show African culture and flora and fauna on them, and the central banks are located in Dakar, Yaoundé, and Moroni — but these are only superficial changes. The banknotes are still made in Paris, the operation accounts are still run by French authorities, and French officials still sit on the boards of the regional central banks and hold de facto veto power. It is a remarkable situation where a citizen of Gabon has a French bureaucrat making decisions on their behalf. Just as if the ECB or the Federal Reserve had Japanese or Russians making decisions for Europeans and Americans.

The World Bank and the International Monetary Fund (IMF) have historically worked in concert with France to enforce the CFA system, and rarely, if ever, criticize its exploitative nature. In fact, as part of the post-WWII Bretton Woods system — where Americans would lead the World Bank, and Europeans would lead the IMF (see Chapter XII) — the position of the IMF managing director has often been held by a French official, most recently, Christine Lagarde. Over the years, the IMF has helped the French pressure CFA nations to pursue its desired policies. A prominent example was in the early 1990s, when the Ivory Coast did not want to devalue its currency, but the French were pushing for such a change. According to Pigeaud and Sylla, "At the end of 1991, the IMF refused to continue lending money to the Ivory Coast, offering the country two options. Either the country reimbursed the debts contracted with the Fund or it accepted devaluation." The Ivory Coast and other CFA nations caved and accepted devaluation three years later.

Contradicting the values of "liberté, égalité, fraternité" ("liberty, equality, fraternity," the national motto of France), French officials have propped up tyrants in the CFA zone for the past six decades. For example, three men — Omar Bongo in Gabon, Paul Biya in Cameroon, and Gnassingbé Eyadéma in Togo — have amassed 120 years in power between them. All would have been tossed out by their people far sooner had the French not provided cash, weapons, and diplomatic cover. According to Pigeaud and Sylla, between 1960 and 1991, "Paris carried out nearly 40 military interventions in 16 countries to defend its interests." That number is certainly higher today.

Over time, the CFA system has served to allow the French state to exploit the resources and labor of the CFA nations, without allowing them to deepen their accumulation of capital and develop their own export-led economies. The results have been catastrophic for human development.

In 2021, the Ivory Coast's inflation-adjusted GDP per capita (in dollars) is around $1,700, compared with $2,500 in the late 1970s. In Senegal, it wasn't until 2017 that inflation-adjusted GDP per capita surpassed the heights reached in the 1960s.[194] As Pigeaud and Sylla note, "10 states of the franc zone recorded their highest levels of average income before the 2000s. In the last 40 years, the average purchasing power has deteriorated almost everywhere. In Gabon, the highest average income was recorded in 1976, just under $20,000. Forty years later, it has shrunk by half. Guinea-Bissau joined the [CFA system] in 1997, the year in which it recorded the peak in its average income. 19 years later, this fell by 20%."

A staggering 10 of the 15 CFA nations are considered among the "least developed countries" in the world by the United Nations, alongside the likes of Haiti, Yemen, and Afghanistan. In various international rankings, Niger, the Central African Republic, Chad, and Guinea-Bissau are often counted as the poorest countries in the world. The French are maintaining, in effect, an extreme version of what author Allen Farrington has called the "capital strip mine."[195]

Senegalese politician Amadou Lamine-Guèye once summed up the CFA system as citizens having "only duties and no rights" and that "the task of the colonized territories was to produce a lot, to produce beyond their own needs and to produce to the detriment of their more immediate interests, in order to allow the metropole a better standard of living and a safer supply." The metropole, of course, resists this description. As French Economic Minister Michel Sapin said in April 2017, "France is there as a friend."

Now, the reader may ask: Do African countries resist this exploitation? The answer is yes, but they pay a heavy price. Early nationalist leaders from the African independence era recognized the critical value of economic freedom.

"Independence is only the prelude to a new and more involved struggle for the right to conduct our own economic and social affairs [...] unhampered by crushing and humiliating neo-colonialist control and interference," declared Kwame Nkrumah in 1963, who led the movement that made Ghana the first independent nation in sub-Saharan Africa.[196] But throughout the history of the

CFA region, national leaders who stood up to the French authorities have tended to fare poorly.

In 1958, Guinea tried to claim monetary independence. In a famous speech, firebrand nationalist Sekou Touré said to a visiting Charles de Gaulle: "We would rather have poverty in freedom than opulence in slavery" and shortly thereafter left the CFA system. According to the *Washington Post*, "In reaction, and as a warning to other French-speaking territories, the French pulled out of Guinea over a two-month period, taking everything they could with them.[197] They unscrewed lightbulbs, removed plans for sewage pipelines in Conakry, the capital, and even burned medicines rather than leave them for the Guineans."

Next, as an act of destabilizing retribution, the French launched Operation Persil, during which, according to Pigeaud and Sylla, the French intelligence counterfeited huge quantities of the new Guinean banknotes and then poured them "en masse" into the country.[198] "The result," they write, "was the collapse of the Guinean economy." The country's democratic hopes were dashed along with its finances, as Touré was able to cement his power in the chaos and begin 26 years of brutal rule.

In June 1962, Mali's independence leader Modibo Keïta announced that Mali was leaving the CFA zone to mint its own currency.[199] Keita explained in detail the reasons for the move, such as economic overdependence (80% of Mali's imports came from France), the concentration of decision-making powers in Paris and the stunting of economic diversification and growth.

"It is true that the wind of decolonization has passed over the old edifice but without shaking it too much," he said about the status quo. In response, the French government rendered the Malian franc inconvertible. A deep economic crisis followed, and Keita was overthrown in a military coup in 1968. Mali eventually chose to re-enter the CFA zone, but the French imposed two devaluations on the Malian franc as conditions for reinstatement, and did not allow re-entry until 1984.

In 1969, when President Hamani Diori of Niger asked for a more "flexible" arrangement, where his country would have more monetary independence, the French refused. They threatened him by withholding payment for the uranium that they were harvesting from the desert mines that would give France energy independence through nuclear power. Six years later, Diori's government was overthrown by General Seyni Kountché, three days before a planned meeting to renegotiate the price of the Nigerien uranium. Diori wanted to raise the price, but his former colonial master disagreed. The French army was stationed nearby during the coup but, as Pigeaud and Sylla dryly note, they did not lift a finger.

In 1985, the revolutionary military leader Thomas Sankara of Burkina Faso was asked in an interview, "Is the CFA franc not a weapon for the domination of Africa? Does Burkina Faso plan to continue carrying this burden? Why does an African peasant in his village need a convertible currency?" Sankara replied: "If the currency is convertible or not has never been the concern of the African peasant. He has been plunged against his will into an economic system against which he is defenceless."[200]

Sankara was assassinated two years later by his best friend and second in command, Blaise Compaoré. No trial was ever held. Instead, Compaoré seized power and ruled until 2014, a loyal and brutal servant of the CFA system.

Farida Nabourema's Struggle for Togolese Financial Freedom

In December 1962, Togo's first post-colonial leader Sylvanus Olympio formally moved to create a Central Bank of Togo and a Togolese Franc. But on the morning of January 13, 1963, days before he was about to cement this transition, he was shot dead by Togolese soldiers who had received training in France. Gnassingbé Eyadéma was one of the soldiers who committed the crime. He later seized power and became Togo's dictator with full French support, ruling for more than five decades and promoting the CFA franc until his death in 2005. His son rules to this day. Olympio's murder has never been solved.

Farida Nabourema's family has always been involved in the struggle for human rights in Togo. Her father was an active leader of the opposition and has served time as a political prisoner. His father opposed the French during colonial times. As of 2022, she is a leading figure in the country's democracy movement.[201]

Farida was 15 years old when she learned that the history of Togo's dictatorship was intertwined with the CFA franc. By that time, in the early 2000s, she had started to get close to her father and asked him questions about her country's history. "Why did our first president get assassinated just a few years after we gained independence?" she inquired.

The answer: He resisted the CFA franc.

In 1962, President Olympio began the movement toward financial independence from France. The parliament voted in favor of beginning such a transition, and of creating a Togolese franc and holding their reserves in their own central bank. Farida was shocked to learn that Olympio was assassinated just two days before Togo was supposed to leave the CFA arrangement. As she put it: "His decision to seek monetary freedom was seen as an affront to hegemony in Francophone Africa. They were afraid others would follow."

Today, she says, for many Togolese activists the CFA is the major reason to seek broader freedom. "It is what animates many in the opposition movement."

The reasons why are clear. Farida said France keeps more than half of Togo's reserves in its banks, where the Togolese people have zero oversight over how those reserves are spent. Often, these reserves, earned by Togolese, are used to buy French debt to finance the activities of the French people. In effect, this money is often loaned to the former colonial master at negative real yield. The Togolese are paying Paris to hold their money for them and in the process financing the living standards of the French people.

In 1994, the devaluation that stole the savings from Fodé Diop's family in Senegal hit Togo hard, too, causing a huge increase in national debt, a reduction in public funding to local infrastructure, and an increase in poverty.

"Remember," Farida said, "our government is forced to prioritize holding our reserves in the French bank over spending at home, so when a shock hits, we have to degrade ourselves, to ensure that a proper amount of cash is in Parisian hands."

This creates a national climate of dependence, where Togolese are forced to ship raw goods out and bring finished goods in, never digging their way out.

Farida said that about 10 years ago, the anti-CFA movement started to gain more traction. Because of mobile phones and social media, people were able to unite and organize in a decentralized manner. It used to just be Ivorians and Togolese struggling separately, she said, but now there is a regional effort between activists.

For decades, there has been the idea of an "Eco" currency, for all of the Economic Community of West African States (ECOWAS) nations, including regional economic powerhouses Nigeria and Ghana. Farida said that the French tried to hijack this plan, seeing it as a way to expand their own financial empire. In 2013, then-President François Hollande formed a commission which created a document for the French future in Africa. In it, they stated it was an imperative to get Anglophone countries like Ghana involved.

Emmanuel Macron's administration is now trying to rename the CFA franc to the Eco, in a continuing process of "Africanizing" the French colonial financial system. Nigeria and Ghana backed out of the Eco project, once they realized the French were going to continue to have control. Nothing has formally happened yet, but the countries currently managed by the BCEAO are on track to switch to this Eco currency by 2027.[202] The French will still have decision-making ability, and there are not any formal plans to adjust the central banking of the Central African CFA nations or of the Comoros.

"It is the high point of hypocrisy for French leaders like Macron to go to Davos and say they are done with colonialism," Farida said, "while in fact, they are trying to expand it."

She said that originally, the CFA franc was created on the basis of the currency plan used by the Nazi occupiers of France. During World War II, Germany created a national currency for the French colonies so it could easily control imports and exports by just using one financial lever. When the war ended and the French regained their freedom, they decided to use the same exact model for their colonies. So, Farida said, "the foundation of the CFA franc is really a Nazi one."

The system has a dark genius to it, in that the French have been able to, over time, print money to buy vital goods from their former colonies, but those African countries have to work to earn reserves.

"It's not fair, it's not independence," Farida said. "It's pure exploitation."

France claims that the system is good because it provides stability, low inflation, and convertibility for the Togolese people. But the convertibility tends to end up facilitating capital flight — when it is easy for businesses to flee the CFA and park their profits in euros today — while trapping the Togolese in a seigniorage regime. Whenever the CFA is converted — and it must be, as it cannot be used outside of a citizen's economic zone — the French and the ECB take their slice.

Yes, Farida said, inflation is low in Togo compared to independent nations, but a lot of their earnings are going to fight inflation instead of supporting infrastructure and industry growth at home. She pointed to the growth of Ghana, which has an independent monetary policy and higher inflation over time than the CFA nations, compared to Togo. By any metric — healthcare, middle-class growth, unemployment — Ghana is superior. In fact, when one zooms out, she said that not a single CFA nation is among the 10 richest countries in Africa. But of the bottom 10 poorest, half are in the CFA zone.

Farida says that French colonialism goes beyond money. It also affects education and culture. For example, she said, the World Bank gives $130 million per year to support Francophone countries to pay for their books in public schools. Farida says 90% of these books are printed in France. The money goes directly from the World Bank to Paris, not to Togo or to any other African nation. The books are brainwashing tools, Farida said. They focus on the glory of French culture and undermine the achievements of other nations, whether they be American, Asian, or African.

In high school, Farida asked her dad: "Do people use any other language but French in Europe?" He laughed. They only learned about French history, French inventors, and French philosophers. She grew up thinking that the only smart people were French. She had never read an American or British book before she traveled abroad for the first time.

In general, Farida said, French Africa consumes 80% of the books that the French print. President Macron wants to expand on this dominance and has promised to spend hundreds of millions of euros to boost French in Africa, declaring that it could be the "first language" of the continent and calling it a "language of freedom."[203] Given current trends, by 2050, 85% of all French speakers could live in Africa. Language is one pillar of support for the CFA franc's survival.[204]

Politics is another. An important part of the CFA system is French support for dictatorship. With the exception of Senegal, not a single CFA bloc country has ever had meaningful democratization. Every single successful tyrant in Francophone Africa, Farida said, has had the full backing of the French state. Whenever there is a coup against democracy, the French support the coup-makers as long as they are friendly to the CFA regime. But the moment anyone has anti-French tendencies, you see sanctions, threats, or even assassinations.

Farida points to the example of Chad and Mali today. Both countries are under threat from terrorism and rebellion. In Chad, late military dictator Idriss Déby was propped up by France for three decades until his death in April 2021. According to the Chadian constitution, the head of the parliament is normally next in line to be the president, but instead, the military installed Déby's son, a general in the army. The French government applauded this illegal transition and President Macron even visited Chad to celebrate this sham.[205] In a tribute speech, he called Déby a "friend" and "courageous soldier" and said "France will not let anybody put into question or threaten today or tomorrow Chad's stability and integrity."[206] The son, of course, will promote the CFA franc.

Mali, on the other hand, Farida said, had a coup a month after Chad's. The junta and the population are not as friendly to Paris and appear to be seeking in Russia a new partner to stymie terrorism. So, the French government has called the coup "unacceptable," is threatening to withdraw troops from Mali to "leave them alone with the terrorists," as Farida said, and is preparing sanctions.[207] Mali is being punished by France for doing the same thing that Chad did. There is despotism and corruption on both sides. The only difference is that Mali wanted to move away from French monetary control, while Chad is still cooperating.

"When you are a dictator, as long as you are working for France, they will continue finding excuses to help you stay in power," said Farida. They did the same in 2005 in her country of Togo, which led to a son taking over from his dictator father and to her own political awakening.

Fodé Diop's Mission to Bring Bitcoin to Senegal

It was not until Fodé Diop had the opportunity to travel to the United States that he could start to look at his country Senegal from the outside.

At first, the 1994 devaluation of the CFA franc had put his academic future in jeopardy. He had an opportunity to go study and play basketball at a university in Kansas, but his family's savings had been destroyed. Luckier than most around him, his family had one more option: His father had book rights for teaching materials that he had created, and he was able to use those to borrow what was needed to get Fodé to school.

One day, a few years after graduating from college, while living in the United States and working on a new video-on-demand site with his brother, Fodé stumbled across a YouTube video of Dr. Cheikh Anta Diop, a Senegalese scientist and historian, talking about how money and language were tools of controlling people's minds and livelihoods.

Fodé had heard about Dr. Diop before — the biggest university in Senegal was named after him — but he had not listened to his critique of the CFA system. It hit Fodé hard. He says it was like the moment in *The Matrix*, one of his favorite movies, when Neo takes the red pill from Morpheus, and breaks out of his pod into the jarringly brutal real world. He finally saw the water that he swam in while growing up.

"This was the first time in my life I started thinking for myself," Fodé said. "The first time when I realized my own country's currency was a mechanism of control."

He said that it is more than just control over currency. Because the French print and control the money through each country's operation accounts, they have data.

"They know what's going where, they have information on all the countries. They have an edge over these countries. They know who is corrupt. They know who is buying property in France. They know what is available. They have first right of refusal on preferential import and export pricing. They have total domination," said Fodé.

He would later reflect on the 1994 devaluation. At the time, he was only 18, so he did not understand what had happened, other than the fact that the family's finances had gotten a lot more difficult.

"They put a bag over your head so that you don't notice your reality," he said.

But in retrospect, there was a big public debate about it. People realized that when they would go to convert to the French franc, they would only get half as much for their money, even though they were doing the same amount of work. The French reasoning, Fodé said, was to make exports cheaper so that the African countries could produce more competitively. But Fodé sees it differently: This allowed France to crack the whip and buy cheaper goods.

Fodé would have two more "red pill" moments. The next came in 2007, when he was working in Las Vegas in the technology scene. He was watching a video of Steve Jobs, who had just announced the iPhone to the world. Fodé was stunned: A mobile phone that had a native touch-screen browser. The same thing that was on your computer was now on your phone. He knew instantly it would change the world. His next thought: How do we get native payments into the iPhone apps, so people with no bank accounts and credit cards could use mobile money?

The final red pill for Fodé was learning about Bitcoin in 2010. He was living in Los Angeles when he first read Satoshi Nakamoto's white paper for a "peer-to-peer electronic cash system."[208] From the moment he read it, Fodé thought: For the first time, we have a weapon to fight back against oppression and colonialism. Money of the people, not controlled by governments. "This," he said, "is exactly what we need."

Years earlier, Fodé had read *Out of Control* by Kevin Kelly. One of the chapters was about e-currencies. He knew that eventually, all money would be digital, part of a great global electronic revolution. But he had never thought too deeply about the transformative power digital money could have — until Bitcoin.

"What is money? Where does it come from? Asking these questions, this is what Bitcoin did for me," he said. "Before that, you don't question it."

Maybe, he thought, one day, France would not have the right or ability to print and control the money of the Senegalese people anymore.

Fodé and his roommate in Las Vegas would stay up late many times over the coming years, thinking about what Bitcoin could make possible for payments, savings, and all economic activity. He learned about what happened when you swiped your credit card, what kind of information this revealed. And what third parties were doing with that information.

He thought that the marriage of the smartphone and Bitcoin would make an incredible empowerment tool. Fodé would frequently go back to Senegal, and each time he would go, he would bring a bunch of phones with him to give away. He viewed them as connections to the outside world for his friends back home.

Over the coming years, he worked at different startups, all in the industry of digitizing different parts of our lives. In 2017, he left Vegas and went to San Francisco. He joined a coding bootcamp and decided to become a computer engineer. Initially, he got very involved with the cryptocurrency scene as a whole, but eventually, he says he "fell out of love" with Ethereum, right around the time he started to go to San Francisco's Socratic seminars with River founder Alex Leishman. He met a lot of the Bitcoin core developers and early Lightning users.

In 2019, he won a transportation hackathon, making a Lightning invoice that would unlock a Tesla. This gave him a big confidence boost that he could help change the world. He decided to go home to Senegal to spread Bitcoin education. On his way, he was gifted a travel scholarship to the Lightning conference in Berlin by Lightning Labs CEO Elizabeth Stark. There, he met Richard Myers of goTenna and developer Will Clark, who were thinking about how to fight internet censorship with mesh networks. Fodé thought: In Senegal, the French telecom Orange controls all the phone networks. Maybe they could figure out a way to circumvent French control over communications and ability to "turn off the internet" through Bitcoin and Lightning.

Senegal's telecom gateways are controlled by France and can be shut down in case there are protests against the country's leader, whom they support as long as he sticks to the CFA system. But it is possible to find endpoints, Fodé said, through other providers. They could be other national phone networks or even satellite connections. Fodé created a box that would pick up on these other signals. Mobile phones could tunnel into that box, allowing users to go online even when the French turned off the internet. To incentivize people running such boxes, he would pay them in bitcoin. For routing data and maintaining these boxes in Senegal, one is paid through Lightning. This is what Fodé is working on today.

"It's very risky," Fodé said. "You can face jail or fines. But with monetary incentives, people are willing."

The next time Orange turns off the internet to protect its ally in government, the people may have a new way to communicate that the regime cannot stop.

Lightning, Fodé said, is everything.

"We *need* instant and cheap payments. We can't do on-chain Bitcoin payments. The fees are just too expensive. We have to use Lightning. There is no other option," he said. "And it works."

This rings especially true in the area of remittances, which, according to the World Bank, are a major source of GDP for many CFA nations.[209] For example, 14.5% of Comoros' GDP is based on remittances. For Senegal, it is 10.7%; Guinea-Bissau, 9.8%; Togo, 8.4%; and Mali, 6%. Given that the average cost of sending a $200 remittance to sub-Saharan Africa is 8%, and that the average cost of sending $500 is 9%, and given that Bitcoin-based remittance services like Strike can reduce fees to well under 1%, anywhere from 0.5% to a full 1% of CFA nations' GDP could be saved by adopting a Bitcoin model.[210] Zooming out, each year roughly $700 billion is sent home by remitters globally. Between $30 billion and $40 billion could be saved, which is roughly the same amount the United States spends each year on foreign aid.

Fodé understands why people in the West might be skeptical about Bitcoin. "If you have Venmo and Cash App, you might not see why it is important. You have all the conveniences of a modern monetary system. But when you go to Senegal, more than 70% of our people have never stepped foot in a bank. Mom never had a credit card or debit card," he said.

He wonders: How are they ever going to participate in the global financial system?

He said the marriage of smartphones and Bitcoin will liberate people and change society. Fodé mentioned *The Mobile Wave*, the book that MicroStrategy CEO Michael Saylor wrote about the handheld revolution, as being "so salient."[211] When Fodé first touched the iPhone, he knew that it was what he was waiting for. The universe was conspiring, he thought. In just a few short years, he saw the iPhone, the Great Financial Crisis, Satoshi's release of Bitcoin, and his own transition to becoming an American citizen.

He said that since he has spent half of his life in Africa, and half in the United States, that he can see a path forward.

"When I go home, I see how people are being held down. But in the same way we leapfrogged landlines and went straight to cell phones, we're going to skip banks and go straight to Bitcoin."

Another effect he is seeing in Senegal is that when people are exposed to Bitcoin, they start saving.

"Today, at home, I'm thinking about how to help people save money," he said. "Nobody saves anything here. They just spend every CFA franc they can get."

Fodé is "forever grateful" for the BTC that Leishman gave him, as he ended up giving it away in small parts to people in Senegal — those who came to events or who asked good questions. People saw its value grow over time.

He has watched what has happened in El Salvador with great excitement. When he stood in a conference hall in Miami in June 2021 and listened to Strike founder Jack Mallers announce that a country had added bitcoin as legal tender, Fodé said that he teared up. He thought this would never happen.

"What began as a store of value, is now evolving to a medium of exchange," he said.

El Salvador (see Chapter V) has some similarities to the CFA zone countries. It is a poorer nation, fixed to a foreign currency, reliant on imports, with a weaker export base.[212] Its monetary policy is controlled by an external power, with 70% of the country unbanked, and 22% of the nation's GDP relies on remittances.

"If it could be a good option for them," Fodé thought, "maybe it could work for us."

But he knows there are major obstacles.

One is the French language. There is not a lot of French information on GitHub, or in the documentation materials for Lightning or Bitcoin Core. Currently, Fodé is working on translating some of this to French so that the local developer community can get more involved.

Could a Bitcoin Beach community eventually happen in Senegal? Yes, Fodé said. That is why he moved back, and that is why he is running meetups, collecting donations through a Lightning tip jar, and building a citizen-powered, Bitcoin-based version of Radio Free Europe.[213]

"They could jail me," he said. "But through the meetups, I'm making it so that I'm not a single point of failure."

He thinks it will be hard to get Bitcoin adoption in Senegal because of the French influence.

"They won't go out without a fight," he said.

As Ndongo Samba Sylla put it, "Today, France faces relative economic decline in a region it long considered its own private preserve. Even faced with the rise of other powers like China, France has no intention of abdicating its mastery — it will fight to the last."[214]

But maybe, instead of a violent revolution, it could be a gradual peaceful revolution over time that kicks out colonialism.

"Not a sudden off switch but a parallel system, where people can opt in over time by themselves," Fodé said. "No coercion."

As for people who think we should just ask the government to protect our rights?

"They don't know that democracies like France have this bad side," Fodé said. "They won't gift us liberty. Instead, we should follow in the footsteps of the cypherpunks and seize our freedoms with open-source code."

When asked about Bitcoin's chances at replacing central banking, Fodé said that the idea "may sound crazy to Americans, but for Senegalese or Togolese, central banks are a parasite on our society. We have to fight back."

Fodé considers Bitcoin "life changing."

"Never before did we have a system where money could be minted in a decentralized fashion. But this is what we have today. It's a solution for those who need it most. For the first time, we have a powerful tool to push back against oppression," he said. "It might not be perfect, but we gotta use the tools we have today to fight for the people. Not wait around for someone to come help us."

The Separation of Money and State

In 1980, Cameroonian economist Joseph Tchundjang Pouémi wrote, *Monnaie, servitude et liberté: La répression monétaire de l'Afrique.*[215] The thesis: Monetary dependence is the foundation of all other forms of dependence. The final words of the book ring especially strong today: "Africa's fate will be forged through money or it won't be forged at all."

Money and currency are buried beneath the surface in the global human rights movement. They hardly ever come up at human rights conferences and are rarely discussed among activists. But ask a democracy advocate from an authoritarian regime about money, and they will tell amazing and tragic stories. Demonetization in Eritrea and North Korea, hyperinflation in Zimbabwe and Venezuela, state surveillance in China and Hong Kong, frozen payments in Belarus and Nigeria, and economic firewalls in Iran and Palestine. And now: monetary colonialism in Togo and Senegal. Without financial freedom, movements and nongovernmental organizations (NGOs) cannot sustain themselves. If their bank accounts are shuttered, notes demonetized, or funds debased, their power is limited and tyranny marches on.

Monetary repression continues to be hidden and not spoken of in polite circles. The reality today for the 182 million people living in CFA nations is that, while they may be politically independent in name, their economies and money are still under colonial rule. Foreign powers still abuse and prolong that relationship to squeeze and exploit as much value from their societies and geographies as possible.

In recent years, CFA zone citizens are increasingly rising up. The slogan "France Dégage!" has become a rallying cry. But the system's loudest critics, Pigeaud and Sylla among them, do not seem to offer a viable alternative. They dismiss the status quo and IMF bondage, only to suggest either a regional currency, controlled by local leaders, or a system where each CFA nation creates and runs its own currency. But just because Senegal or Togo gets monetary independence from France does not guarantee that they will perform well or that the country's leaders will not abuse the currency.

There is still the threat of domestic dictatorial misrule or new capture by Russian or Chinese foreign powers. It is clear that people are in need of a money that actually breaks the wheel, one that they can control and that cannot be manipulated by governments of any kind. Just as there was a historic separation of Church and State that paved the way for a more prosperous and free kind of human society, a separation of Money and State is underway.

Could citizens of CFA nations, over time, with increasing access to the internet, popularize Bitcoin to the point that governments would be forced to de facto adopt it, as happened in Latin American countries like Ecuador with "dolarización popular"?[216] History remains to be written, but one thing is for sure: The World Bank and IMF will resist any trends in this direction. Already, they have come out swinging against El Salvador.[217]

In June 2021, the actor Hill Harper was quoted in *The New York Times* regarding his activism for Bitcoin in the African American community.[218] He said, quite simply, "They can't colonize Bitcoin."

Farida Nabourema agrees. "Bitcoin," she said, is "the first time ever that there is money that is actually decentralized and accessible to anyone in the world regardless of their skin color, ideology, nationality, amount of wealth or colonial past."

She said it is the people's currency and even goes a step further.

"Maybe," she said, "we should call Bitcoin the currency of decolonization."

Chapter VII

Can Bitcoin Be Palestine's Currency of Freedom?

One day in July 2021, I spoke to a Bitcoin user inside the Gaza Strip.

He asked to remain anonymous and go by the name Uqab — the Arabic word for "eagle" — as he took a large personal risk to talk to me.

We spoke on Telegram and had to time our call, as Uqab only had a few hours of electricity per day. For him, our chat was in the middle of the night. A Palestinian friend helped translate the call live. As we spoke, it was hard to fathom what life was like on the other end of the line.

Uqab was talking to us from Rafah, a city in the southern part of Gaza, a war zone only a few weeks removed from being heavily bombed by the Israeli military. I felt like I was speaking to someone from a different planet.

He spoke of roads destroyed, buildings vaporized, power cut, and supplies restricted. Maps of Israeli missile strikes make Gaza look like Swiss cheese and give a sense of the structural damage.[219]

Uqab asked me to consider how bad things have been economically around the world, even in the United States, because of the pandemic and ensuing lockdowns, and said, "Now imagine what it's been like for us."

A Checkpoint That's Always Open

The Gaza Strip is a piece of territory roughly five miles wide and 28 miles long, sandwiched between Israel's southwestern corner, the Egyptian Sinai, and the Mediterranean Sea. Originally the site of a Palestinian community flooded by refugees fleeing from what is now Israel after the 1948 Arab–Israeli War, it is today one of the most densely populated places on Earth. Gaza is less than half the size of Austin, Texas, but has more than twice its population. Think Hong Kong but besieged in a desert, with crumbling infrastructure.

Over the past four decades, the two million inhabitants — half of them under the age of 18 — have suffered from a near-total civilizational collapse.

In 2006, Hamas — which was founded on a mission to destroy Israel and does not recognize its right to exist — won the Palestinian elections, in what was widely seen as a protest vote against the extreme corruption and ineptitude that the ruling Fatah party had displayed in the 12 years since the creation of the Palestinian Authority.[220] The elections were not deemed legitimate by many international actors — the United States and European Union, for example, consider Hamas a terrorist group — and Fatah clung to power in the West Bank.[221] Gazans, meanwhile, fell under the dictatorial rule of an Islamist police state. In retaliation, in 2007, the Israeli and Egyptian governments closed off Gaza from the outside world.

A 15-year-old living in Gaza today is the survivor of four major wars between the Israeli Defense Forces (IDF) and Hamas, the most recent taking place in the spring of 2021.

Between May 10 and May 21, 2021, Hamas fired more than 4,300 rockets toward Israeli cities and towns, and the IDF responded with more than 1,500 missiles of their own. This battle was the worst between the two since 2014. A UN report published in July 2021 estimated the damage at between $280 million and $380 million, and projected a recovery budget anywhere from $345 million to $485 million.[222] Amid the rubble, 800,000 Gazans remain without access to clean drinking water. They can only exit into the outside world officially through two checkpoints, and those had been turned on and off during the violence, too.

In 2012, the UN published a paper predicting that Gaza would be "unlivable" by 2020.[223] That prediction is tragically accurate. According to a World Bank report published in June 2021, before another spate of bombings, the unemployment rate in Gaza was 48% and 64% for those under the age of 30.[224] One out of every two Gazans — including more than 400,000 children — live in poverty, and more than 80% of households are dependent on food handouts or some kind of social assistance.

According to a 2017 International Monetary Fund (IMF) report, war between Israel and Hamas at the end of 2008 destroyed more than 60% of Gaza's capital stock and the bombings in 2014 destroyed 85% of what remained.[225] In the 25 years between 1994 and 2018, Gaza suffered a 44% decline in real GDP per capita, with Gazans going from having 96% of the average income of their West Bank counterparts to having just 30%. This all despite having one of the world's highest birth rates, at more than 3.5 children per family in 2019, down from nearly seven children per family in 1990.[226]

Outside investment in Gaza has withered from 11% of total Palestinian GDP in 1994 to just 2.7% in 2018.[227] In the aftermath of the 2008 to 2009 war between Hamas and Israel, it was estimated that more than 90% of the strip's factories closed. Extreme restrictions on trade with Israel took a heavy toll.[228] Gaza's sole power plant only operates at a fraction of its capacity, given an inability to import enough fuel and parts.[229] The agricultural sector has collapsed, as farmers lost their main Israeli market for goods and were forced to sell to the much smaller Gaza population at lower prices.[230] In some cases, they had to destroy their crops.

In 2020, a UN report considered a counterfactual where Gazans did not face additional restrictions after 2006, and where instead their economy continued to grow at the same rate as the West Bank's.[231] In that "dream" world, per capita income would be 105.5% higher, reaching $1,539. Instead, in the real nightmare that Gazans live in, it is well below $1,000.

Gaza's economic disaster is not new and is not simply a result of the last 15 years of war and authoritarianism. Rather, it is an outcome of policies that began many decades ago. In 1987, Harvard scholar Sara Roy published a landmark paper using years of fieldwork and interviews to reflect on the economic toll of 20 years of military occupation in the Gaza Strip since 1967.[232] To describe what she saw, she coined a new term, "de-development." This was the "deliberate, systematic, and progressive dismemberment of an indigenous economy by a dominant one, where economic — and by extension, societal — potential is not only distorted but denied."

Gazan incomes and economic output rose significantly from 1967 to 1987, driven by remittances from work in Israel and abroad. But Roy observed that this flow of capital was largely used to purchase consumer goods from Israel, with two-thirds of disposable income going to private consumption by the mid-1980s. This resulted in "increased levels of consumerism within the Gaza Strip with little, if any, of the economic benefits derived from such consumerism accruing to the Strip."

Roy noted that the high percentage of Gazan labor in Israel was not a sign of a society "experiencing typical patterns associated with the process of industrialization (or modernization) in which labor gradually shifts from agricultural to non-agricultural activities ... rather, for Gaza's labor force, the decision to seek employment inside Israel is a function of the lack of comparable options inside Gaza's domestic economy." By 1987, Roy could observe that the distinguishing features of Gaza's economy were "the erosion of its own internal economic base and its resulting dependency on Israel."

In 1991, Israeli Defense Minister Moshe Arens created the Sadan committee, tasked with exploring how Gaza's economy could be improved.[233] The conclusion was telling: "In promoting the economic interests of the [Palestinian] population, the focus was on wage earners and on the short run. Regarding wage earners, priority was given to increasing their income by employing them in the Israeli economy. Only rarely did the policy opt for the development of infrastructure and the encouragement of the creation of factories and employment within the Gaza Strip itself. No priority was given to the promotion of local entrepreneurship and the business sector in the Gaza Strip. Moreover, the authorities discouraged such initiatives whenever they threatened to compete in the Israeli market with existing Israeli firms."

And so, the staggering plight of Gazans can be seen as the result of decades of external policies. First, a forced reliance on the Israeli economy and discouragement of sovereign industrial development under Israeli military occupation. Then, a closure of that economic lifeline, as Gazans were over time prohibited from working in Israel and, eventually, cut off from the outside world. And finally, the destruction of their infrastructure through war.

In early 2021, the Biden administration sent Secretary of State Antony Blinken to the West Bank to meet with Palestinian president Mahmood Abbas and promised $75 million in new aid to help rebuild Gaza.[234] But regional history shows that much of these gifts are pocketed by the elites and fail to improve the lives of the average person. Aid alone cannot fix a dying capital stock.

Through it all, Gazans continue to show incredible persistence. A shop owner named Ashraf Abu Mohammad was quoted by *Reuters* during the May 2021 conflict as saying, "Life will return, because this is not the first war, and it will not be the last war. The heart is in pain, there have been disasters, families wiped from the civil registry, and this saddens us, but this is our fate in this land, to remain patient."[235]

But patience has its limits. When I spoke to Uqab, it was clear that he was not going to wait around forever. He told me that he wants to escape and build a better life for his family. And through Bitcoin, he has found a way out.

He said there has been rising demand for bitcoin in Gaza over the past three years, mainly among the youth. Gazans might be physically trapped and economically cut off from the outside world, but Uqab called Bitcoin, "a checkpoint that's always open."

"It has allowed some people to get out of poverty," he said. "They are just investing bit by bit, gradually, but it's working." He even said that Gazans have been "buying the dip" recently, accelerating their purchasing as the bitcoin price went down in the summer of 2021.

Some receive bitcoin directly through mobile apps from friends or family abroad. Others use Telegram groups to coordinate in-person meetups to trade cash for bitcoin, or they take cash to brick-and-mortar shops and make the exchanges there. At these stores, Uqab said, the authorities take a cut and keep lists of who is buying and selling. No one yet, he said, has been arrested for Bitcoin use. To store bitcoin on their phones, Gazans might use Binance or

Payeer as custodial solutions or Blue Wallet, which has native Arabic language support, as a noncustodial solution.

Despite warnings from officials, more Gazans join the Bitcoin network every day.

"We have a saying," Uqab said: "If the government says something is haram, that means it's halal."

We spoke about a lot of things:

Why Uqab prefers bitcoin to shekels? "Everything in Gaza is monitored, but you could have a lot of bitcoin; and your family wouldn't even know."

Can the IDF or Hamas stop people from using Bitcoin? "We're too smart for this, we'll always find a way out".

Could Satoshi have predicted that people would be using Bitcoin in Gaza? "Definitely not".

Had he heard about El Salvador making bitcoin legal tender? "It was a big win, they cheered when they heard the news."

Might Gazans adopt Bitcoin faster than Israelis? "They may not take the risk that Gazans are willing to take."

What's wrong with the banking system? "We all know charging interest to people you loan money to is sinful."

In Gaza, Uqab told me, there is no Venmo, no PayPal, and no easy way to transact with the outside world. The financial infrastructure is collapsing just as badly as the physical and social infrastructure. But today, he can do with Bitcoin what was impossible before: Send and receive money to and from family abroad, quickly, directly, with barely any fees.

For international payments, Uqab said previously a remitter in the Gulf or the United States would have to send money through a bank account in a country like China or Thailand, with the money eventually landing in a currency office in Gaza.

"Many middlemen would take their cut," he said, leaving the recipient with only a percentage of what was originally sent. Also, he said, today, the Western Union offices have started to ask for proof of blood relations; interrogations and confiscations are frequent.

"With Bitcoin," Uqab said, "I don't need to pass any tests or check any boxes. I can just use it."

In 2021, he can receive or earn money directly, across borders, and be his own bank in a new financial system.

"It's so much better," he said, proudly telling me that he feels at least on some level "peer to peer" with others in the world.

"With Bitcoin, we're getting on with our lives," he said. "Inshallah, more Palestinians will discover this technology."

Uqab hasn't been able to leave Gaza yet. But at least for now, he is able to save in cyberspace, keeping his money safe from the authorities. It's a big innovation, the kind that Palestinians desperately need.

In the constant coverage of their political suffering — trapped by Israeli military occupation, Hamas's terror tactics, the corrupt Palestinian Authority, and a largely uncaring world — their monetary and economic situation often goes untold. But money lies at the very root of their struggles.

Palestinians do not have control of their currency. Their lack of economic sovereignty has deeply damaged their growth and prospects for the future. But many like Uqab are turning to Bitcoin as a way to seize financial freedom.

A History of Financial Repression

More than 30 years after her 1987 paper on Gaza, Sara Roy reflected that "events have reduced the Palestinians to a humanitarian issue, deprived (and undeserving) of political and economic rights and dependent on the international community for sustenance, where relief not progress becomes the primary if not the only political option."[236] She wrote that "Palestinians see the present as better than the future."

Many reasons for this despair are tied to their financial and economic situation, where Palestinians have become deeply dependent on the outside world, yet cut off at the same time. But the topic of money itself is marginalized and sometimes ignored in the present discourse. For example, in an exhaustive, book-sized report on Israel and Palestine published in April 2021 by Human Rights Watch, the issues of currency, banking, remittances, and trade go virtually unmentioned.[237] The Paris Protocol — a hugely important document signed in 1994 that still determines the rules of money and economics for Palestinians — was completely missing.

To dig deeper, we have to ask new questions. Why is the Palestinian economy so dependent on the Israeli economy? Why do Palestinians use the shekel and not their own currency? Why can't Palestinians easily order goods on Amazon or receive money from abroad? To learn more, I spoke to Palestinian political economist Alaa Tartir.

Tartir, who now lives in Switzerland with his family, was born in Ramallah, Palestine, and credits his days working as a teenager for his interest in money. When he was 14, he started long shifts at a grocery store to support his family and save up for his education. He could take nothing for granted and was entirely self-dependent. This motivated him to keep working for seven years until he finished a degree in finance and accounting.

All the while, he grew up studying the economic system around him. He was "dealing with aristocrats and elites," he said, and began to understand how the Palestinian Authority exploited its position and siphoned off aid and other revenue to enrich itself, while colluding with the Israeli government to leave the average Palestinian in the cold.

Tartir walked me through modern Palestine's economic and monetary story, which is usually ignored or, at least, takes a backseat to the more well-known political story.

"It is basically hidden," he said, "even though the dominance of the Israeli actor over the Palestinian actor is entrenched in everything from the use of the shekel to the way that the Israeli government collects our income abroad to how we have no central bank."

He said money is arguably the driving force behind why the Palestinians are where they are today, where occupation, corruption and war have led to de-development, civilizational stagnation, and the erosion of capital stock.

We started in the years after Israeli's military occupation began in 1967, when its policies initially appeared to help Palestinians from an economic perspective. Trade opened up with other Arab nations, and Palestinians were able to increasingly work in Israel for higher wages than what they could make at home.

But this was with a bigger agenda. In the 1960s, 1970s, and 1980s, the Israeli government designed an occupation system that incentivized Palestinians to work in Israel and prevented them from developing a manufacturing base, increasing dependency on Israeli imports. In the two decades from 1968 to 1987, the industrial share of GDP in the Occupied Palestinian Territories (OPT) (The West Bank, East Jerusalem, and Gaza Strip) fell from 9% to 7%. In 1970, there were 59,000 agricultural workers in the OPT, making up 5.4% of the population, compared to just 54,000 or 2.3% of the population in 1993.[238]

Tartir explained that in the 1970s and 1980s, dependence on Israel became near total, as its products exceeded 90% of OPT imports, making Palestinians the second-largest buyer of Israeli goods after Americans.[239] As Israeli economic scholar Shir Hever wrote, "The main source of income to the Palestinians became remittances from Palestinian workers … by 1974, a third of the Palestinian workforce was already employed in Israel … many Palestinian farmers abandoned their farmlands in order to work in Israel, and Israeli authorities took advantage of this and confiscated land that remained uncultivated for a certain period of time."[240] This is evidenced by how "Palestinian agricultural productivity [fell] sharply from 53% of GDP in 1967 to 13% by the late 1980s."[241]

By the mid-1980s, Palestinian economic growth began to slow. A collapse in the oil price and extreme inflation in Israel brought Palestinian remittances from abroad crashing down. In 1987, after enormous political frustration, and after their rising quality of life stalled out, the Palestinians rose up in a decentralized movement aimed at self-sovereignty, known as the Intifada.

According to political scientist Tariq Dana, the Intifada was "economic warfare" in two parts: "The first sought to harm Israeli economic interests in the OPT through tactics of civil disobedience such as commercial strikes, boycotting of Israeli products, withholding tax payment, and refusing to work in Israeli marketplaces and settlements ... the second involved the Palestinians embracing domestic models of household and neighborhood economies to ensure survival and self-sufficiency."[242]

Initially, Tartir said, the Israeli government profited from the occupation. Taxes collected outweighed expenditures; Israel was flooded by low-wage workers; it obtained a captive market for low-quality exports; and it could exploit, at below market prices, the OPT's natural resources.[243] The Intifada succeeded in making the occupation much more expensive for Israel — after the early 1990s, it no longer made a profit and became a costly enterprise — but the uprising did not succeed at achieving real independence for Palestinians.

The Paris Protocol

On April 29, 1994, delegates from the Palestinian Liberation Organization (PLO) and the Israeli government met in France to sign a rarely-discussed document called the "Protocol on Economic Relations," also known as the "Paris Protocol."

This meeting was part of the Oslo Accords, an internationally supported peace process through which Palestinians received political autonomy. Oslo marked an end to the Intifada and a start to the Palestinian Authority (PA) and its state-building process. It sparked the age of foreign aid for Palestinians, as previously donors were reluctant to fund Israel when it was a straightforward occupying power. Most notably, it won PA President Yassir Arafat and Israeli prime ministers Shimon Peres and Yizhak Rabin the Nobel Peace Prize for "efforts to create peace in the Middle East."

Why would the Israeli government give up total control over the OPT, a position it held for the previous 25 years? Palestinian resistance and international and domestic pressure were primary factors, of course, but Tartir thinks a key reason was the ability to be seen as "gifting" political autonomy to the PLO through the creation of the PA, while actually retaining economic control behind the scenes through the Paris Protocol.

In 2021, the Paris Protocol still steers Palestinian monetary, fiscal, tax, agricultural, insurance, industrial, and labor policy, as well as tourism and trade with Israel. It was supposed to boost Palestinian trade, allow the PA to establish a formal public sector and generate tax revenue from its citizens, and increase job opportunities.

But according to Tartir, the Oslo process has only fueled a consumerist culture and increased dependence. "Individual freedom and economic sovereignty," he said, "were sacrificed by Arafat and his cronies for their personal gain."

The protocol was supposed to be temporary — meant to last only five years until 1999 — but remains in effect 29 years later. The document decreed that Palestinians would not have a central bank, nor their own currency. Instead, they would get the "Palestinian Monetary Authority" (PMA), which was misleadingly named, because it did not have any.

Israel would control Palestinian monetary policy and its banking system. The Israeli new shekel would be mandatory legal tender in the West Bank and Gaza Strip. Banks would denominate deposits and loans in shekels. The PMA would have discretion over reserve requirements but little else.[244] Any change to this system would require a vote from the Joint Economic Commission — an organization that, over the years, fell into dormancy and Israeli control.[245]

By signing the Paris Protocol, the Israeli government cemented the following:

Control over the amount of customs duties, VAT, and import taxes collected on goods heading into the West Bank or Gaza, and the deduction of a 3% "processing" fee for payments cleared to the PA.

The ability to make Palestinian goods artificially expensive, preventing them from competing with Israeli goods, forcing Palestinians to import, and allowing Israel a specialized market to export high-margin, low-quality goods that could not be sold elsewhere.

Control over trade policy, giving Israel veto power on what goods enter the West Bank or Gaza, limiting anything considered "dual use" that could be utilized by the military, including medicine and fuel. This is enforced with the help of the Egyptian government.

The ability to collect income taxes and social transfers from Palestinians working in Israel or the settlements, which the Israeli government "clears" once a month to the PA, enabling it to delay payments, collect interest on the capital in its banking system, and even use it to pay debts.[246]

Social security taxes, union fees, and security taxes were imposed on Palestinian workers, but they did not receive the benefits.

The collective impact of the Paris Protocol reforms can be seen in one simple yet shocking statistic: Palestine's manufacturing sector declined from 19% to 10% between 1994 and 2011.[247]

Tartir said that this foreign dependence puts Palestinians in a difficult situation because it is so hard to actually get funds from abroad back home. "If I want to transfer any amount of money from Geneva to Ramallah," Tartir said, "it has to go through an Israeli correspondent bank."

"As a Palestinian exporter or importer, you can't do anything alone," he said. "You need to rely on an Israeli counterpart to help you execute your trade. You can't have your own space at Israeli ports. This element of enforced counterparty not only increases the cost of every transaction but also benefits the Israeli economy. But we have no choice."

On average, between 1997 and 2017, Israeli-controlled clearance payments and foreign aid flows made up 72% of the PA's total revenue.[248]

Tartir also points to the lack of fintech in Palestine. "In Ramallah, we have no PayPal, no TransferWise, no Venmo, no Revolut. If you want to receive money from abroad, you have to go pick up the cash from Western Union," he said.

He explained that even Western Union used to be more flexible and available at stores all over the West Bank, but due to counter-terrorism measures, these payments are now only receivable through one or two banks. They can take time — often days or even weeks if they are flagged as suspicious by the PMA — and they are hugely expensive: A $500 remittance could cost $30 or $40.

But that's the best option if he wants to send money from Europe to the West Bank today. A bank wire is a much more difficult process, he said. And, either way, sending anything over $10,000 is "pretty much impossible."

A 2019 UN report estimated that the total fiscal cost of occupation for Palestinians from 2000 to 2017 was $47.7 billion, or three times the 2017 GDP of the OPT.[249] The report concluded that 3.7% of Palestinian GDP annually leaks to the Israeli treasury as a result of the mechanisms set up by the Paris Protocol.

What was pitched as a step toward Palestinian independence was really a set of rules and policies which increased Palestinian dependence on foreign aid and the Israeli economy. Israel gave responsibility over millions of Palestinians to the PA but did not give up control of monetary policy, banking, natural resources, transport, and borders.

As a result, even though the 1990s were boom years for Israel, the Palestinian economy contracted. Despite hope from the Oslo peace deal, the Palestinian standard of living fell during the following decades, according to some estimates, declining as much as 40% by 2008.[250]

In September 2000, triggered by Ariel Sharon's visit to the Al-Aqsa Mosque and a drinking water crisis in Gaza, a second Intifada began. The Israeli reaction was harsh and ultimately devastating for the Palestinian economy.

According to the World Bank, between 2000 and 2003, Israeli restricted the number of West Bank Palestinians permitted to work in Israel by 53% and Gazans by a staggering 86%. As a result, Palestinian per capita GDP dropped by 40%, surpassing the decline felt during the 2001 financial collapse in Argentina and the US Great Depression in the 1930s.[251]

The Dependency Problem

Taken all together, the Paris Protocol restrictions have led to a chronic Palestinian balance-of-payments deficit. Typically, when a nation finds itself in such a situation, it has a few options. First, it can print more money, devaluing the currency. But Palestine has no monetary discretion, no central bank, no way to do debt monetization, and no way to print money. A second option is drawing down reserves. But given its lack of monetary independence, it has few reserves. Third, would be to borrow through debt financing. But since Palestine is not a nation, few want its debt. So, the fourth option is foreign aid.

Palestine has become dependent on foreign aid to function. If the aid checks do not arrive, the government often cannot finance the public budget. Since 1993, more than $40 billion has been spent in the West Bank and Gaza Strip by international donors, making Palestinians one of the highest per-capita recipients of aid in the world.[252]

According to Tartir, "Palestinians have been forced to live in an aid-development paradox: large amounts of aid associated with a downward decline in socioeconomic and human development indicators. In cases like Gaza, those declines have been dystopian."

Despite all of the aid, unemployment and poverty and debt are up; per capita income is down; the economic base deteriorated; costs of living and food insecurity are up; and the promised foreign investment has not materialized.

A 2010 analysis by Nikki Tillekens showed that 71% of aid to Palestinians ended up in the Israeli economy.[253]

"Of the more than 12 billion dollars of foreign aid given to the Palestinians between 2000 and 2008," she wrote, "8.7 billion dollars ended up in the Israeli economy."

International donors are, Tartir said, whether they know it or not, helping to preserve this status quo.

Each year, Washington supplies Israel with $3.8 billion of aid, remaining by far Israel's primary market for exports and source of imports.[254] This makes for a bizarre situation where even though the Palestinians are highly dependent on aid, Israelis receive much more of it per capita. Before 1999, US foreign aid covered the entire cost of the occupation.

Today, the United States still heavily subsidizes the occupation in an arrangement Shir Hever called a "profitable venture" where Israel receives payments in dollars but builds walls and pays troops in shekels. As a result, the foreign currency reserves in the Israeli central bank increase, which can be used to pay for trade deficits or to strengthen the shekel, which has appreciated against the dollar 25% over the past 20 years. Hever argued that the Israeli government goes to great lengths to protect this mechanism, even theorizing that a main motivation behind its attack on Gaza in 2008 was to stop an outflow of shekels that was pouring into Egypt through underground tunnels, in effect draining Israeli reserves.[255]

The US government also supports the Egyptian military dictatorship, the Jordanian king, and the Saudi tyranny, who all work in concert with Israel to oppose threats from Iran and its allies in the region. Even with their nuclear arsenal, Israelis are understandably wary about the Iranian threat of annihilation, as it is not an idle one. Especially when one considers Israel's history, where it was attacked upon its independence from all sides. So, it would be naive for Palestinians to expect outside support for Israel to end anytime soon.

Supporters of the status quo insist that it is just a matter of time, and that with continued gradual improvements in Palestinian standards of living, peace will one day come. This idea dates back to the 1970s and the Carter administration, which thought that "happy" Palestinians, "who had steady employment and a functioning administrative structure, would be willing to negotiate for a settlement while under occupation." The result of this philosophy was to de-link economic aid from sovereignty.[256]

Many Israeli, American, and European officials and donors vehemently disagree and say that they are doing their best to help support a vulnerable Palestinian population under the thumb of corrupt and violent leaders who pose a threat to regional stability.

Tartir also blames the PA for preserving the status quo. As we speak, he said, it is repressing protestors because it does not want anyone to disrupt the deal it has, where its inner circle benefits from cooperating with the Israeli government in running a broken rentier state.

Yasser Arafat's Legacy of Corruption

Fadi Elsalameen is a Palestinian democracy advocate. As we spoke in a series of phone and in-person conversations in the summer and fall of 2021, he told me that Palestinians were protesting in huge numbers against President Mahmood Abbas, who has ruled the west Bank for 16 years. Elsalameen called him "extremely corrupt."

Yasser Arafat's kleptocracy was legendary: He was estimated to be worth billions, large chunks of which he plucked out of flows of income coming from the backs of Palestinian workers in Israel and diverted to his own bank accounts, or to French accounts belonging to his wife.[257]

Elsalameen said that Abbas has now followed in Arafat's footsteps, where Abbas and family have used their political power to build an empire in industries like insurance, telecommunications, construction, and tobacco.[258] According to leaked documents from the Panama Papers, Abbas and his two sons "used power and influence to control the two major Palestinian economic boards (Arab Palestinian Investment Company, Palestinian Investment Fund) and built a West Bank economic empire worth more than $300 million."[259]

Abbas's son Yasser owns Falcon Tobacco, which holds a monopoly over the sale of US-made cigarettes in the West Bank. According to Elsalameen, Abbas raised taxes so high on West Bank tobacco producers, to benefit his own import business, that they collapsed. Critics have accused Abbas of pilfering hundreds of millions of dollars of Palestinian state money for personal gain.[260] A 2016 poll showed that 95.5% of Palestinians viewed him as corrupt.[261] He continues to rule by decree.

"I hate Hamas more than Abbas," Elsalameen said, "but we have to target the head of the pyramid scheme here in the West Bank."

Elsalameen said that a reliance on foreign aid has made it so that the PA is less accountable to the people, and has also created a special elite class, separate from the rest of society. Public revenues, he said, have propped up this system for decades. In 2015, "only 16% of the PA's annual budget was spent on education, nine percent on health and one percent on agriculture," according to *Al Jazeera*, but 26% was spent on the security sector, which, Elsalameen said, often targets Palestinians.[262]

Protests last summer broke out around when Abbas had activist Nizar Banat, one of his fiercest critics, killed.

"His thugs," Elsalameen said, "went at night and abducted Banat from his home and beat him to death with clubs. Abbas gave them complete immunity. So the family of the victim said: 'We're going to protest until he leaves.' And then everyone else joined them on the streets."

Thousands marched across the West Bank and demanded an "overthrow of the regime," Elsalameen said, in scenes that reminded some of the Arab Spring a decade ago. But Abbas continues to survive. Elsalameen said Abbas stays in power by telling the Israelis, Americans, and the World Bank: If you do not have me in power, you're going to have Hamas.

"That's how Abbas gets them to protect him," he said. "He is their client."

Elsalameen pointed to the failed protests and said that politics is proving of limited use to the Palestinian struggle. "You can only get so far with the ballot box," he said.

When asked about Bitcoin, he said, "Yes, we can start fighting back peacefully with Bitcoin. It's something that any young Palestinian can do. You give up price stability, perhaps, but in return you get freedom."

A challenge, he said, is that "we have to get people to know about it." It's a new, weird concept, he said. But once people understand, he has no doubt they will use it. "It's an upgrade over today," he said, "where people keep cash under a mattress, or where they wait a month to receive a payment from their family abroad."

Bitcoin could also fight corruption, he thinks.

"Today, if you bribe the payment authorities, they will let your wire go through faster," he said. "They grow fat on this. That could end with Bitcoin."

He noted that in the young generation, many Palestinians are already buying bitcoin.

"They don't have the S&P 500," he said.

Elsalameen thinks the fact that both the Israelis and the PA are criticizing Bitcoin is a good thing.

"That's how you know it's going to help the average Palestinian," he said.

From Banking to Bitcoin in Ramallah

With average daily wages at 264 shekels in Israel, compared to 123 shekels in the West Bank, who could blame Palestinians for seeking a higher income elsewhere, even if by doing so they deepen their own dependence?[263]

Given this reality, I asked Alaa Tartir what a decolonial Palestinian economy would look like.

"It's a future project," said Tartir, depressingly. "It's nothing very close."

He did say that there has long been an idea in the Palestinian discourse of a "resistance economy" which would allow them to stay, resist and gain sovereignty. After the second Intifada, the Arab-Israeli author Azmi Bishara "lamented the lack of a single Palestinian bank, insurance company or printing press, and called on Palestinian investors to 'begin to think of local economic ventures with their own structures, market, and labor.'"[264]

But, Tartir said, they have always been reliant on the shekel and the Israeli financial rails and "have always lacked the tool to make this happen."

A Palestinian former banker named Abuwedad thinks Bitcoin can be this tool. He did not want to give his real name for our interview but spoke to me from his home in Ramallah, where he recently left his job after seven years in the industry. By the time he quit, he was a deputy financial manager for a major bank servicing the West Bank and Jordan. He left because he had grown sick over his personal role in spreading what he considers a financial disease hurting Palestinians: too much borrowing.

"The whole system," he said, "has been based for the last 15 years on making people borrow much more than what they can afford."

Even worse, he said, the loans are not used to start businesses or build infrastructure but are spent on weddings, cars, or apartments downtown. According to policy researcher Yara Harari, "Over the past 10 years, car loans have jumped sixfold from $40 million in 2008 to $250 million. Thus, Ramallah … could easily be mistaken for a prosperous city with middle-class neighborhoods full of plush villas and shiny BMWs. But this is just a facade."[265]

Abuwedad said that with all the easy money — and with no Robinhood, no E-Trade and no access to the world's top stock markets — people have piled into real estate. Between 1994 and 2016, 80% of Palestinian capital formation was in buildings.[266] This has made costs "surreal." It could be $100,000 for a small apartment, he said, or $1,000,000 for 1,000 square meters of land, all in a place where the GDP per capita is somewhere around $3,500.

He said that banks are guilty of helping Palestinians increase their reliance on Israel, and decrease their own sovereignty. This is as a result of reforms brought in 2007 by then-Palestinian Prime Minister Salam Fayyad, which Abuwedad said "prioritized consumerism over independence."

The laws "required banks operating in Palestine to extend 40% of their credit locally… credit facilities skyrocketed from $1.3 billion in 2008 to $7.1

billion in 2018, a 450% increase," according to *Political Economy of Palestine*, a new collection of essays edited by Alaa Tartir and others.[267]

"Consider a member of the Palestinian security forces making $600 per month," Abuwedad said. "They can now take a monthly loan 5 times or even 10 times their salary, and with 10% down in cash buy a fancy 120 square meter apartment in Ramallah."

The banks are happy, of course, as they can make $200,000 over 25 years on every $100,000 they give out. But the people are now indebted, oftentimes for their entire lives. This is the reality now, Abuwedad said, for huge segments of Palestinian society that have borrowed to finance not just apartments but all kinds of personal goods.

Very little borrowing, he wrote, goes into industry, agriculture, or entrepreneurship. In 2008, only 7% of credit was used for agriculture and manufacturing versus 33% for "cars, credit cards, and consumption goods."[268]

"It's the same policies that many decades ago forced us away from creating an industrial base and made us reliant on external powers," Abuwedad said, "just dressed up in new clothes of "state building" and "economic empowerment."

Today, all Palestinians still look forward to freedom, he said, but the system "makes it much more difficult to focus on that ultimate goal and distracts them with immediate financial concerns." People, he said, "are living paycheck to paycheck to pay back loans and enrich the bankers instead of saving and investing for their future."

After leaving his job in banking, Abuwedad worked for a tech company in Ramallah for a few years, then tried to start a business with friends in the online gaming industry. He believes Palestinians can be competitive in eSports — even though they are not today — and that gaming can help with cooperation, team-building, increasing personal dignity, and connecting with people abroad. However, there are so many obstacles, mainly, that the internet is not good enough (despite it being blazing fast a few miles away in Israel) and that computers are so expensive.

Abuwedad points to a laptop that might cost $1,500 in the United States or in Israel, and said that if he wants to buy the same thing in Palestine, it will cost as much as $3,500. At first glance, one might assume that because Israelis and Palestinians use the same currency, that inflation of the shekel would damage them equally. Abuwedad walked me through why that is not the case.

"When Palestinian imports arrive in Israel," Abuwedad said, "they get taxed, then they cost money to store as they have to wait to be sent into the West Bank, as truck schedules are very restricted. Along the way, inventory often gets stolen. Then, local sellers mark up the goods to cover their own taxes and profits. By the time the laptop is sold in Ramallah, it could be two-to-three times more expensive than in Tel Aviv, even though everyone is using the same currency."

Another account said that it took on average "38 days" for Palestinian traders to import and sell goods, while their Israeli counterparts could do it in 10 days.[269] This led to an average cost per transaction of three times as much in Ramallah as in Tel Aviv. This aggressive inflation, Abuwedad said, is true for many consumer products.

"If we could import directly," he said, "then it would be much cheaper." He blamed the Paris Protocol, which he said is "outdated" and has not been updated in almost 30 years despite the fact that the world has changed dramatically.

Israeli and Palestinian inflation tracked together through the 1980s, when the shekel crash decimated Palestinian purchasing power, and through the 1990s; but they split after the second Intifada in October 2000. Israel experienced deflation, but the Palestinians experienced stagflation with a fall in income and a rise in prices. Palestinian purchasing power began to massively trail Israeli purchasing power. Shir Hever notes that by 2008, "The same product would have been 32% more expensive in a Palestinian city than in an Israeli city."

Abuwedad's plans to get out of this trap through starting a company were foiled by the COVID-19 pandemic, which he said hit the West Bank particularly hard, depressing economic activity. In the time since, he has gotten very into Bitcoin. He said there is a whole community in the West Bank and Gaza now getting involved. I mentioned to him that global adoption of Bitcoin in 2021 is roughly around the same level as it was for the internet in 1997 — about 200 million people or 2% of the population. He thinks that's probably the percentage of Palestinians who are using Bitcoin, and said that will grow quickly in the coming years.

But how do Palestinians buy bitcoin?

"We always find the holes," Abuwedad said.

He told me about a loophole, where the Palestinian Monetary Authority will block transactions from local bank accounts trying to buy cryptocurrency on exchanges. But there's one exception, the tether stablecoin (USDT). He thinks that because tether is linked to the dollar, they have let it slide, and so purchases of tether on platforms like Binance go unblocked. Abuwedad said that almost everyone he knows gets into cryptocurrency through tether. From there, he said, they may buy bitcoin as a savings instrument or stay in tether as a "checking" account. He said that some people also go around the banking system entirely and use Telegram or Facebook groups to coordinate to buy tether or bitcoin in a peer-to-peer way.

Abuwedad seems to know that tether is not an ideal solution. But it works for now, he said. We discussed the idea that in the near future, Palestinians could have Lightning wallets that are "pegged" to a fiat currency like the dollar and could use those instead of having to rely on tether. He did not know much about Lightning, but during our WhatsApp call, I showed him how to download a Muun wallet and sent him $5 via Lightning.

"That was really fast," he said, impressed by the instant transfer from Boston, where I was staying, to Ramallah. I told him there were virtually no fees either and that got him even more excited. We took a moment to reflect on the fact that it is such a struggle for Palestinians to move money from one place to another and discussed how game-changing Bitcoin is: From thousands of miles away, I sent him money and we did not have to deal with any customs police, delays, red flags, confiscations, or VAT. The Israeli government did not get a cut and neither did the PA.

He thinks stable Lightning wallets could be huge for Palestinians: a bank account where you do not need any ID, where you control your own funds, where you can transact instantly anywhere in the world for virtually no fees, and where you can choose to peg the value to the dollar or keep your money natively in bitcoin. "That's the dream," he said.

Abuwedad considers Bitcoin a peaceful protest against a corrupt, exploitative, and centralized financial system: one that he saw from the inside during his career as a banker. The obstacle, according to Abuwedad, is that only a small number of Palestinians are using Bitcoin today.

"Most see it as an investment," he said, "and not as a currency."

It will take time, he said, for it to become a mass movement. Education, he said, is very important.

"People have a lot of questions, but over time, they learn, and they use," he said.

He's seen reports lately of the Palestinian Authority launching its own digital currency, but he does not think people will trust it. If anything, he said, it may encourage more people to use Bitcoin.

"If we want to make Bitcoin our way to say no to the world, to live free from the Oslo and Paris agreements, then we need to start using it in daily life. And that will take time," he said.

"We all know," he said, "that the international community will not give us freedom. So, we must take it on our own."

He told me that he chose the name Abuwedad as Wedad is the name he would call his daughter, if he eventually has one. And maybe, he said, she will grow up in a Bitcoin world.

The New Resistance Economy

Kefah Abukhdeir is a third-generation Palestinian American. She grew up in Atlanta, Georgia, settled with her husband in East Jerusalem, and works as an educator.

Abukhdeir's family originally left Jerusalem when it was under Ottoman rule, fleeing conscription to the United States and South America, but retained ties to the homeland. Her father returned to Palestine and became an outspoken dissident against the presence of the Jordanians in the West Bank in the 1960s. Eventually he left for good to the United States, where he went to Georgia Tech and started a family in the American South. Like her family before her, Abukhdeir went back to the West Bank to Birzeit University in the late 1990s to learn Arabic. She ended up earning an education degree and eventually moved to East Jerusalem.

"If you want to break a Palestinian mother's heart," she said, "tell her that her child is going to study business or agriculture." To achieve actual independence, she thinks, these two fields are critical, but it is discouraged or even shunned. It is a result, she said, of indigenous economic progress being seen as a "waste of time."

Abukhdeir has spent the last decade working in education with Palestinian youth, with US State Department programs and through EduReach, an organization that provides for teacher training and extracurricular programs for kids. There, she faced a dilemma: To be more competitive, the students have to learn English and go to school in Israel. She knows this continues to prolong the situation where Palestinians remain dependent on the world around them, and that it boosts the economy in Israel, but she wants the best future for the children, who want to be as employable as possible. "We stay up all night debating this," she said.

"I started to feel guilty because I felt like I was facilitating brain drain," she said. "If the kids are successful, they'll go to college in Israel or the US, and they don't want to come back." They are then overqualified for jobs in Palestine. Best case, they could end up working for an NGO or foreign entity, like her. "We aren't really part of the local economy," she said. "We aren't helping to reinvest."

Her experience encapsulates the dilemma for many Palestinians since 1967. You could stay at home, or you could go work in Israel for higher wages and do more for your family. But you made a trade-off, bringing economic activity and development there instead of back home.

"Independence is financial," Abukhdeir told me. "If we don't have financial freedom, nothing is going to change."

Abukhdeir pointed out that the currency usage in Palestine has varied over time. People still use the Jordanian dinar, as well as US dollars, but lately, she said, the shekel has become even more popular, even in Gaza.

"Easily 80% of your daily transactions are in shekels," she said. This means that nearly every transaction a Palestinian makes "is supporting and deepening reliance on Israel."

Growing up in Atlanta, she said that she learned a lot about the American civil rights movement and studied similar movements in South Africa and Ireland.

"One of the first things they'd do," she said, "is set up an independent economy. But we don't have that. We just have red flags, confiscations and taxes that pay for benefits that we don't even receive."

Recently, Abukhdeir started spending time at tech hubs in Ramallah and Jerusalem. There, she said, she was introduced to "tech colonialism." Here, Israelis would come into recruit the best and the brightest, but there were no Palestinian companies recruiting.

"We're creating a labor force for the ongoing occupation," she said. "Tech is important because we need a plan that does not require raw resources. We can't own land, we can't manufacture — so what can we do?"

To make a change, Abukhdeir is looking at Bitcoin. She is part of a movement that will try to map the Palestinian business ecosystem, both Palestinian-owned businesses in Israel, as well as enterprises in East Jerusalem and the West Bank, and encourage new practices.

The idea is, if you're a Palestinian-owned business, you can offer to take bitcoin for payment. It would, she said, spark curiosity, launch a circular economy, encourage more people to learn about Bitcoin, and teach them more about how money works.

"This," she said, "is how we could end our reliance on the shekel."

Today, Abukhdeir has teachers working for her in Gaza. She says that paying them is hugely complicated. "I can't use PayPal, even though I'm a dual Israeli-American citizen. Even with my financial privilege, it's hard to do," she said.

She describes how she might take money out of her Israeli account through an ATM, deposit it in a Palestinian bank — which she could only open with her American passport — and then she can make a wire transfer to the teacher's account. This takes time and is expensive. But with Bitcoin, she said, she can send value instantly to the teacher in Gaza.

She said that she's still putting the future picture together in her head.

"With Bitcoin, you could build a company that's totally independent, where you don't have to use a PA bank, and where you don't have to rely on the shekel and the Israeli economy," she said.

Abukhdeir thinks that change will ultimately come only through "huge amounts of violence or huge amounts of economic activity" and thinks the latter is the only way to find success. "We can't settle for a half-baked solution," she said, pointing to how the Oslo process failed.

"We need to escape completely," she said. "If we don't opt out of the currency, we are just going to end up strengthening the system."

The Israeli Bitcoin Community

It is clear that some in the Palestinian community view Bitcoin as a way forward. But what about their Israeli counterparts? For background, I spoke to several Israeli Bitcoiners on the condition of anonymity.

Some are worried about the political environment in Israel right now. Some say it's "not that bad," but one entrepreneur told me that it is risky to do anything that could be described as "left-wing" (such as helping Palestinians through Bitcoin) and that it is getting harder and harder to speak one's mind.

"The sentiment is getting worse by the day," he said. "It reminds me of bad days in world history."

He went on: "It makes it hard to think about a bright future here. It's a huge dilemma about whether to even stay in the country."

But while he said connecting with Palestinians about Bitcoin use has not been a topic or priority at the meetups in Tel Aviv so far — "never," he said — he thinks it could be successful.

He said Bitcoin continues to build bridges, not walls. And when he stopped to think about how Israelis could actually extend freedom to Palestinians, Bitcoin could be a way.

"It's not fake freedom," he said, "like the kind we have tried to give before."

"I'm here for coexistence," the entrepreneur said. "I want a single state solution. I want one country with bitcoin as the currency, with the same rules for everyone. How Bitcoin can help create this atmosphere of co-existence is very important. It's not about creating two states: it's about reducing the power of the state."

An Israeli Settler's View on Bitcoin

Many Israeli Bitcoiners are relatively progressive and even sympathetic with the idea of helping Palestinians with open-source money. But what about nationalist Zionists? Or even settlers? Surprisingly, at least one of them is trying to promote Bitcoin in Palestine.

Jonathan Caras is an American tech entrepreneur and Bitcoin advocate who has been living in the West Bank for 10 years.

"I can see Ramallah from outside my window," he told me as we spoke by video chat.

Today, some 14 million individuals — approximately half Jews and half Palestinians — live between the Mediterranean Sea and Jordan River under the economic control of the Israeli government.

On one side in the state of Israel there are nine million citizens living in a robust, if eroding, democratic society. On the other, there is a military occupation of nearly five million Palestinians, now entering its 54th year. A 700-kilometer barrier — which is in many places a literal concrete wall — has been under construction for two decades and separates the two.[270] Caras and hundreds of thousands of other Israeli settlers live east of this barrier.

According to the Israeli civil rights group B'Tselem, "More than 2.6 million Palestinian subjects live in the West Bank, in dozens of disconnected enclaves, under rigid military rule and without political rights.[271] In about 40% of the territory, Israel has transferred some civilian powers to the PA." However, it reminds us, even there "the PA is still subordinate to Israel and can only exercise its limited powers with Israel's consent."

Sixty-one percent of the West Bank's territory is classified as Area C — comprised of vast open spaces and farmland — and is directly controlled by the Israeli military. A 1995 agreement decreed that resource-rich Area C would be "gradually transferred to Palestinian jurisdiction" by 1997.[272] But that has not happened. Instead, Palestinians have been prevented from harvesting or investing in this land, and Israeli settlers and companies have increasingly colonized the area.

Israel utilizes many resources in Area C, including solar power for more than 10,000 Israeli homes, water sources and farmland.[273] At the same time, it confiscates Palestinian property. In the past 20 years, Israeli forces have, for example, uprooted more than one million productive Palestinian trees.[274] Israel and Jordan make $4.2 billion per year selling minerals like potash and bromine from the Area C regions around the Dead Sea. A World Bank report states that Palestinians could increase their GDP by almost 10% if they were allowed to invest in this operation, too. In total, the report concludes that Palestinians could increase their GDP by 35% if they were allowed to harness Area C for agriculture, minerals, mining, construction, tourism, and telecommunications.[275]

The Israeli military has closed off most of the West Bank to Palestinian civilian access, and has installed checkpoints and barriers to stifle human movement in the remaining Areas A and B. A dizzying array of restrictions — imposed in the name of counter-terrorism — limit the ability of Palestinians to move, build, go abroad, marry, buy property, work and vote to participate in the system that governs them.[276] The technology used to enforce this system is sold by Israeli companies like Candiru, Cellebrite and NSO Group to governments around the world.[277] Marketed as tried and tested in the West Bank and Gaza, these surveillance products are highly sought after and considered world-class.

Hundreds of thousands of Jewish settlers now live permanently in West Bank settlements east of the Green Line, the border established as separating Israel and Palestine after the 1948 war.[278] These settlers are financially incentivized and subsidized to move there by Israeli policies, including tax and housing benefits. In total, there are more than 280 Israeli settlements and a variety of industrial zones in the West Bank, with more than 60 outposts created in the past 10 years, all in contravention of international law. The maps of this shift in control are striking.[279]

When the Oslo process began in 1993, there were a little more than 100,000 Israeli settlers in the West Bank, not counting East Jerusalem. In 2021, there are more than 475,000.[280]

Caras is one of them. He said he is a "religious Zionist settler." His goal is to "reinstate the Kingdom of David and build Solomon's Temple." Twenty years ago, he first came to Israel, and realized that "the best way for me to fulfill my Biblical obligation is to settle on an empty hilltop in the West Bank."

In the past few years, Caras has given a number of lectures about "how technology can promote mixed interaction and co-existence." He said that Bitcoin allows humans to cross borders that previously were impassable: legal, financial, and ideological.

"It allows us to come together," he said. He sits on the Judea and Samaria Chamber of Commerce and interacts frequently with Palestinians as part of his role.

He said that if he does business with a Palestinian, that could be a danger to their life. "If I want to start a business with my neighbor, his children could be killed," said Caras. "So, Bitcoin allows us to work together and keep him safe."

He tells me that he's seen cars get burned to the ground as a warning message for doing business with Israelis.

Caras argued that Palestinians have actually benefited from the strong shekel, comparing their plight with that of Lebanese, Syrians, Egyptians, and others in the region who have suffered from high inflation or hyperinflation. He says Hamas and the PA are corrupt, but that the shekel has partially protected Palestinians from their misrule by providing a reliable unit of account, medium of exchange, and store of value.

When I mentioned to him that Palestinians still suffer from significant price inflation, he said "a glass of water is always going to be more expensive in the desert than at Niagara Falls" and said this doesn't have to do with the money, it has to do with control over the borders and goods and services.

"In the West Bank, Palestinians can't just get stuff on Amazon," he said. "There's always going to be a price discrepancy."

He said the restrictive economic regime that holds Palestinians back is "stomached" by the Israelis and the international community because of violent threats from Palestinians. "As long as Hamas and the PA are aiming to annihilate the Jewish state, there isn't a hope for Palestinians to have the same prices as in Tel Aviv," he said.

Ultimately, though, from a religious perspective, Caras thinks that the shekel and all fiat money will be "viewed as unethical and immoral from an Islamic Judeo-Christian perspective."

He said that "fiat is rent-seeking, clearly a form of theft, you are paying interest to the government for building your own family's wealth."

He contrasted this to commodity-based money, like gold and bitcoin, where "every member of society is equal underneath heaven."

With Bitcoin, "we all know what the rules are and we know that we can participate without people changing the rules in the future," he said. "This is not the case when we work in a fiat system, where it's by nature a two-party system. There's the oligarchy of fat cats who set the monetary policy and control the flow of funds, and then the peons and serfs who are subject to its enforcement. It's built into the name 'fiat' that we are not equals."

Caras believes we are "in a messianic era" and that "Biblical prophecies are unfolding" and there's "a lot of evidence" that Bitcoin falls under those prophecies.

When asked if he thinks the Israeli government will try to ban or restrict Bitcoin as a tool of terror or resistance, he said the Israeli people know that technological innovation and opportunity far outweighs the risks. He said that if Hamas is trying to circumvent banking restrictions by collecting funds in bitcoin (as the Israeli government has recently alleged, seizing bitcoin on exchanges that it claimed was connected to Hamas), then that is more easily regulated than Caras "paying a gardener or web developer in bitcoin."[281]

He said the new Israeli prime minister has a background in cybersecurity and entrepreneurship and said a ban is unlikely.

"Banning Bitcoin," Caras said, "is as ridiculous as banning marijuana. If I have a seed in my pocket, I can plant fields of crops. If I have 12 words in my head, you can't stop me."

Caras pointed out that Bitcoin is already much larger by market cap than the shekel today.[282] He thinks countries are going to be forced to add bitcoin to their balance sheets as a reserve asset and make it legal tender, or try to ban or fight Bitcoin, a battle they will lose and have to buy in later at a higher price.

He is a big critic of central bank digital currencies (CBDCs) and talked about how cash is helpful because it is unstoppable and private.

"I would vehemently oppose replacing cash with a CBDC: it's a form of control," he said. "It can hurt your business if Twitter freezes your account for 72 hours. It can literally kill your business if there is no cash in society and the government doesn't like who they saw you holding hands with on a security camera and so they freeze your account."

But cash, he said, is still subject to debasement, and it hurts people's ability to save for the long term.

"It will allow for a generation that believes in their ability to invest in themselves and to put money away every month that can be time locked, that can be used as collateral," he said. "This will have a socioeconomic impact, eventually, on a personal and national level for Palestinians and Israelis."

"I put my money away for my children in Bitcoin," he added. "I have more faith in Bitcoin than the Central Bank of Israel over the next 20 years. And I'm a big supporter of Israel. Think about that.".

Caras does agree that paying someone in shekels is a power dynamic.

"That resonates with me," he said, which is why he always offers to pay people in bitcoin first. "Even if they are just going to dump it," he said, "first they'll have to create a wallet and begin to understand it."

When asked if he thought Israel might lag behind Palestine in the adoption of Bitcoin, he said he is lobbying the Israeli government to be on the cutting edge. But if Palestinians made the switch to a Bitcoin standard first, he thinks it would cause Israel to "chase after them."

Caras said he does not view himself as unbiased, and he knows that some Palestinians will call him a war criminal and a "physical representation of all of their hardships." But, he said, he's still been able to sit down and geek out about Bitcoin with Palestinians.

"We all want financial sovereignty," he said. "I am interested in prosperity for everyone, not just the Jews."

The Fight for Sovereignty

Many Palestinians are trying to push back against Israeli settlements, and some view Bitcoin as a possible tool that can aid this effort. To learn more, I spoke to Zaytoon, who works for the Palestinian Social Fund, an organization that is crowdfunding from the Palestinian diaspora to seed agricultural activities in the West Bank.

Zaytoon said Palestine is "totally dependent on foreign aid and imports. Our production capacity has dwindled. We don't have sovereignty." He believes that the future is in "producing our own food." His plan is to grow cooperatives across West Bank villages, and launch a new governance paradigm, not dependent on foreign aid or the Palestinian Authority, but one "that the individuals and communities own."

It is a left-wing vision, for sure. I mentioned to him that there's also a libertarian Bitcoin community in the United States that is trying to achieve agricultural self-sufficiency, to go "off grid," raise animals and crops, and seek freedom and distance from the federal government.

"At the end of the day," he said, "we are all human. We are occupied by Israel and what we are seeing now is that an agricultural solution is necessary. The Americans you speak of might be occupied instead by consumerism, but they seek the same thing. It's two sides of the same coin."

Achieving agricultural independence is hard. Israeli settlements, Zaytoon said, are expanding.

"They are cutting us up geographically into Bantustans," he said. "First they take the hilltops as vantage points, and then they go for the areas with the most fertile soil — for example the region around the Dead Sea — these places are great for growing produce all year round."

According to B'Tselem, only one-eighth of the land under Palestinian control is even under cultivation because of Israeli's strict permit regime.[283]

"We must start with what we have," he said: "the land around our houses. We can start to build a resistance economy that is more and more decentralized."

Agricultural self-sufficiency was the spirit of the first Intifada, Zaytoon said, but that was sacrificed by Yasser Arafat and his PLO cronies for money and personal gain.

"We have to try again," said Zaytoon.

A big problem Zaytoon and his team face is that any money going into Palestine is inspected by Israel. The financial borders are controlled. Money gets delayed, taxed, trimmed, and sometimes confiscated.

"Whenever they deem us a risk, they can freeze our assets in seconds, even if we are in Canada," he said. So, he said, they are planning to raise money in bitcoin, and sidestep the whole restrictive system. His team is currently working on setting up a BTCPay Server, an open-source payment processor.

But Zaytoon wants to make it clear that an anti-colonial currency is, by itself, an incomplete solution.

"Monetary freedom must go hand-in-hand with building our production powers," he said. "At the end of the day, any currency is an alias to resources, and we have to generate our own resources from nature and build them into valuable products that can be used in our society to further innovation and education and healthcare and food security."

"In doing so, Palestinians should use a currency that *we* control, not one pegged to the Israeli economy or the petrodollar or anything else," he added.

The Future of Bitcoin in Palestine

In July 2021, the Israeli government publicly announced the seizing of bitcoin funds connected to Hamas.[284] It seems certain that the IDF will begin to demonize Bitcoin as a tool of terrorists and, perhaps, make it harder for Israelis and Palestinians to use.

Given that the Israeli government has prioritized centralizing as many economic flows as possible under its control into and out of Gaza and the West Bank, any money moving outside "official channels" will likely be deemed suspicious. This could be a deterrent to future adoption.

But already today, Paxful and LocalBitcoins have vibrant peer-to-peer marketplaces in Palestine.[285] If Bitcoin could become adopted by hundreds of

Palestinian businesses, and hundreds of thousands of individuals, then it could become a remarkably powerful peaceful protest.

There is a possibility here for Palestinians — or any vulnerable population, whether trapped by foreign occupation, domestic authoritarianism, a collapsing economy, or a structural lack of opportunity — to adopt Bitcoin as a new currency. Millions of individuals are already making this choice in Turkey, Argentina, Nigeria (see Chapter I), Iran, Lebanon, and beyond.

More than two-thirds of Palestinians are under the age of 30 and more than 70% have internet access.[286] Young people are more comfortable with the idea of mobile money and will be looking for technological solutions to their problems. It is a risk, but adopting Bitcoin as a circular economy could very well give Palestinians a leg up on their neighbors and position them relatively well for the next century.

El Salvador has provided a national template of how Bitcoin can be used not just as a savings instrument to invest in the future, but also as a payment network that can allow citizens to connect with anyone in the world instantly.

Could Palestine be the El Salvador of the Middle East? President Nayib Bukele is, after all, Palestinian.[287] His grandparents originally emigrated to El Salvador from the Jerusalem and Bethlehem areas during the fraying of the Ottoman Empire. His father even converted to Islam and "became a prominent imam in San Salvador and a vocal defender of the Palestinian cause."

Bukele has been quoted as saying that he is very proud of his Palestinian origins, saying he "would like to see a thriving Palestinian state."[288] It is ironic that a person of Palestinian descent would be the first world leader to adopt bitcoin as a national currency.

There is no question that the Israeli government, American government, Palestinian Authority, World Bank, and United Nations would all oppose such a move. They are all too invested in the status quo. So, any adoption would have to come from a people power movement.

As for traditional attempts at reform, in 2021, there was discussion of restarting the Joint Economic Committee (JEC) — the organization created at the time of the Paris Protocol, which would ultimately have the power to make a new currency for Palestinians. The JEC has not met since 2009 and has largely been used to oversee operations in the OPT, but Israeli and PA ministers are planning to revamp the JEC and "remove obstacles" to PA economic activity.[289]

Palestinians have seen this movie before. An Israeli government push to help the PA has typically not done much for the average person in the West Bank or Gaza, beyond siphoning more money to PA leadership and introducing new controls on the ground. The stated goals this time are to issue 17,000 more permits to Palestinian laborers to "work in construction and industry in Israel" and to bolster the Palestinian Fuel Administration.[290] Again, any reform here is likely to deepen Palestinian dependence on the Israeli economy and put the PA on additional life support.

Recently, the news broke that the Palestinian Monetary Authority is mulling a "central bank digital currency," a new kind of asset meant to replace banknotes and coins with a digital central bank liability that individuals would hold on their phones. Critics have been blunt: "It's not going to replace the shekel or the dinar or the dollar. It's certainly not going to be a store of value or a unit of accounting," said Barry Topf, a former senior advisor to the Bank of Israel.[291]

Palestinians have not been able to mint their own cash — per the Paris Protocol — but even if they could, there's no guaranteeing that the Palestinian Authority would not abuse its power and create massive inflation. Its track record on fiscal matters is poor. Topf might be right.

Moreover, the creation of a "Palestinian" currency (digital or otherwise) runs the risk of prolonging the power imbalances that exist today with the Palestinian economy. Would it provide financial "inclusion" — or global financial exclusion?

Even worse, transitioning the Palestinian economy to a digital one — whether it's controlled by the PA, World Bank, Israel or anyone else — would be disastrous for the small amount of freedom that Palestinians do receive from cash and their informal economy, where they can save and transact outside of government control. A CBDC would enable greater blacklisting, confiscation and surveillance, no matter who is in charge of design.

Activism Beyond Virtue Signaling?

A lot of the online activism for Palestine can be classified as "virtue signaling." What does posting #FreePalestine actually achieve? Usually, very little. But by helping someone understand how to use Bitcoin, one can help them achieve a degree of real freedom: the ability to protect value from confiscation and to connect with anyone in the world.

For a people whose history is so filled with confiscation, Bitcoin gives Palestinians a way to take the fruits of their labor and time and lock it into an asset in cyberspace, beyond the control of Hamas, Israel, the PA, or the World Bank, and secure it with math. It is a peaceful protest, a digital shield, that could lead to big change.

This has been underscored by the many interviews that I conducted to inform this chapter. Beyond those whose stories were told, I spoke to a half-dozen other Palestinians for background. They all seemed to echo a few things.

First, as one said, "If we're not taking matters into our own hands, then no progress will be made." There is a tremendous (and understandable) lack of trust of the authorities on all sides, and a realization that the status quo will continue unless something new is tried.

Second, if only a few people are using Bitcoin, then everyone seems to agree that the authorities would go after them and put them in jail. But if 100,000 people are using it, then there is nothing they can do. Building a movement is paramount.

Third, if critics on the left do not get it and continue to attack Bitcoin from their position of privilege, then, said one, they "seem to be more interested in talking about the problem than actually fixing it." They went on: "Where's their solution?"

The left traditionally dislikes or ignores Bitcoin. Left-wing critics and economists often call it useless: a Ponzi scheme, a tool for criminals, an environmental disaster, and so on. Amnesty International and Human Rights Watch continue to be silent on Bitcoin. Yes, they have done admirable work to detail the suffering of the Palestinians, but why not speak up about a technology that so many of them are already using for empowerment? The same can be said for the international community in general. If they actually want to get involved in changing the situation on the ground, it has to involve changing the money. And Bitcoin is one way to do that.

The Bitcoin silence is perhaps most sadly reflected by a search for the term on the websites of the establishment, Palestinian economic think tank MAS or the Israeli civil liberties group B'Tselem: zero results. It is clear that Palestinians will continue to adopt Bitcoin. But it remains unclear if their supporters around the world will help them in this regard.

Today, Palestinians have no monetary independence, are increasingly forced to use the currency of their occupier, are unable to increase their capital base, have become more consumerist and debt-saddled, are entirely reliant on foreign aid and, in Gaza, face civilizational collapse.

When Sara Roy reflected recently on "what is to be done," one of her conclusions was that "knowledge production is itself a form of resistance."

There is nothing to lose by sharing information about Bitcoin, which has already helped so many Palestinians. Perhaps the world's largest open-source money project can help, where everything else has failed.

Fix the Money, Fix the World

In the Bitcoin community, there is a saying: "Fix the money, fix the world."

Obviously, money is just one part of our social fabric. But it is a very important part, and at the end of the day, if Palestinians are not able to fix their money, they will not be able to fix their world.

At the end of my call with Uqab, he told me that many people were becoming so desperate in Gaza that they were selling their homes for bitcoin. It was the same for businesses. "Any enterprise that opens in Gaza is doomed to fail," he said, "so the owners would rather sell it than keep it."

He said their calculation was the following: Real estate is "going to zero" in Gaza, so worst-case scenario, if bitcoin crashes, "it is the status quo for us."

But if bitcoin continues on its historical trajectory and gains value versus fiat currencies? "Then we have a door to freedom."

"I'm saving up for my kids," he said, right before we hung up. "Bitcoin is going to be my ticket out of here."

.

Chapter VIII

Inside Cuba's Bitcoin Revolution

Lucia is a 30-year-old medical worker and Bitcoin user living in Matanzas, a city of about 150,000 people sitting about 50 miles east of Havana on Cuba's northern coast. Named after an aboriginal rebellion against Spanish colonizers, the word *matanzas* literally translates to "slaughter." The settlement later turned into a 19th-century epicenter of slavery and sugar plantations. Today, like all Cuban cities, it is ground zero for a financial and human crisis.

Since early 2021, the Cuban people are suffering through their worst economic struggle since the early 1990s, when the Soviet Union collapsed and the regime lost its main lifeline. At the time, longtime dictator Fidel Castro told citizens they needed to unite together to get through a "Special Period." The era was marked by food shortages, blackouts, thousands fleeing to Florida on risky rafts, and a spectacular devaluation of the Soviet ruble–pegged peso. Between 1991 and 1994 the Cuban economy contracted by 35% and quality of life deteriorated dramatically.[292]

Tensions peaked in the summer of 1994, when an anti-government protest known as the Maleconazo uprising broke out in Havana.[293] Without its Soviet subsidy, the state ration system was failing to support the population, and important goods were all of a sudden only available for purchase with dollars, which were increasingly expensive for Cubans to obtain with their peso wages and pensions. In a desperate move, the regime violated its founding collectivist philosophy and imposed a series of unprecedented taxes on the population. In response, tens of thousands of protestors gathered at the Malecon waterfront, calling for an end to the government.[294]

The internet did not exist, so the regime was able to quell the movement through police brutality while ensuring that most Cubans barely knew anything had happened. State television and radio made a brief mention of a small gathering of delinquents and troublemakers. But in reality, the Maleconazo was a staggering display of dissent, the biggest on the island since the revolution.

When the money system breaks, it can threaten a regime's survival.

Monetary Purification

Today, Lucia and other Cubans talk of a new "Special Period." As a result of currency reform and social frustration from decades of repression and bureaucracy, there are again shortages, blackouts, extreme inflation and protests.

The big difference is that today, with widespread mobile phones and internet access, everyone knows what's going on. On July 11, 2021, the biggest anti-government protest since the 1959 revolution broke out, not just in Havana but in cities all across Cuba.

With a firsthand view into the medical system, Lucia told me that the human support network in Cuba is collapsing. The pandemic had overwhelmed hospitals in Matanzas, she said, and dead bodies piled up on the streets. It is incredibly hot in the summer and Cubans were going many hours a day without electricity. Food — especially beef, fish, chicken, and eggs — remains scarce or even impossible to find. New American regulations, passed by then-President Trump right before he left office, have cut Cubans off financially from their families in the United States.

"It's hard to get food, it's hard to get medicine, it's hard to get bathroom supplies, the power grid is broken, the pandemic is peaking, tons of elderly people are passing away, the healthcare system is collapsing, we have no oxygen or fans," Lucia said. "This was too much. This is what put people out on the streets."

Lucia told me that at the very root of the state's failures and the unprecedented citizen uprising is a crisis of money.

In January 2021, the Communist Party of Cuba conducted what it described as a "monetary purification." Since 1994, the government issued two kinds of currencies: the CUP, or Cuban peso — pegged to the dollar at 24 to 1 — and the CUC, or Cuban convertible peso — pegged to the dollar at 1 to 1.

Public sector salaries and pensions were always paid out in pesos, but for years, citizens needed to obtain CUCs to buy key items like medicine, any food beyond the basics, clothing, cleaning supplies, and electronics. The regime designed the system to suck value out of the population, selling CUCs for 25 pesos at state-run money exchanges called *cadecas*, while only buying them back for 24 pesos. The regime knew it would have to keep printing and inflating pesos for the staffing of its centrally planned economy, even as its agricultural and industrial sectors collapsed. The dual-currency system gave it life support, propping up purchasing power for the elite and well-connected.

Lucia described the system's output as creating a reality where she could buy a cup of coffee, a bus ride, or even a small meal for an incredibly cheap price in pesos, but a pair of shoes or a phone plan, priced in CUC, could cost an entire month's salary. This put state workers — including teachers, police officers, and medical workers like her — at a severe economic disadvantage compared to anyone exposed to the tourist industry, like waiters or taxi drivers.

In tragic irony, unskilled workers were often far better off financially than highly educated ones, and many of the latter dropped out of their careers to clean tables or pick people up from the airport to get access to the CUC economy. The dual-currency system institutionalized inequality, creating clear classes of haves and have-nots. For many people like Lucia, this as much as anything else showed that the revolution was a sham.

More than 1.5 million Cubans have fled their home since Fidel Castro and his troops captured Havana in 1959, and many ended up in the United States. In the 1960s, Castro and his cronies triggered the human and capital flight by enforcing a planned, communist economy in Cuba, nationalizing businesses, confiscating land, and reducing the role of the private sector practically to zero.

Many Cuban Americans still have family on the island and find ways to send them dollars. It is estimated that as much as $3 billion is remitted into Cuba each year.[295] To convert dollars to CUC, one had to pay a fee of 10%, at a minimum, to the state. The system was designed to suck in hard foreign currency and provide Cubans with "fake dollars" or even worse, pesos.

Fidel Castro ceded control to his brother Raúl in 2006, and since then, the regime has made a series of half-hearted economic reforms to stay alive. As Anthony DePalma wrote in his modern history book, *The Cubans*, the communist government toyed with capitalism "the way a tiger plays with its prey: tapping it lightly one minute, squeezing the life out of it the next.[296] Socialist officials urged would-be Cuban capitalists to go ahead and open their small businesses, then they erected layers of burdensome regulations to limit profit and handicap success. Their real goal was not to lift millions out of poverty. It was to prevent anyone from making millions."

Starting in 2011, Raúl spoke openly of the need for monetary unification, but he ruled for another seven years without taking any action. The Cuban economic disaster he presided over can be summed up in one statistic: As of 2015, Cuba's GDP per capita was roughly the same as it was in 1985, despite having much higher economic potential with 13% more citizens.[297]

In 2018, longtime communist bureaucrat Miguel Díaz-Canel took over the Cuban presidency, ending nearly 60 years of Castro family tyranny. Like Raúl, Díaz-Canel presided over changes to the planned economy — like mass layoffs of state workers and permitting tiny businesses to operate privately — but continued to parrot Fidel's rallying cry in his speeches: *"¡Patrio o muerte! ¡Socialismo o muerte! ¡Venceremos!"* ("Homeland or death! Socialism or death! We will be victorious!")

As DePalma wrote, "Fidel and Che are dead. Raúl's tomb already has his name on it, and the new president is as unrecognizable around the world as the leader of any small country. The mythology of the revolution means very little to Cuban youth, who, with their tattoos, smartphones, and seething nihilism, see the old men of the Sierra as impossibly out of touch with their own reality. The foreign aid Cuba relied on for so long — first from the former Soviet Union, then from Venezuela, and additionally from sympathetic nations around the world — has dried up, and, to quote Margaret Thatcher, Cuba has run out of other people's money. At the bottom of every prescription, it now prints the line: healthcare in Cuba is free, but it costs money."[298]

Lucia agrees and said the revolution has run out of steam. Díaz-Canel is no Fidel and cannot put protests down with personal charisma or a secret police force operating in a world with no internet. He was forced to act, and the "monetary purification" is one of those actions.

As of January 1, 2021, the CUC was officially phased out. Cubans were given six months to exchange their CUCs for pesos at the official exchange rate. This constitutes a massive time theft, considering Cubans worked hard for those CUCs and are now being liquidated out of dollar positions into tiny amounts of rapidly depreciating currency. Even before January, CUCs were traded at a 15% discount to the dollar.

Over the eight months that followed, the monetary reform caused a massive devaluation in the peso. Cubans lost 75% of their purchasing power since the end of 2020, as the price of $1 has gone from the official rate of 24 pesos to costing as much as 90 pesos on the black market as of January 2022.

The official Cuban annual median salary in 2018 was approximately 9,300 pesos, or around $372.[299] Lucia told me that a pound of rice in 2020 cost her 6 or 7 pesos, but as of summer 2021, it ran more than 50 pesos. Two kilos of chicken once cost 60 pesos but now cost more than 600. Economists often say inflation is not a problem as long as wages rise at the same time, but wages have barely budged or have even declined in dollar terms.

The government extended the window for Cubans to redeem CUCs for a few more months, but use evaporated, as the currency has essentially been replaced by the MLC, which stands for *moneda libremente convertible* or "freely convertible currency."

Introduced by the regime in 2019 as the future monetary system of the island, the MLC functions like a reusable gift card. There is a plastic MLC card that one can pick up from a bank, and two different apps that one can download on a mobile phone. There are no MLC banknotes, coins, or ways to earn interest. Functionality is pointed at citizens giving their account information to contacts abroad, who send hard currency, which the regime seizes and replaces with MLC credit for Cubans to spend at government-run stores.

In a comically cruel twist, Cubans — who largely remain paid or pensioned in pesos — cannot buy MLC with pesos. The only way to officially "top up" your MLC account is with foreign hard currency. You must have family or contacts abroad send funds to your account. Initially, this could be done with dollars, but after the Trump administration cracked down on remittances to Cuba in the wake of a scandal in which American diplomats fell ill after apparently being exposed to sonic weapons, that option is gone, so MLC is now mainly generated through pounds, euros, and Canadian dollars.[300]

In an evolution of the trend started 25 years ago with better goods only being available in dollar stores, today's MLC stores are basically the only place to buy good food, medicine, cleaning supplies, appliances and other essentials. The peso stores face constant shortages, and have very few and very low-quality goods. Cubans who have family abroad are able to get MLC top ups and buy things to keep their lives going, but Cubans who do not must take their pesos and buy MLC in the black market. As of publication of this book, the real exchange rate is around 90 pesos for one MLC.

Through the MLC system, the Cuban regime is essentially able to print pesos to obtain hard currency. It is a giant rug pull on the Cuban population and a major reason for 2021's historic protests.

Lucia said that the government's official line is that the MLC system is necessary for the state to attract hard currency so that it can buy things on the international market to keep the system going and feed the people — a stunning admission of the revolution's failure.

Finding Freedom Through Bitcoin

I met Lucia on Telegram, through a mutual friend who runs a Latin America Bitcoin chat group. In early 2020, she started buying bitcoin with her state salary. She uses Telegram groups to find people willing to sell her bitcoin in exchange for MLC or pesos. She does transactions in person — at a café, for example — where she sends MLC from her mobile account to the seller, or hands over peso banknotes stamped with the faces of revolutionary figures like

Che Guevara in exchange for a transfer of bitcoin to the Blockstream Green wallet on her phone.

Since Lucia started "stacking sats," the fruits of her labor have grown significantly and her purchasing power has increased dramatically. Since the spring of 2020, bitcoin has risen from below $4,000 to more than $40,000. If Lucia had kept her savings in pesos, she would have lost almost everything. Bitcoin has changed, and saved, her life.

Lucia told me that she is not a technologically savvy person. At first, she did not think Bitcoin would be relevant for her ("I don't like math," she said) but in early 2020, she started watching RT for a few hours every Tuesday, Thursday, and Saturday. Since it is trusted Russian propaganda, the Cuban regime broadcasts *RT* (formerly *Russia Today*) on state television. One show on *RT*, however, is called the *Keiser Report* (produced by Max Keiser and Stacy Herbert) and evangelizes Bitcoin use. Likely permitted to air because its tone is very critical of US foreign policy, the show has acted like a Trojan horse of sorts, reaching a large number of Cubans and Venezuelans through state programming and onboarding them into the new Bitcoin economy. Ironically for Lucia, it was socialist state propaganda that showed her how to obtain personal freedom, not the hundreds of millions of dollars that the United States has spent on democracy promotion in Cuba since the 1990s.

Captivated by what she heard on *Keiser Report* about a new form of digital money, Lucia started researching Bitcoin. She eventually joined a Telegram group, first in English and then in Spanish, filled with other Latin Americans who follow the show. These communities gave her a full education in how to use Bitcoin.

"They taught me how I could be my own bank," Lucia said.

Through conversation one day, Lucia discovered that one of her friends was also into Bitcoin, and they started talking about it on a regular basis. Lucia also joined several Cuba-focused Bitcoin groups on Telegram, continuing to expand her knowledge. She bought and then sent $10 of bitcoin to a friend abroad, and the two marveled together at how they did not have to use a bank, provide any identification, or use the official system in any way. Even the currency itself, they realized, was not produced by a state or corporation but by an online community. They did not even know who created Bitcoin, and it did not seem to matter.

"This is groundbreaking," she told me. "What papers did I have to fill out? None at all."

Lucia told me that many people receive bitcoin from abroad and then convert it to MLC or pesos to buy food or supplies. In her case, she uses it to invest for her future. She calls it her "personal reserve" and best option for saving money.

She said that the US embargo is still very painful for Cubans.

"A lot of people will deny this reality," she said, "but we can no longer buy MLC in dollars. We do not have access to American financial apps. Our families in the US have a very hard time sending us dollars."

"Bitcoin," she said, "helps ease the pain."

Lucia looks to Bitcoin as an alternative to the dollar system.

"If we are free from the dollar," she told me, "then we have freedom."

Several Cubans that I spoke to for this story demonstrated a similar lingering patriotism, despite the betrayal of the revolution.

"The embargo puts our government against a wall," Lucia said, arguing that Bitcoin can give independence not just for people like her at an individual level, but for the Cuban society as a whole.

She credits curiosity for her new Bitcoin life.

"Curiosity is what moves people. That's what motivated me to become a medical worker," she said. "It animates all human beings."

This curiosity is now driving her to learn about Bitcoin and spread it to others.

"People have so many questions," she said. "Who makes it? How does it work? Where do you get it? It's good to take advantage of these teachable moments."

She told me that she is now personally teaching others in Matanzas and in her wider circles about how to use Bitcoin.

But learning is tough. Because of desperation, she said, a lot of Cubans have fallen into MLMs and pyramid schemes. The state, she said, conflates Bitcoin with the schemes, so people are in general fearful of getting involved. Bitcoin is hard to learn about, she said. It is unlike anything that people have ever seen before. Its abilities are hard to believe. Using it properly takes time and research.

"Adoption is happening," she said, "but it will take time."

Lucia concluded our conversation by telling me how important it is for Cuban women to use Bitcoin, saying that it is "vital that women learn to assert their financial freedom." Even though Cuban society might be relatively advanced in the area of women's rights, she said, there is still a broader culture of machismo and misogyny. Even in this context, most men do not even understand financial independence, she said, "so imagine how hard it is for women."

"Bitcoin allows you to control your money, your spending, and by extension, your life. As a woman," she said, "my future is finally in my own hands."

Cuba's History of Economic Misery

By the end of the 1950s, Cuba was one of the richest countries in Latin America. As currency researcher Boaz Sobrado wrote, "Cuba had more in common with US states like Louisiana and Florida than Hispanic countries like Mexico and the Dominican Republic. Cuban income per capita exceeded Mexico's by 70% and the Dominican Republic's by 300%. Its income per capita was even greater than that of ex-colonial powers Spain and Portugal."[301]

Sobrado pointed to the Havana Hilton as a "symbol of Cuba's mid-century opulence."[302] It was Latin America's tallest and largest hotel, boasting 630 guest rooms, 42 suites, a casino, six restaurants and bars, an arcade, an outdoor pool, and an expansive underground garage system. At first glance, then, Cuba seemed like an unlikely place for a socialist revolution. But behind the glamor of old Havana was a deeply broken society.

Dictator Fulgencio Batista ruled the island with an iron fist and with strong support from the US government and private sector. Cuba's annual income was an impressive $353 per capita in 1958, but most rural workers earned less than $100, and had very few public services and very weak infrastructure.[303] Foreign governments and corporations controlled the economy, owning around 75% of the arable land, 90% of essential services and 40% of the sugar production.[304]

During the 1950s, Fidel Castro led a socialist movement that challenged the Batista regime. By the end of the decade, his guerrilla tactics, directed from mountainous and rural areas, had drained a huge amount of funds and energy from the capital. In 1958, the US government placed an arms embargo on Cuba, as Batista began to lose all foreign support. On January 1, 1959, Castro's forces captured Havana.

"El Comandante" promised a people's revolution, but his rule quickly descended into tyranny, complete with concentration camps, thousands of arbitrary executions, secret police, a surveillance state on par with Eastern Germany or North Korea and political prisons. The Cuban gulags were especially cruel. Their horrors, once hidden, were eventually brought to light by testimonies of survivors in books like Armando Valladares's *Against All Hope*.[305]

As Anthony DePalma wrote,

> Cubans who dared to think differently feared more than anything else their ever-present neighborhood CDR (Committee for the Defense of the Revolution). The president of each local CDR was the person to whom neighborhood snitches reported. They kept track of who had not attended a May Day parade, who listened to the baseball game while Fidel was speaking on the radio, who had an illegal satellite dish hidden under a barrel on the roof, and passed along the information to Fidel's feared Stasi- and KGB-trained Interior Ministry. The CDR president had what some called the power of *fusilamiento del dedo*, literally, 'to execute with a finger' by pointing out and denouncing anyone suspected of counterrevolutionary activities. Simply allowing someone to use your telephone to call a relative in Miami could trigger a denunciation and ruin a life. The surveillance network was so pervasive that Cubans grew fearful of voicing any complaint. Even in their own homes, they refrained from mentioning the name Fidel, in case anyone was listening. Instead, they stroked an imaginary beard when they dared to criticize el comandante.[306]

Beyond being brutally repressive and invasive, the new government was also completely inexperienced when it came to actually running an economy. They followed the Soviet example of a planned financial system and quickly became dependent on the USSR as an export market. Economists were replaced by loyalists, regardless of their background or proficiency. It is said that when Castro chose Che Guevara as head of the Cuban central bank, it is because Guevara rose his hand after Castro asked if anyone was an economist, thinking Fidel asked if anyone was a communist.[307]

In the early 1960s, in a back-and-forth series of retaliations, the Eisenhower and Kennedy administrations placed trade restrictions and eventually a total blockade on Cuba, while Castro and his troops nationalized hundreds of millions of dollars in US property and businesses.

The revolution was disastrous for Cubans' personal savings. As president of the central bank, Guevara switched the peso peg from the dollar to the ruble, devaluing extant pesos by 75%. Then, pre-revolutionary banknotes were demonetized. If the new authorities declined to accept your old money, you lost everything.

Various American plans and attempts to oust Castro failed, and the regime persisted. It became structurally dependent on the Soviets for oil, loans, weapons, technical training, and as a market to sell their main export of sugar, which Moscow purchased at a subsidized price above market rates.[308]

Over the next few decades Cuba's economy grew, in large part due to the relationship with the Soviets. But even during communist Cuba's most prosperous times, in the late 1970s and early 1980s, making ends meet was still difficult, and thousands tried to leave. In 1980, more than 125,000 Cubans fled to the United States on around 1,700 vessels and rafts in an event known as the Mariel boatlift.[309]

When the Soviet Union dissolved in the early 1990s, the Castro regime lost as much as $5 billion in annual subsidies, and Cuba's sugar exports crashed by 80%. The peso suffered a devaluation from 5 per dollar to 150 per dollar.[310] Castro asked the Cuban people to make a collective sacrifice to get through the "Special Period," not unlike the way Kim Jong Il asked the North Korean people to stay strong and committed during the "Arduous March" in the late 1990s when millions perished.

During the "Special Period," many Cubans could only afford or find enough food to eat once per day. Their *libreta* (ration book) promised things like beef and chicken, but these items disappeared. Fidel had promised that everyone would be able to have a glass of milk each day but even that went missing.

According to DePalma, Cubans "flattened and tenderized grapefruit rinds and fried them as if they were steaks. Banana peels ground up and mixed with spices became another pale substitute for meat."[311] Each family received around nine eggs per month. The food shortages were accompanied by blackouts "so routine and long lasting that lightless nights became the norm, as Cubans celebrated the brief periods when the lights came back on as fleeting phenomena that they excitedly called *alumbrones*."

Industry collapsed. For example, by the end of the 1990s, fishing fleets all but disappeared.[312] Today, Cubans consume just 25% of the seafood that they did in the late 1980s.[313] In a nation where one is never more than 60 miles from the water, Cubans joke about being an "island without fish." A country that once produced 80% of its food now imported 80% of it.[314] Sobrado wrote that Cuba's domestic consumption has "never recovered to pre-1990 levels," a tragic summary of a starving state.[315]

Times were so grim that in 1993, Castro was forced to make the enemy dollar legal tender to attract hard currency. Cubans began to make dollar deposits at banks with remittances from abroad. Thiers' law (the opposite of Gresham's law in economics, where bad money drives out the good) was in full effect, as good money drove out the bad. Sobrado estimated that as many as half of all day-to-day transactions were done with dollars, a rate similar to present-day Venezuela. To stop this trend and prevent full dollarization, the regime rolled out the CUC "dollar peso," which they said was backed by an equal amount of dollars in the Cuban central bank.

Out of desperation, Castro also allowed family restaurants or "paladares" to operate as small private businesses. This was part of a wider opening process that included allowing European companies to operate Cuban hotels, permitting some citizens to run independent farms, and restoring Christmas as a national holiday — a move seen as a quid pro quo for the eventual visit of Pope John Paul II. The combination of small reforms and increased foreign investment led to a relative recovery out of the "Special Period."

In the early 2000s, Venezuelan president Hugo Chávez began to support the Cuban state with some of his new oil profits, providing a new lifeline. But while the government was bailed out, times for the average citizen continued to be extremely difficult. Sobrado wrote about a Cuban expression: *dice que hay pollo* (they say there is chicken), which the crowd in the streets would shout when chicken became available at stores. *Libretas*, he said, used to have a provision for fish but that ran out and was substituted with chicken — *pollo por pescado* — and in the past few years, the chicken ran out, too.

In November 2004, facing another economic collapse, the Cuban government withdrew US dollars from circulation. State-run stores, enterprises, and banking moved entirely to the CUC system. Dollars had to be converted into CUC upon arrival in Cuba, allowing the regime to seize the hard currency, tax it and replace it with something they could print unbacked. The big picture effect was that dollars once held by citizens were now held by the communist central bank.

In the CUC era, the dual currencies allowed the government to provide a very basic level of some cheap goods and services but created a system where one needed CUCs for anything beyond the bottom-rung tier of items. For example, one might be able to purchase a low-quality loaf of bread for 1 peso at a state-run bakery — if there was any left — but for 1 CUC, you could get a much nicer loaf at a fancier store. Tourists in recent decades only used CUCs and shopped at the fancy stores with the much higher prices, and thus always poured a lot of hard currency into the regime's coffers.

The dual currencies also allowed for accounting alchemy that benefited state-run enterprises. For example, as Sobrado noted, a well-connected elite could buy a ticket to fly out of Cuba paying a few hundred pesos, instead of a few hundred CUCs or dollars. This also meant that some state enterprises could buy imports at the "peso" price, while selling at the dollar price. There was a chronic exaggeration of assets and underestimation of liabilities. These financial tricks were done at the expense of the peso and the average worker.

Many Cubans have another gig beyond their state job, which might give them access to CUCs (or today, MLC) and earn them enough to survive. One can often make more than their entire monthly state salary or pension in one day on the black market. Sobrado said that some even have what he calls negative salaries: "People sometimes bribe their boss so that they do not have to show up. This way they can work at their income earning hustle all day."

DePalma wrote that "almost every Cuban — whether an entrepreneur with a small business or a parent searching for dinner — became a criminal in one way or another. Inventando (the Spanish verb for 'inventing') largely replaced the word 'stealing' in Cuban vernacular, and the rules of civil society changed so that stealing was condoned, so long as what was being stolen came from the state and not from a neighbor or a friend. In the new Cuba, inventando was a way of leveling the playing field and making up for the miserable dollar-a-day salaries that the state workers received."[316]

The cumulative decay of Cuba's economy is hard to imagine, but the fact that the 2018 sugar harvest yielded just one million tons, the same as the harvest in 1894, helps paint the picture. Once the largest sugar exporter on the planet, Cuba has been forced to import from France.

"Historic" reforms of the system announced by Raúl and Diaz-Canel ended up being small tweaks. Entrepreneurship does not grow well in a climate with no wholesale market, with strict limits on the number of employees one can hire, where licenses are expensive, taxes hefty, and credit scarce. By 2017, despite many much-hyped reforms, a pair of jeans still cost a month of state income, and rations ran out after only a few days. The vaunted healthcare system allowed a cholera outbreak and was tilted toward special care for elites.[317] Education remained propaganda. In 2014 and 2015, the Obama administration opened up American restrictions, boosting local enterprise with a wave of new tourists. But President Barack Obama also ended the wet-foot, dry-foot immigration policy, and a few years later President Trump reversed the opening.[318]

According to DePalma, the small economic reforms that the government offered Cubans over the past 15 years were not "freedom to better themselves, but permission to eke out a level of survival the government could no longer provide. On top of the limitations, it slapped onto their entrepreneurial vision and capacity to amass wealth, the government required would-be capitalists to buy their licenses for relatively hefty fees and pay heavy taxes. The goal, as outlined by the government, was to make Cuba a rich country without rich people."

Cuba's Human Rights Crisis

As part of my research for this chapter, I spoke to a human rights defender with a background in accounting and finance, living in Havana. She did not wish to be named ("I want to keep a low profile," she said) but spoke openly about a variety of sensitive topics in our video chat. We will call her Verita.

Her concern is understandable. Cuba remains a one-party communist state. Diaz-Canel's regime continues the climate of fear built by the Castros. Other political parties are illegal, dissent is suppressed, and civil liberties are severely restricted. According to the rights watchdog Freedom House, "The regime's undemocratic character has not changed despite new leadership in 2018 and a process of diplomatic normalization with Washington, which has stalled in recent years."[319]

Cuba earns just 13 out of a possible 100 points on the Freedom House 2021 democracy report, with only 1 out of 40 points on political rights, and 12 out of 60 on civil liberties.[320] The constitution forbids independent media, and "the country's independent press operates outside the law, its publications are considered 'enemy propaganda,' and its journalists are routinely harassed, detained, interrogated, threatened, defamed in the official press, and prohibited from traveling abroad."

Cubans are banned from posting content on foreign servers, including social media platforms, and in general cannot share anything "contrary to the social interest, morals, good customs, and integrity of the people." Private universities and schools have been illegal since the 1960s, and teachers are promoted based on ideological loyalty, not academic performance. Independent labor unions are outlawed, and Cuban workers cannot strike, protest, or collectively bargain. A popular revolutionary saying goes, "*Dentro de la revolución, todo. Contra la revolución, nada*" — "Within the revolution, everything. Against the revolution, nothing."

Verita is part of Cuba's community of human rights defenders. Born largely in the 1990s in the wake of the "Special Period," they live under constant attack. In 2003, at just around the same time as the regime was forced to modify the currency system to keep society afloat, it launched the "Black Spring" crackdown, rounding up dozens of poets, authors, and journalists. To this day, the sisters, wives, and daughters of these political prisoners march in Havana every Sunday for their freedom and are known as the *Damas de Blanco* — the Ladies in White.

Independent outlets like *14ymedio*, founded by blogger and philologist Yoani Sánchez, and *Diario de Cuba* continue to report, but work remains difficult. One of Cuba's leading human rights advocates, Oswaldo Payá, died in a car crash in 2013, an incident widely believed to be state murder. Going onto the street and protesting continues to carry huge risk, as hundreds of disappearances and lengthy prison sentences for protestors in 2021 demonstrate.[321]

In 2018, an Afro-Cuban group of academics, artists, and journalists known as the San Isidro Movement, formed to protest Decree 349, a communist law requiring artistic activity to be pre-authorized by the government.[322] In November 2020, the group launched a protest in support of one of their members, the rapper Denis Solis, who had been convicted of "contempt for authority."[323] State police raided the protest, but the regime was forced to promise more rights for artists, and the seeds were sown for last month's uprising.

Black Cuban communities have been at the center of these protests. It is estimated that up to 90% of white Cuban families have relatives abroad as a remittance stream, but only 30% to 40% of Black Cuban families have the same option. Guillermo "El Coco" Fariñas, a well-known Black dissident, calls the situation a "powder keg about to explode."

At first, Verita, who is also Afro-Cuban, was extremely formal, literally reading from a speech that she had prepared for the first part of our conversation, where we talked about the economy. She kept repeating the government line that "devaluation does not impact inflation" and that the peso-to-dollar exchange rate remains 24 to 1. Later in our chat though, she opened up and told me that, in reality, the exchange rate was at the time as much as 70 to 1. It was clear that Big Brother is very much still alive in her mind.

Verita explained that the MLC system was a government strategy to stockpile hard foreign currency and avoid the flight of dollars and euros. It was also, she said, a way for the government to tax the informal sector which had been leaking huge amounts of value out of Cuba.

For example, a few years ago, if you wanted to buy an air conditioner, you would likely hire someone (sometimes known as a "mule") in a place like Panama, and they would bring it to you and you would pay them in dollars, which would permanently leave the Cuban economy, without the regime getting a chance to take a cut. With the MLC system, the regime stocks the stores with appliances like air conditioners, so that it is actually easier for citizens to buy them there as opposed to with a mule. This way, instead of leaking hard currency out, the regime actually accumulates it, as citizens ask family, friends, and colleagues to top up their MLC accounts so they can buy the air conditioner.

As a result, Verita said, the peso is in the process of demonetizing. Out of the three main functions of money, it has essentially lost the functions of store of value and unit of account — which have now leaked to the MLC or dollar — and really only lives on as a medium of exchange for individuals when interacting with the government, or when buying things on the street.

When I asked her if the government had a plan to stop the peso inflation, she gave me a look that I will never forget: She turned her head, smiled slightly, and looked at me in disbelief.

"Plan?" she asked. "No. There is no plan."

In her estimation, the Cuban economy would need to grow 5% per year for the next 12 years to recover from its current trauma. But, she said, it actually contracted by 11% in 2020 and will shrink even more in 2021 and 2022. It will be, in her words, "a disaster."

The Embargo's Ongoing Impact

To learn more about the impact of the American embargo on Cubans, I spoke to Ricardo Herrero, a son of Cuban exiles and the executive director of the Cuba Study Group. He explained that as of 2021, because of US sanctions, Cubans cannot access a wide range of popular American products like PayPal, Stripe, Cash App, Zelle, Coinbase, GitHub, Adobe, Dropbox, Lyft, Uber, or Amazon. He called the embargo "the most rigid and expansive sanctions regime towards any society on the planet."

Herrero works to help push the US government to relax some of these restrictions. He said his job is difficult, especially because of the Torricelli and Helms–Burton Acts, which were passed in the 1990s, formalizing restrictions on American trade, business, and travel to Cuba in order to destabilize the Castro regime at a time of weakness and promote democratic opposition.

Unlike previous Cuban policy between the Kennedy and Clinton years, in the new era since 1996 when Helms–Burton was passed, the embargo has been codified into law and cannot be lifted by executive order. Centered on American claims of business and property considered stolen by the Castro regime during the revolution, Helms–Burton expanded extant restrictions on US companies and tries to prevent any company in the world from doing business in Cuba. It threatens, for example, to prevent a corporation from entering or doing business with the United States if it chooses to do business with Cuba.

US Presidents Clinton, Bush, and Obama waived part of the act, so some foreign entities have been able to do business with Cuba, with mixed results.

As Sobrado dryly noted, the Havana Hilton, which was renamed the Habana Libre during the revolution, was eventually handed over to Spanish hotel chain Meliá Hotels International. As of 2020, the famed hotel stood empty.

Before leaving office, President Trump designated Cuba a state sponsor of terrorism and introduced 243 new measures to strengthen the embargo.[324] President Biden has yet to rescind them. Herrero said that Helms–Burton is the deterrent that explains why you do not see Starbucks, Zara, or McDonald's in Cuba. It is why Cuba does not receive loans from the International Monetary Fund (IMF) or the World Bank. It is why the Juragua Nuclear Power Plant was never finished. During the Obama opening in 2015 and 2016, some American payment companies tried to explore establishing payment services between the United States and Cuba, but once Trump won the election, it was clear the opening would be rolled back, and plans were put on hold.

The embargo, Herrero said, gives "political oxygen" to the Cuban government's revolutionary narrative.

"It's the big bogeyman," he said. "Without it, the regime would suffer an ideological collapse."

The embargo mixed with an inept, repressive government is an especially tragic combination. This was illustrated recently when a diabetic British citizen was unable to find insulin in Havana, due to the medical shortages. His wife tried to ship him some from London, but DHL returned the package, scrawling "US sanctions on Cuba" on the label. He died in a hospital soon after.[325]

"The combination of the American sanctions on Cuba, Cuba's mismanagement of scarce resources, and the Covid-19 pandemic is a lethal brew," his wife said.

Herrero still places most of the blame for the suffering of the Cuban people squarely on the regime's shoulders and said that they play a duplicitous game. The regime blames the embargo for all or most of the crises in Cuba, but they have "never missed an opportunity to miss an opportunity to lift it."

It continues to use the embargo as a scapegoat and as a tool to draw international sympathy for their cause.

"They paint themselves," Herrero said, "as a David against the imperialist Goliath."

Under the Obama opening, US companies flew in to strike deals, but the Cubans allowed very few to get signed. Herrero explained that this was partly because of their Soviet mentality: "The bureaucrats were trained to be enemies with the yankees and to oppose capitalism."

They were, when presented with the opportunity to connect Cuba with the world, unable to seize it. For the past decade, the Cuban regime has talked about private enterprise and decentralization of the economy, but in reality, it has been all talk, no action.

Anthony DePalma explains in his history of Cuba that the regime constantly reminds citizens "of the imperialist peril from the north, yet it also demands that the empire drop its embargo so that Cuba can do more business with America and its allies.[326] The regime has used the perpetual threat of American intervention as a cover for every misstep, failed program, food shortage, or power blackout over the last six decades, but it also depends on the billions of American dollars that exiles send back in remittances to keep Cuba afloat. State-run media presents the United States as a hellhole of drug addiction, mass murder and runaway consumerism, while portraying Cuba as an egalitarian paradise run by a government that can do no wrong. And yet, when Cubans compare their own lives with what they hear from relatives in Miami or with what they see on the internet, they know it isn't so."

Nearly everything the regime promotes about its economy is a veil of ideology covering up exploitation. As of 2018, Cuba's top source of revenue was shockingly not the tourism industry but rather the export of more than 50,000 healthcare workers each year to more than 60 countries.[327] Cuba's educational system is designed to produce a surplus of doctors, nurses, and technicians — an "army of white coats" — who are sent abroad in a PR scheme. Herrero said the program is a way to "weave the revolution" into a solution, where the government proudly announces that we will send brigades around the world to save the downtrodden, who have been ignored by imperialist powers. In reality, the state confiscates 75% of the salaries of these workers, raking in more than $11 billion per year, making a form of indentured servitude Cuba's biggest export.[328]

Meanwhile, Cubans abroad find it hard to simply send money to their families. Herrero said one way was to make a bank wire to someone in Panama who would "duffel bag" cash to Havana. Another way would be to rely on a hawala-type system. One could give $100 to someone in Miami, and they would call their business partner in Havana and have them deliver $100 minus a cut to one's family. Western Union transactions from the United States to Cuba were also an option until November 2020 when the Trump administration shut them down.[329] The company closed 407 locations across the island, which seems staggering, but Herrero said that most Cubans already found the service too expensive.

As an example, Herrero detailed a Western Union transaction from 2020, where someone sent $1,030 to a family member in Cuba. The fee was $77.25, so the total paid by the sender was $1,107.25. The amount that was delivered to the recipient in Cuba was $1,000. The double-digit fee was split up with 1.5% staying in the United States as a clearance fee, 4% going to Western Union, 1.5% going to Fincimex (the now-sanctioned Cuban state payment processor), and 3% burned by the "exchange rate" conversion, which the government pockets.

Even if the United States opens up Western Union again, recipients would only receive $1,000 at the "official rate" of 24 pesos to $1. So, the receiver would get 25,000 pesos, even though the real value of the remittance is 90,000 pesos. The regime would keep the difference.

Americans, Herrero said, could actually top up MLC accounts directly with dollars until mid-2020. But the Trump administration's new sanctions closed this channel. Combined with flight closures and reduced tourism, Herrero said this was a "double whammy" that caused a dramatic reduction in dollar flows to Cuba. This, he said, is right when Bitcoin started taking off.

"There is no currency," he told me, "that would have helped you navigate the oscillations of US–Cuba policy over the last five years better than Bitcoin."

"It's hard for anything to grow in Cuba," he added, "but if you've been investing in bitcoin over the past few years, you have been growing."

Bitcoin as a "Cheat Code" for the Cuban System

Herrero told me about Erich García Cruz, a popular Cuban Bitcoin personality. He called Cruz a "one man CNET," as he often appears as a guest on state TV and runs his own popular YouTube channel reviewing different kinds of technology and payment systems. I reached out to Cruz to learn more.

"I've lived in Havana since the day I was born," Cruz told me. He was comfortable using his name for this interview, as he said he is already a "very popular, very known" person.

Cruz said the recent protests have been triggered by a lack of food, a lack of medication, by people suffering from hunger, trying to survive in brutal conditions, during a pandemic, with government bureaucracy, and with high inflation.

"The Cuban people are tired," he said. "They want a better life."

"The system isn't working," Cruz said, "so people are turning to Bitcoin to escape."

Cruz's business, BitRemesas, is a solution to the giant problem that people have when trying to send remittances from the United States to Cuba. Again, because of the embargo, US banks cannot wire dollars to Cuban accounts.

There is no TransferWise, no PayPal, no Revolut, not even Western Union anymore.

The mule method still works — of wiring money to someone who will physically go into Cuba and give cash to your family — but this is expensive and time consuming. Cruz said one can also make a transfer to a bank in Spain, for example, where then the remittance can be sent directly to someone's MLC account. But again, expensive and time-consuming.

The better option, Cruz said, is to use Bitcoin.

"It has become a way to connect to the outside world," he said. "The number of Cubans using Bitcoin is exploding."

Cruz estimates that at least 300,000 Cubans have used bitcoin or cryptocurrency at least once and that maybe 100,000 use it on a regular basis. This is 2.5% of the island's population, precisely in line with global estimates that 200 million of the world's 7.8 billion people have used Bitcoin.

Cruz said that any Cuban businesses not using Bitcoin today to interact with the international financial system will learn the hard way, and adapt and adopt.

"All externally-facing companies will be forced to use Bitcoin," he said. "We have a saying in Cuba: You have to get in the bus, because the bus is leaving the town."

He thinks Bitcoin adoption is already greater per capita in Cuba than in Europe or Canada, but told me that he was not always a Bitcoin believer. In fact, until March 2020, he thought it was a scam. There were always friends and colleagues, he said, trying to introduce him to cryptocurrency, but they were trying to get him to do it so that he could then send the BTC to pyramid schemes like Arbistar or Trust Investing.

"I was very skeptical," he said.

In March 2020, Cruz made a popular video where he exposed Trust Investing, and showed how it was a pyramid scheme. As part of the reaction to the video, people encouraged him to look at other investing options. One was Bitcoin. He pledged to himself to try and become an expert on the topic.

In April and June 2020, he went "down the rabbit hole" and "discovered the holy grail." Through the lens of Bitcoin, he told me, "You start seeing the actual limitations that Cubans have and the freedom that Bitcoin provides. You see the world from a different perspective."

"We can't access the traditional payment solutions. We're stuck. Well, if that's the case," he said, "then I will make my own payment provider using Bitcoin, and we'll develop a business around this opportunity."

On September 1, 2020, Cruz launched BitRemesas so that Cuban families can transact easier between the U.S. and Cuba. The process is simple: Someone in the United States sends bitcoin or other cryptocurrencies to a wallet managed by BitRemesas (he told me it is a two-of-three multisig, for additional security) — then the company sells the digital assets for MLC or pesos and delivers it to the recipient.

He describes a "negative bid" system, where his company will advertise a newly received $100 remittance of bitcoin in a local network: One trader will offer $95, another $94. BitRemesas will sell to the lowest bidder and take the spread as their profit. The trader will deliver the money to the recipient. The big improvement this holds over other ways of sending money to Cuba, he said, is that the receiver gets close to the real exchange rate. Going through the official system, he said, results in being stuck with the 24 peso to $1 rate.

He said the Cuban people are "smart and intelligent" and are storing value in bitcoin because they trust it more than the peso.

"If you can buy satoshis with pesos and can wait three years, you're growing your purchasing power in a huge way," he said.

"I don't like to speak about politics or the government or whether they have the right or wrong policies," Cruz said. "I'm just trying to teach my fellow Cubans how to live with Bitcoin and cryptocurrency."

He credits Satoshi Nakamoto for his new life and new business.

Cruz said he has no special political information, but he said the government is researching cryptocurrency as part of its current five-year plan and could eventually adopt a Bitcoin strategy. For example, it could start accepting bitcoin at MLC stores, or allow citizens to use bitcoin to top up MLC accounts, or to sell tourist offerings or even exports for bitcoin. In September 2021, two months after I first spoke with Cruz, the Cuban government publicly instructed the island's central bank to acknowledge and legalize cryptocurrency.

"Adopting Bitcoin would be a smart move, a good way to accumulate the hardest currency" he said. "But we are talking about the Cuban government, so I don't know."

Cruz remains very critical of the US embargo, which prevents him from accessing a variety of services otherwise available to people living just a few hundred miles away in Miami, Florida.

"But fighting the embargo," he said, "is a fight you cannot win."

"In Cuba, there are two options," he added. "You can leave Cuba and escape the Matrix, or you can stay and play the game. Bitcoin is a cheat code to play the game. Now, I choose to stay."

Building a Bitcoin Economy in Havana

Jorge works for a Bitcoin company in Havana. He discovered Bitcoin in March 2018, when he took advantage of Cuba's expanded internet access to start trading and stacking sats online for various tasks. For much of Jorge's life, however, connecting to the outside world had been close to impossible. The web had been heavily restricted, and information could only get to Cuba in quiet ways.

As an intern at the Human Rights Foundation, I helped participate in a 2007 program where we would send foreign books and films into Cuba's pre-internet "underground library" system. From an office in New York, I would burn copies of subtitled films like *V For Vendetta* and *Braveheart* onto DVDs, which were disguised as music CDs, and sent to Cuba with Latin American citizens who would head to the island through Mexico. They would drop off the *samizdat* content — along with medical supplies and other technology — with our contacts, who would run private screenings in their homes on portable DVD players with three or four other people at a time and host discussion groups afterward.

For many years, this — along with picking up radio signals from Florida — is how Cubans accessed outside information. A few years later, "paquete" was born: A system where some Cubans would use illegal satellite equipment to download foreign content and upload it to hard drives, which were then disseminated through communities where people would pay per item to transfer what they wanted to their own USB sticks to watch or read at home.

In 2014 and 2015, Wi-Fi started to pop up across Cuba at hotels and public access points. Paquete grew dramatically at this point, with some people getting paid to simply stand around and download content all day. In 2017 and 2018, data was introduced to mobile phones. Internet access has increased dramatically in recent years, but it's still censored and slow and surveilled.

"There's no great firewall," Jorge said, "but our experience is not as smooth and shiny as the open web."

When we spoke, he used a VPN.

The power of the internet in Cuba was on full display last summer, when a July 10, 2021, Facebook post in the small town of San Antonio de los Banos helped ignite national protests the next day.[330]

"Tired of having no electricity?" the post asked. "Fed up of having to listen to the impudence of a government that doesn't care about you? It's time to go out and to make demands. Don't criticize at home: let's make them listen to us."

Jorge could not have predicted the 2021 July 11 movement, but either way, he was thrilled to connect to the world online. Bitcoin's new form of digital money was one of the most interesting things he found on the web, but he did not know how to actually "give use" to the new digital currency beyond saving. That is when he found Bitrefill.

Through this online service, he started to top up his phone using bitcoin. On the Bitrefill platform, Cubans can buy mobile phone vouchers — along with other things like app store and gaming coupons — directly with bitcoin that they earn, buy or receive from abroad via platforms like BitRemesas. In Jorge's case, he'll store his bitcoin on the Muun or Blue Wallet apps on his phone. He said these two are his favorite: Both apps are free, open-source, Lightning-enabled, and available to Cubans in Spanish language formats directly from the Google Play store. From there, it's just one step to buying things with Bitrefill.

Through the platform, some Cubans have found arbitrage opportunities in an otherwise extortionate financial system. For example, in order to lure hard currency, state-run telecoms company ETECSA will sometimes provide extra credit if one tops up their mobile phone with euros or pounds. The promotions are so good that some Cubans will pay middlemen to top up their phones from abroad. But a Cuban can sit at home, earn or buy bitcoin, and then top up anyone's phone from the Bitrefill service, making a tidy profit.

Jorge said that he even taps into an informal market for meal delivery using bitcoin. He places an order via a peer-to-peer service and the prepared food shows up at his doorstep. He pays in bitcoin, a cypherpunk Cuban version of Uber Eats. He said that between his business, his meals, and other various items, he buys almost everything he needs today with bitcoin. For Jorge, living in a Bitcoin economy is not a future dream, it is the present day.

Using bitcoin so comprehensively to live is not widespread, Jorge said, and he admits he is one of the very early adopters. But, he said, either way it is very easy for him to exchange bitcoin for MLC or pesos and buy whatever he needs.

When asked if Bitcoin was a fad, or something that he might stop using at some point, he said, "I'm not going back. I can't imagine my life right now without Bitcoin."

He pointed to friends who are doctors or lawyers, whose savings were getting eaten by inflation before finding bitcoin, or others who are entrepreneurs and are building their entire lives around bitcoin right now, just like him.

When I spoke to Sobrado, the currency researcher whose work informed much of this essay, he told me about a business he ran in Cuba before the pandemic. He built a team that would service, for example, taxi drivers and apartment owners, to make it easier for them to accept foreign payments.

Sobrado's company would allow foreigners to pay for their Havana airport pickup online. Sobrado would receive their euros into a foreign account, and then he would sell those euros for bitcoin, which could be sent to his team in Cuba in minutes, and sold there for CUC or pesos. His team would then drop off the cash with the drivers.

Sobrado provided a similar service with Cubans using Booking.com or Airbnb, which have special OFAC permission to operate on the island.

"Let's say you are a Cuban apartment owner," he told me. "You get a license to do business, and you rent out your place online and the first guest comes. The way your guest pays Airbnb is through a remittance company called Va Cuba. On the Cuban end, what this means is that some dude shows up on your doorstep and asks around for you and if you happen to be home, he will hand you an envelope of cash. This dude would often be late, he would give the official exchange rate, it was a mess. So instead, what we would do is pay you directly and immediately, at the real price, using Bitcoin as a rail."

If Bitcoin didn't exist, Sobrado said these businesses wouldn't have worked. He would have had to raise prices by at least 5%, and the profit margins would have disappeared. Sobrado said the best months in terms of overall revenue were late 2019 and early 2020. During the pandemic, he said, "the whole thing died," but it is yet another example of how creative minds are using Bitcoin to improve lives, make things more efficient, and earn money even in a dreary police state.

In writing about Cuba's internet adoption in 2017, the author Antonio Garcia Martinez said that an important word to know is *resolver*: "While literally meaning 'to resolve,' in practice it's closer to Silicon Valley's notion of 'life hacking,' but without the humblebraggy lifestyle posturing."[331]

"Need to navigate the endless hurdles involved in getting a small business license? *Resolver*," he wrote. "Cubans are the kings and queens of *resolver*. It's the only thing that kept them afloat since the Special Period."

However, Martinez wrote, "Arrayed against the forces of resourceful *resolver* lies another important word: *complicado*."

"Want to talk to the dissident journalists who scoff at Cuban censorship and are routinely harassed and jailed? *Es complicado*," he wrote. "Want to get a passport and visa to travel abroad? *Es complicado*."

According to Jorge, Bitcoin is the embodiment of *resolver*. It is a workaround, a way to defeat *complicado*.

As Martinez wrote, *resolver* "almost always" beats *complicado*, "especially when there is real money to be made."

Even though Martinez made this observation in Cuba's pre-Bitcoin days, it could not be more true today, when citizens are turning to bitcoin over pesos in search of "real money."

Jorge told me that Bitcoin is no magic solution to all of Cuba's problems and notes that people are facing an incredibly difficult time for a variety of reasons. He looks to El Salvador's national Bitcoin adoption and said that services used there like Strike (which connect Bitcoin to the local banking system) are not available in Cuba and likely will not be because of the embargo.

But, Jorge said, people are learning more about Bitcoin, getting enthusiastic and saving up. After so many years of the government rug pulling citizens with the CUC and MLC systems, today, Bitcoin users are rug pulling the government by exchanging pesos or MLC for bitcoin, a superior form of money that has appreciated dramatically over the last decade. Maybe, Jorge said, the people will finally get the last laugh.

I asked Jorge about the many Western critics of Bitcoin, who say it is just for criminals and that it has no social value. He laughed in disbelief. Many people's lives "have been improved dramatically" through Bitcoin, he said.

"This technology goes around blockades and government restrictions, it allows you to move value without trusting anyone, it connects you to the world, and it allows you to empower yourself and do things that are otherwise impossible," he said. "It has created hope for those who want change."

A New Cuba Is Coming

Much like other closed regimes like North Korea and the Soviet Union, technology and outside information is having a massive impact on Cuba. There is no way a protest movement like July 11 could have scaled nationwide without people being able to digitally organize and connect with one another.

When I spoke to Antonio García Martinez last summer, he told me that "the internet is going to nuke 62 years of Cuban communism."

On the island, he said, "The internet is a machine for destroying the consensus elites, who depend on a monopoly of information."

"If the internet stays on," he said, "the Cuban government will eventually fall."

But after nearly 20 years of economic reforms, and a half-decade of a connected population, the Cuban communist party still holds onto power. Even the advent of the internet has not been enough to shake its grip. Its stubborn, conservative nature has sadly worked and kept it alive for many decades. While Bitcoin might be a good way for it to accumulate the hardest currency on Earth, the dinosaurs in charge may not think this is a risk worth taking.

On the US side, the Biden administration has ordered a "review" on remittances to Cuba, trying to determine how those in the United States can best send money to their family on the island without supporting the regime.[332] The answer, of course, is Bitcoin, but given Treasury Secretary Janet Yellen's animosity for the new currency, it is unlikely they will be willing to admit this and begin operationalizing it in their foreign policy.

While speaking to Cubans during this tumultuous time, one thing is clear: A growing number are not going to wait for their government to unroll some new reform, or for the Biden administration to soften its sanctions. They are seizing their own financial destiny through Bitcoin.

More than 100 years ago, the great Cuban poet José Marti wrote that "rights are to be taken, not requested; seized, not begged for."[333] This could be the motto of Cuba's new Bitcoin movement.

Perhaps the recent political protests will be enough to show the world that Cubans are tired of living under dictatorship but not enough to end the regime. Over the decades, many predicted the fall of the Castro tyranny, only to be proven wrong.

In the meantime, Cubans will continue to peacefully protest by opting out of the exploitative peso, and the MLC system, and into Bitcoin. After six decades of economic misery, there is finally a way out.

Whether it is through individuals like Lucia in Matanzas, stacking sats quietly every day, or Cruz or Jorge in Havana, who keep innovating and onboarding the masses, Bitcoin is now a thoroughly Cuban movement, a *resolver* that seems unlikely to be stopped.

Chapter IX

Finding Financial Freedom in Afghanistan

Roya Mahboob — the first female Afghan tech CEO, one of *TIME*'s most influential people in the world and one of the first entrepreneurs to introduce Bitcoin to Afghanistan — was seven years old when the Taliban first took over her country and invaded her hometown in 1996.[334]

One day she was playing with her bicycle in her front yard, wearing her favorite red scarf, when a bunch of armed men showed up in a jeep, screaming at her father in a language she did not understand. After that, she was not allowed to go outside and play anymore.

"My family took my scarf away and forced me to wear a black dress," she said, "just like all the other girls."

A few days later, the Taliban returned. Its members rolled down her street, armed to the teeth, and went home by home, going into each house by force, looking for any signs of books or television sets.

"If they found any books, they would take them out to the front yard and set them on fire," Mahboob said. "If they found any VHS tapes, they would set those on fire too."

She said the most jarring part was that she could no longer go to school. Instead, she was forced to go to the mosque, and study the Quran, and sit through lectures from a mullah who could not even read. For her, all paths to knowledge had been closed, and all bridges to the outside world had been burned down.

Shortly after the Taliban conquered Afghanistan, Mahboob's family fled into Iran. She told me that her father was a secular leader and that it had become too dangerous for him to raise a family in a new land of religious fundamentalism. She grew up in Iran a stranger in a strange land and as a second-class citizen. But over time, she got used to the new country, and when her father decided to move the family back to Afghanistan in 2003, she was terrified.

When she finally arrived back in the city of Herat one night, however, she remembers things were surprisingly calm. Iranian state TV had portrayed Afghanistan as a place of death and destruction, but Mahboob found her home region stabilized. Now a teenager, she was still forced to wear a hijab, but she found the restrictions much looser than under the Taliban. Yes, there were foreign troops everywhere, but compared to today, she said, there were many new economic opportunities and the security situation was much safer: "There was a sense of hope in the air."

Discovering the Internet

One of the things that intrigued Mahboob most about her new life in Herat was the internet cafe. Living in Iran, she had never been allowed to go to a library or bookstore. Her schooling was limited and based mainly on Islam. Getting other kinds of information was a struggle. Upon arriving in Herat, she heard about a shop that had small boxes that could communicate with each other. If one typed into them, she heard, they would provide lots of information. One could even talk to other people through electronic messages. But, she said, women were not allowed in this kind of shop.

"One day," she said, "I forced one of my male cousins to take me inside." The cafe owner would not let them in, but she was persistent, and one early morning he relented. She fell in love with the computer immediately. She learned that the United Nations had started a local computer course for women, and the teacher told Mahboob that if she could get 15 girls to enroll, they could start a class. She rallied her cousins and friends to make it happen. After a six-month course, she was hooked on the web.

The next year, in 2004, Mahboob entered Herat University and took up computer science. Over the next four years, she learned how to code, and her desire to change the world through technology grew.

Unknowingly, Mahboob had tapped into the philosophy of a group of coders who were thousands of miles away: the cypherpunks. They believe that the best way to change society is through technology, not through government (see Chapter II). Their philosophy is to innovate without permission. In this sense, Mahboob was one of them.

She continued her studies, eventually working her way up to coordinator of the university's IT department, where she helped build the campus network architecture. She learned English, mainly to communicate with the teachers, and started working on the Silk Road project, a NATO initiative that helped all the key universities in Afghanistan get linked up with fiber optics.

In 2009, Mahboob met with Paul Brinkley, the US deputy undersecretary for defense. The Americans wanted to build a tech incubator in Herat. By that time, Mahboob had helped create an association of young girls interested in technology and software. According to Mahboob, Brinkley asked her, "Why not start a company? We can hire you."

Mahboob's Citadel

With contracts from the US government and multilateral organizations, Mahboob built Citadel Software.

Why the name?

"In Herat," Mahboob said, "there is a beautiful citadel that looms over the rest of the city. It is impressive, even breathtaking." Mahboob said that her company wanted to be a castle of software programming and a place where women could safely pursue their careers.

Little did she know, she was already on the same page as many Bitcoin users, who often talk of the idea of a citadel where they can retreat into a space of freedom without external control. "I'll see you in the citadels," says the popular Bitcoin podcaster Stephan Livera at the end of every one of his episodes.

Mahboob founded her own "citadel" and became the first female tech CEO in Afghanistan. To launch, she used some of the money she had saved while working at the university and for the Afghan Ministry of Education. Of course, she had less access to commercial finance than men, but the meeting with Brinkley was her breakthrough. The US government would pay Citadel to consult on the strengths, weaknesses, and different approaches to building technology systems in Afghanistan.

After a few months, Citadel also started to win contracts from the Afghan government. At the end of 2011, an Italian businessman saw a documentary about Citadel. He was so moved that he reached out and eventually financed the company, giving Mahboob private investment by the end of 2012.

"Citadel was 85% female," Mahboob said. "For every woman at Citadel, this was her first job."

Because it was a mostly female environment, conservative families were more comfortable with allowing their daughters to work there as opposed to male-dominated organizations.

At the same time, Mahboob started a platform called WomanNX, which helped Afghan women in high school and college work from home, getting paid based on their contributions. Work ranged from uploading short videos to writing articles or translating documents.

At first, Mahboob paid her employees and the WomanNX contributors in cash. The problem was that the women wanted to send the money to family and pay vendors in different parts of the country. They used the hawala system, an 8th-century money transfer process that relied on brokers and a web of trusted intermediaries.

This ancient platform seemed dated and slow to Mahboob and the women, many of whom already had Nokia cellphones and had started to create and use their own Facebook accounts. Even worse, sometimes the money did not make it through the hawala system, and it was hard to verify that the whole amount reached the recipient.

So, Mahboob researched the idea of mobile money. As it turned out, cellphone-based payment systems like M-PESA, which worked so well in Kenya, never took off in Afghanistan. PayPal was still not available because of US sanctions. And the women did not have bank accounts, so she could not wire them the money. The women had to have their father's or husband's permission to open an account, and this was often not granted.

Mahboob's employees wanted digital control over their time and earnings.

"If I gave them cash," she said, "their fathers or husbands or brothers might find out and take it away."

Enter Bitcoin

In early 2013, Mahboob's Italian business partner told her about bitcoin. He said it was a new kind of money that could be sent from phone to phone without a bank account. Unlike the local Afghani currency, which was steered by the government, bitcoin floated on the open market. When Mahboob first learned about bitcoin, it was trading at around $13. By the early summer of 2013, it broke $70.

"At first, I did not think the girls would trust Bitcoin," Mahboob said. "It was too hard to understand."

But her business partner encouraged her and said: "Let's try it — what do we have to lose?"

And so Mahboob taught her employees and contractors how to install Bitcoin wallets on their phones, how to receive funds and how to back up their savings. If the girls ever wanted to spend the bitcoin, Mahboob or her sister Elaha would buy it back from them with cash.

"I began to understand Bitcoin as a digital upgrade of the hawala system," Mahboob said. She and the women liked to get paid in bitcoin because they could keep it on their phone, and no one needed to know how much money they had.

"The girls were happy to finally have a money that the men in their lives could not take from them," Mahboob said. "It gave them security, privacy, and peace of mind."

Elaha started a business that bought bitcoin from the women for cash when they needed to purchase things. Some shops in Herat even started accepting bitcoin as a means of payment for clothing.

During the late summer and fall of 2013, bitcoin's price skyrocketed to more than $1,000. Citadel had put all of its cash assets into bitcoin. Business was booming, and the women could not believe their new wealth and economic freedom.

Mahboob felt invincible.

But in November 2013, bitcoin crashed, losing 60% of its value relative to the US dollar. Citadel's assets were decimated. Worse yet, its employees' savings evaporated.

"Our competitors went on the attack," Mahboob said, "arguing that Citadel was run by frauds who stole money from young girls."

Mahboob decided to offer to buy back the bitcoin from all of her employees and contractors — more than 150 in all — at pre-crash prices. To salvage what remained of Citadel, Mahboob converted almost all of the company's bitcoin to US dollars.

Following the crash, 2014 and 2015 were hard years for Citadel and Mahboob. She had to lay off a lot of employees, and WomanNX lost popularity. She did not close shop, but she did scale down the business, giving her more time and energy to help young women learn vocational skills through software. In 2014, she launched a nonprofit organization called Digital Citizen Fund (DCF) to educate women on how to use computer technology. By 2016, DCF became her primary focus.

"By then," she said, "many Afghans had lost their trust in Bitcoin. But I could not forget its potential. It stuck in my mind and would not go away."

Later in 2016, she created a curriculum through DCF to teach women across many schools how to use Bitcoin, set up a wallet, and understand how the network's "blockchain" ledger system worked. As of August 2021, thousands of women in the Herat area have learned about Bitcoin and attained more financial freedom because of Mahboob and the DCF.

Mahboob said the girls liked that they could receive, save, and spend bitcoin without needing a bank account. It only took a few minutes to set up a wallet and write down a seed phrase to back up their savings, in case they lost their phone. They could send the money anywhere in the world in minutes.

"The volatility," she said, "was the price you had to pay for the rest of these benefits."

Perhaps most powerfully, Bitcoin could not discriminate by gender. Despite the 2013 crash, the technology was too interesting to ignore.

A Refugee's Escape

A few of the women did keep their bitcoin from 2013. One of them was Laleh Farzan. Mahboob told me that Farzan worked for her as a network manager and in her time at Citadel earned 2.5 BTC. As of the exchange rate in late 2021, Farzan's earnings would now be worth *more than 100 times* the average Afghan annual income.[335]

In 2016, Farzan received threats from the Taliban and other conservatives in Afghanistan because of her work with computers. When they attacked her house, she decided to escape, leaving with her family and selling their home and assets to pay brokers to take them on the treacherous road to Europe.

Like thousands of other Afghan refugees, Farzan and her family traveled by foot, car, and train thousands of miles through Iran and Turkey, finally making it to Germany in 2017. Along the way, dishonest middlemen and common thieves stole everything they brought with them, including their jewelry and cash. At one point, their boat crashed, and more belongings sank to the bottom of the Mediterranean. It's a tragic story familiar to so many refugees. But in this case, something was different. Through it all, Farzan was able to keep her bitcoin, because she hid the seed to her bitcoin wallet on a piece of tiny, innocuous-looking paper. Thieves could not take what they could not find.

Once Farzan got to Germany, she sold some of the bitcoin for $2,500, making ten-times her initial earnings in dollar terms. Bitcoin helped her start a new life. Reflecting on the countless refugees in recent history, and thinking about how most of them could only bring the clothes on their back with them as they fled, Mahboob thinks Bitcoin could make a difference for so many.

As another example, Elaha saved some of the bitcoin she made back in 2013 and held onto it until 2017, eventually spending it on her college tuition when she was admitted to Cornell University. For the girls who were patient, bitcoin became an enormous treasure.

Today, Roya Mahboob says she uses bitcoin as a savings account and as an investment for the future. The bitcoin she obtained in 2013 for around $100 has increased in value by 400 times. She often uses it to send money from New York, where she spends a lot of time, to friends and family and vendors in Afghanistan.

In the past two years, she said, many hawala system brokers have started to learn about Bitcoin. She explained to me that in Herat there are more and more people willing to buy bitcoin in exchange for cash, and that in Kabul it is even more prevalent. The data supports Mahboob's observations: When adjusted for purchasing power and internet penetration, the firm Chainanalysis reported in late 2021 that Afghanistan had the seventh-highest, peer-to-peer exchange trade volume in the world.[336]

Mahboob said that as Bitcoin becomes easier to use, it will get more adoption. Since 2013, she said, wallets have improved in a staggering way with regard to usability and design. The DCF plans to continue offering classes to Afghan women and girls today on how to use Bitcoin.

"Thousands of graduates," Mahboob said, "have built the knowledge for economic sovereignty that they would not otherwise have."

Mahboob does not see Bitcoin as a Western innovation or a Silicon Valley creation, but rather as a global tool of financial freedom that can empower women. So many girls and women in Afghanistan do not have an ID or a bank account, she said.

"Bitcoin gives them power. They can learn how to mine it, code it, or trade it," she said. "When they earn money, they can convert that into radical self-reliance and power that they can use to escape the traditional role of Afghan women in the home."

Mahboob does not know if Bitcoin's mysterious inventor, Satoshi Nakamoto, realized how powerful it would become. To her, it is the most world-changing invention since the internet.

"It is more than just an investment," she said. "It is a revolution."

Economic Collapse

As of late 2021, Mahboob said, Bitcoin is more important than ever for Afghanistan.

In the wake of the fall of Kabul to the Taliban, Afghans are in dire economic straits. Already before the transition, as many as 14 million Afghans did not have enough food to eat and 2.5 million people had already fled the country. All of a sudden, bank accounts were frozen, economic activity slowed, and remittances halted.[337] ATMs were empty — after withdrawals spiked from hundreds per day to thousands per day — and financial exchanges were shuttered.[338]

The afghani has fallen to a record low, breaking more than 100 per dollar. Earlier in 2021, the rate was 78 per dollar, and 10 years ago, 58 per dollar. As of January 2022, the rate is 105 per dollar. Normally propped up by a flow of US currency, those shipments sustaining the afghani have stopped arriving.

Further exacerbating the situation, the US government has pressured the International Monetary Fund (IMF) to stop the release to Afghanistan of $460 million of special drawing rights, a kind of credit that can be exchanged for hard currency, and has confiscated more than 99% of the country's foreign reserves, which sit in New York. The German government has suspended $300 million in aid.[339] The World Bank announced that it is freezing its aid mechanism, which has committed more than $18 billion to Afghanistan.[340] Development assistance — which reached $4.2 billion in 2019 — could trickle to zero. Instead of being supported with aid, the Afghan economy could be strangled by sanctions.

Western Union and MoneyGram — two of the world's biggest money transmitters — cut off services, and websites like GoFundMe have been blocked from fundraising efforts for "compliance" reasons.[341] Remittances are a key lifeline for the country, making up nearly 4% of the economy or around $800 million annually. But now Afghans are in the cold, greeted by these kinds of statements when they try to receive money from abroad:

> Western Union understands the urgent need people have to receive funds, and we are committed to resuming operations for our customers in Afghanistan as conditions permit. We will continue to monitor the situation closely and we will keep all appropriate stakeholders apprised of further developments.[342]

WasalPay is a service that Afghans use to top up their phones, but the company's CEO is inundated with requests, and has run out of cash. He does not know how long he can stay in business.[343] Asef Khademi, who was working on a World Bank project to digitize payments in Afghanistan, says all progress has stopped since the Taliban took over.[344]

"They might just destroy it," he told *MIT Technology Review*. "They might just burn all of these technologies. Who knows?"

Mahboob pointed out that while the Taliban could crush local businesses or shut down financial modernization plans, they cannot stop Bitcoin.

Afghanistan's former central bank head Ajmal Ahmady — who fled during the fall — has predicted capital controls, currency devaluation, price inflation, and tough times for the poor.[345] He said the Taliban have access to just 0.1% to 0.2% of the country's savings. This, combined with the slowed remittance and aid flows, will crash the currency and cause prices to rise. Ahmady said that there are already reports of wheat prices doubling in Kabul.[346]

There could even be a demonetization event if the Taliban finds the existing currency, installed by the American-backed government in 2002, as not Islamic enough. After all, when the Taliban came to power in 1996, its economic chief declared the legacy currency "worthless" and halted production of new notes.[347]

In this dire climate, experts are predicting hyperinflation and an economy that could contract as much as 20%.[348] People holding afghanis are trying to exchange them for dollars or goods, driving prices up more and more. In a country where only 10% to 15% of the population has a bank account, a quick erosion of the afghani's purchasing power would be devastating. Some say that opium production or intervention from Russia or China could prevent economic collapse, but Ahmady called that an "over-optimistic scenario."[349]

"This is always how it is," Mahboob says. "The poor suffer, no matter what the elites do."

Bitcoin Fixes This

Mahboob said that in the chaos of last summer's transition, her parents fled Afghanistan but were not able to bring their money with them. Earlier in 2021, she flew to Kabul to see them. She tried telling her mother to start converting some of her afghanis into bitcoin. But her mother is traditional, the process seemed unnecessary and she procrastinated.

Mahboob wishes she had been more persuasive. Had her parents put at least some of their money into bitcoin, they could have taken their savings with them when they fled.

"Bitcoin fixes this," Mahboob said.

She thinks Bitcoin could have helped many other Afghans during this time — whether they fled and needed to take their savings with them, or stayed and needed an alternative to the afghani — and remains committed to teaching as many people as possible about it in the coming years.

She told me that she is negotiating with the Taliban to try and keep her educational programs going.

"Giving up," she said, "is not an option."

Mahboob has already spoken to Taliban spokesperson Timothy Weeks about keeping technology and finance classes for girls going in the Herat area. Weeks is a former professor from Australia who was kidnapped while teaching in Afghanistan, and beaten, and jailed for three and half years in a small cell.[350] In 2019, he and an American prisoner were freed in exchange for three Taliban commanders. Upon his release, he seemed to have developed Stockholm syndrome and has sided with his former captors, now going by the name Jibra'il and running point for the Taliban on digital issues. He is savvy enough to use apps like Signal. Mahboob said he seems open to her ideas.

One objective would be to try and convince Afghan Islamic scholars that Bitcoin is halal.[351] Mahboob thinks that an approach framing bitcoin like a digital hawala system based in gold — concepts that have been a part of Afghan society for thousands of years — could work.

"Religious scholars currently criticize Bitcoin as gambling," but, she said, "it depends on how you frame it." For example, Islamic finance experts like *Heaven's Bankers* author Harris Irfan argue that Bitcoin is halal, while fiat is haram.

Mahboob has helped many young women — including some of the stars of Afghanistan's female youth robotics team, which she founded and mentored to worldwide fame — get out during the transition.[352] But millions of young women remain in the country and will need ways to connect with the outside world.

Moving forward, Mahboob does not want to retreat to a passive state of simply condemning the Taliban from abroad. She experienced its rule and knows how brutal it is for women's rights, but she said, "We have to work on the ground and push for action, not just write articles criticizing the new government."

In negotiations so far, Taliban leaders have told her team that in Herat, women will be able to continue to go to school once female-specific buildings are established.

Data is hard to trust in Afghanistan, but estimates say that out of a country of nearly 40 million, there are around nine million internet users, with close to a quarter of the population online and 90% living on less than $2 per day.[353] Mahboob said that these numbers seem low and said that a much higher percentage of people, at least young people, have internet on their phones and that a much higher percentage make more than a few dollars per day, especially through side jobs.

Most of the young generation, she said, have cellphones with internet access. And the Taliban is allowing people to remain online, at least for now. Mahboob's goal is to convince the Taliban to allow women to participate in the digital economy.

Bitcoin, she said, is a big part of this plan.

A Legacy of Corruption

Mahboob said that over the past 20 years, Afghanistan has seen many achievements, especially with regard to women's rights, elections, and education. The number of Afghan girls attending first grade rose from zero in 2001 under the Taliban to more than 60% in the past decade.[354] But the government's fatal sin, she said, was corruption.

She blames the collapse on the "selfish behavior" of men like former-President Ashraf Ghani and his predecessors.

"The elites only thought about their own interests," Mahboob said.

Ghani taught at top American universities, worked at the World Bank, gave a TED Talk, wrote a book on fixing failed societies, and started an NGO called the "Institute for State Effectiveness," but then lost Kabul to the Taliban and fled the city, allegedly stealing $170 million in cash along the way.[355]

Afghanistan hosted the longest war in American history, leaving more than 240,000 people dead, but the operation has faced very little scrutiny.[356] US lawmakers never actually voted to declare war in Afghanistan, and the $2.2 trillion cost of the war was only questioned once in 20 years by members of the US Senate Finance Committee.[357]

The United States faces an astonishing $10 trillion in debt from 20 years of forever wars in Afghanistan and Iraq: $2 trillion in debt-financing to pay for the wars, $6.5 trillion to be paid on interest by 2050, and $2 trillion for expected expenses related to benefits for four million war veterans.[358] Much of the war money was wasted, as hundreds of millions of dollars of equipment has been destroyed or is now under Taliban control.[359]

Mahboob is critical of the way the West "supported" Afghanistan. Tens of billions of dollars was invested in her country, but little was actually given to Afghans, with most given to American NGOs and companies to do implementation, bringing that money back to the United States instead of having it soak into the local society. Out of the $144 billion that was invested in Afghanistan since 2002, an astonishing 80% to 90% ended up back in the US economy, siphoned through "a complex ecosystem of defense contractors, Washington banditry, and aid contractors," according to *Foreign Policy*.[360]

Who benefited most from the war? Undeniably, the lives of Mahboob and millions of other Afghan women improved. But the country's elites, like Ghani, and the military-industrial complex, led by companies paid billions by the US government such as Fluor and Amentum, profited most handsomely.[361] A cynical interpretation would be that the war operation was only sustained for so long to keep funds going to certain companies and interest groups — and not to build serious lasting infrastructure — explaining why the government in Kabul fell so quickly.

One former US soldier said that "the Afghan army wasn't real.[362] The Afghan Civil Authority was never real. They never collected taxes. There were no courts outside of police robbing people. None of it ever existed ... it was just a big jobs program funded by American money, and the moment it looked like the money would go away, everyone went home."

Mahboob thinks there could be a different kind of future, where Afghanistan is actually independent, and not just something so dependent that it collapses without foreign support.

A New Chapter

Mahboob said that before the fall of Kabul, she was thinking about reducing her time with her nonprofit activities and going back to working entirely on the business side. But now, she realizes that education is more important than ever.

"With everything that has happened during the transition, I can see that our fight has just begun," she said. "We need to hold the Taliban accountable."

Even with all that she has accomplished, Mahboob said that she regrets not doing more Bitcoin education.

"If we had done more," she said, "so many more could have benefited."

She vowed to double down in this area, telling me that in DCF programs moving forward, financial literacy and "being your own bank" will be key components, and Bitcoin will be a core part of the curriculum.

"Democracy is over," Mahboob said. "That chapter has closed and a new chapter has started. We are upset, yes, but we will not give up. I'm going to keep fighting."

"The women are going to make it," she promised.

Chapter X

The Humanitarian and Environmental Case for Bitcoin

Bitcoin is typically thought of as an investment and a strictly financial innovation.

But what if some of its greatest impact over time ends up being in the humanitarian and environmental spaces?

This chapter explores some of the major challenges in the realm of international development and argues that donors should be looking at bitcoin payments and mining as tools to reduce corruption, diminish dependency, and help renewable energy overcome adoption obstacles worldwide.

***

In his searing 2010 essay "Alms Dealers," Philip Gourevitch tells the history of humanitarian aid.[363] The industry, he wrote, was largely born in 1968 from Western compassion triggered by the televised starvation of children in Nigeria's breakaway Biafra province. The impulse to help those less fortunate in the world around us has become a vast $200 billion foreign aid industry.[364]

The 22 wealthiest governments provide approximately 60% of that sum, with private nongovernment organizations (NGOs), companies, and foundations funding the rest.[365] Around a third of government foreign aid is classified as development assistance, a third as humanitarian relief, and a third as military or security support.[366] In total, over the past six decades, more than $4 trillion of aid has been sent from rich countries to poorer countries.[367]

This is a staggering sum, and, on its surface, a seemingly impressive display of altruism. Public figures like Jeffrey Sachs and Peter Singer argue that aid is a moral imperative. But not everyone agrees on the overall impact. As Gourevitch asks, "Does the modern humanitarian industry help create the kind of misery it is supposed to redress?"

In the end, he credits humanitarianism with doing a lot of good; but there are three striking flaws with international development that prevent it from more fully achieving its mission.

First, aid is usually directed through and distributed by local governments. At that point, these often-autocratic regimes often siphon a portion of the funds or goods off to their cronies or troops, or develop patronage networks. When aid is not outright stolen, fees can be trimmed at every point along the path to the intended recipient. Significant percentages of aid get extracted by middlemen as it makes its way from Washington, DC, or Brussels, Belgium, to farmers or refugees halfway around the world.

In his critique, Gourevitch wrote that there is a "deeper decadence of a humanitarianism that paid war taxes of anywhere from fifteen per cent of the value of the aid it delivered (in Charles Taylor's Liberia) to eighty percent (on the turf of some Somali warlords), or that effectively provided the logistical infrastructure for ethnic cleansing (in Bosnia)."

Second, aid is often structured in a way that creates dependency. From shoes being dropped out of a helicopter only to ruin demand for local production to entire nations whose food and basic goods industries have been so destroyed by the competition from free alternatives that they permanently rely on imports from abroad, aid has at times stymied the economic and political independence known to governments and citizens in places like the United States, France, or Japan.

Gourevitch described the "ignoble economies that aid feeds off and creates: the competition for contracts, even for projects that everyone knows are ill-considered, the ways in which aid upends local markets for goods and services, fortifying war-makers and creating entirely new crises for their victims."

A third related problem is that aid is not leveraged enough to help communities and developing nations become *energy independent*, because there is rarely a clear path to economic sustainability for renewable energy farms, whose harvest points are often far from population centers, and lacking grid infrastructure.

Could Bitcoin help humanitarians overcome these three challenges?

On the one hand, it seems obvious how this new digital currency can help connect donors to recipients, in a peer-to-peer way, that cannot be stopped and could significantly reduce "middleman" corruption.

On the other, and in a way that has yet to be widely discussed, it seems possible that financing bitcoin mining, as opposed to other forms of aid, could actually help lift communities and nations out of dependence on foreign powers and expand electrification.

Cutting Out the Middleman

The overwhelming majority of aid comes from Western governments and individuals and is sent to or through governments in emerging markets. Many of these governments are corrupt or authoritarian, and they decide how to distribute the aid. Some more peer-to-peer efforts exist like GiveDirectly, but in general, the opportunity for reform — and for donors and philanthropists to send aid directly to communities and individuals in need — is massive.

When aid is given today, it passes through a string of third parties. According to scholars, "The history of foreign aid has been inextricably linked with corruption."[368] Reports suggest a "leakage rate" of 15% for aid heading to the most poverty-stricken nations and that "a large fraction of aid money never reaches a developing country."[369] A recent study found that "as much as a sixth of foreign aid intended for the world's poorest countries has flowed into bank accounts in tax havens owned by elites."[370] In 2012, then-UN Secretary General Ban Ki-moon said that "corruption prevented 30% of all development assistance from reaching its final destination."[371] As an example, in one Oxfam study, researchers could only verify that 7% of $28 million in US aid meant for Ghana made it to its destination between 2013 and 2015.[372]

In her book, *Dead Aid*, Zambian economist Dambisa Moyo argued that foreign assistance can actually hamper growth and, in some cases, does more to line the pockets of bureaucrats than sustainably improving life for the average citizen.[373] Aid can also spark a negative feedback loop of more waste, as when recipient governments are "too weak or too unscrupulous to handle aid resources, donors need to devote a surpassingly high amount of resources to oversight and controls."[374] Even when aid workers are honest, they are often stuck, unable to complain about corruption for fear of getting kicked out of the country they are working in by local strongmen. This results in a "historical lack of openness among aid agencies about corruption issues."[375] Many governments, ranging from Myanmar to Venezuela, have acted as a block, using their control of borders and financial systems to prevent aid from flowing to their citizens, for fear it could rescue or strengthen opposition groups.

But humanitarianism could be done more directly.

As a personal example, someone reached out to me, at the beginning of the Myanmar revolution in February 2021. They wanted to provide aid to the democracy movement, but the banking system was practically shuttered, and there was no easy way to wire dollars. After doing some digging, we were introduced to an aid worker-turned-activist, who was also a Bitcoin user. He could easily accept a donation, save it in BTC, and then sell it into the peer-to-peer markets when he needed to spend the collapsing local kyat currency on goods. An address was sent over Signal, and a gift was made in minutes. No barriers, no middlemen, and no possibility for corruption along the way. It is just one small example, but it is a glimpse of what the future could hold.

The key to Bitcoin as a successful humanitarian payment rail is either local liquidity (so that the recipients can easily cash out into fiat when necessary) or circular economies. The former has expanded dramatically across the world in the past few years, and the latter is already being built.

Today, if you want to support a humanitarian project in any country in the world, from Iraq to Senegal, all it takes is for the recipient to have a smartphone. From there, they can receive bitcoin directly on a free, open-source Android app like Muun or Blue Wallet, and then, when necessary, shave it off over time into fiat through peer-to-peer markets like Paxful, LocalBitcoins, or informal Telegram channels.

Aid, donations, and remittances can now be sent to individuals in El Salvador, for example, with the help of Strike.[376] The Lightning Network–powered platform — developed by Jack Mallers, Rockstar Dev, and others — became, three weeks after launching in spring 2021, the number-one finance app, number-one top app, and number-one overall app in the country. This growth was powered by the "Bitcoin Beach" circular economy and community, which is now having spillover effects and sparking other nascent communities, not just in El Salvador but even in neighboring countries like Guatemala. By late 2021, bitcoin became legal tender in El Salvador (see Chapter V), and anyone around the world can now send money instantly and cheaply to citizens of that country either through open-source wallets like Muun or through the state-provided Chivo wallet, which subsidizes the exchange rate.

The idea of Strike as a humanitarian tool is very compelling. Any American, for instance, could pay any Lightning invoice with their debit card, with the funds delivered in bitcoin instantly, with final settlement anywhere in the world, directly to a recipient's phone. Leveraging Lightning — which has tiny fees, settles instantly, and has barely any energy footprint — seems like an especially promising way forward, especially in a world where payment processors act as rent-seeking middlemen, skimming 2% to 5% of online gifts.

Ultimately, one of the biggest obstacles to effective international development has been the fact that there are so many third parties between the donor and the intended recipient. Often, they are kleptocratic governments or exploitative, monopolistic corporations. With Bitcoin, there is a new model to cut straight through this mess and connect grantors and grantees in a peer-to-peer way.

The Extractive Society

In their book *Why Nations Fail*, economists Daron Acemoglu and James Robinson break the world down into two kinds of societies: inclusive and extractive.[377]

Inclusive societies, such as South Korea or the United States, "are those that allow and encourage participation by the great mass of people in economic activities that make best use of their talents and skill and that enable individuals to make the choices they wish."

This contrasts with extractive societies, which depend on absolutist political institutions for their survival.

"Inclusive political institutions, vesting power broadly, would tend to uproot economic institutions that expropriate the resources of the many, erect entry barriers, and suppress the functioning of markets so that only a few benefit," but in extractive societies, those in power are able to counteract these forces and "enrich themselves and augment their power at the expense of society."

In general terms, aid flows from inclusive societies to extractive ones. Acemoglu and Robinson told the tragic story of the Democratic Republic of the Congo (DRC), which has, for centuries, suffered under highly extractive institutions. From the Kingdom of Kongo to the genocidal reign of King Leopold, and from later-stage Belgian colonialism to the dictatorship of Mobutu and today's rare mineral wars, elites and foreign powers have plundered the country's vast natural resources, skimmed incredible profits, destroyed the environment, and decimated the population.

Mobutu, for example, owned a palace with an airport big enough to land a Concorde jet (which he rented to fly back and forth to Paris) and bought castles across Europe and even owned large tracts of Brussels. Meanwhile, Congolese citizens under his reign suffered from hyperinflation, abject poverty, rampant violence, and a near-complete lack of consistent electricity.

"Modern DRC," Robinson and Acemoglu wrote, "remains poor because its citizens still lack the economic institutions that create the basic incentives that make a society prosperous. Political power continues to be narrowly concentrated in the hands of an elite who have little incentive to help the people."

Aid does not fundamentally change this and, sometimes, helps prop up the oppressors who keep their people down in the first place.

What if a new type of humanitarian aid could break this model of dependency, instead of aiding and abetting it?

A Bootstrap for Independence

Billions of people in developing nations face the stranded power problem. In order for their economies to grow, they have to expand their electrical infrastructure, a capital-intensive and complex undertaking. But when they, with the help of foreign aid or investment, build power plants to try and capture renewable energy in remote places, that power often has nowhere to go.

In many countries across Africa, for example, there are vast solar, wind, and hydro resources. These forces could drive economic activity, but local communities and governments usually lack the resources to invest in the infrastructure to kickstart the process.

Foreign donors and investors are not keen to support projects that do not have a pathway to sustainability or profits. Without strong transmission lines to deliver energy from harvest points to population centers, power plant builders could wait years before they can run without foreign subsidy.

Here is where Bitcoin could be an incentives game changer. New power plants, no matter how remote, can generate immediate revenue, even with no transmission lines, by directing their energy to the Bitcoin network and turning sunlight, water, or wind into money.

As local authorities or customers gradually link up to the power plant and are willing to pay more for the energy than what miners can afford, the Bitcoin load is lowered, and communities can grow. In this way, economic activity and renewable grids can be bootstrapped by bitcoin mining. And international aid could provide the spark.

Bitcoin Mining in the Congo

In 2014, the European Union helped finance a 15 megawatt (MW) hydroelectric plant on a small tributary of the Congo River in the DRC. The facility is nestled in what is, after the Amazon, the second-largest tropical rainforest in the world. It is owned and operated by Virunga National Park, which aims to preserve thousands of animal and plant species including the endangered Mountain Gorilla, as well as support the five million people who live near the park's borders.

The dream of powering parks like this with hydro energy is compelling. As *The New York Times* wrote in a 2017 profile, these plants in Virunga "may save a park and aid a country."[378]

But, as is typical, due to the difficulty of grid construction, the park's management has not been able to use all of the power right away. In 2020, it decided to start mining bitcoin with the surplus energy.

Normally, generating revenue right away from a remote power plant in the mountains or jungles or deserts is nearly impossible, because the energy may not be connected immediately with customers. But with Bitcoin, the facility can still profit even without distribution lines or local demand.

Seb Gouspillou — a French Bitcoin miner whose company is now working to transform running water into bitcoin in the Virunga region — said the hydro mines, and his firm's other projects, like solar farms in South Africa, are good examples of this mechanism in action.

As local demand rises, his miners will turn off. This works because of the energy market: As of 2021, Bitcoin miners needed prices in the range of 2 cents to 5 cents per kilowatt (kw) to run profitably. But practically every other electricity user will pay more, from 5 to 6 cents/kw for industrial users and 10 to 15 cents/kw for residential users in developed nations, to a staggering 20 to 40 cents/kw range in Africa. If there is ever competition for the energy that the bitcoin miners are buying, the miners turn off their machines, perhaps to turn them back on later in a real-time response to grid loads. This relationship is poorly understood by many, leading to a popular but incorrect assumption that Bitcoin is "wasting" energy that could be used for other projects.

Gouspillou's company built and operates the Virunga mining facility — in what looks in videos like containers of computers in the middle of the jungle — and they trained local staff, who run daily operations.[379] The farm connects by satellite internet to mining pools, and the company deposits the park's share of bitcoin revenue directly into its online account on an ongoing basis.

This is a new economic lifeline for the park, which according to Gouspillou only receives around $100,000 per year from the Congolese government, but has a monthly operating budget of around $1,000,000.

There is another Virunga hydro project in the works, a 30 MW dam, on a different river nearby, to be financed by the European Union. This time, the park is already planning to use some of that energy for bitcoin mining as a bridge. Eventually, these dams could support the millions of people who live around the park territory, and constitute an "ambitious attempt not only to protect Virunga — Africa's oldest national park — from threats including armed rebels, deforestation and oil prospectors, but to jump-start the local economy and potentially help stabilize one of the world's worst conflict zones."[380]

Hundreds of millions of people today still live without access to electric grids, and most are located in sub-Saharan Africa. As of 2019, just 8.7% of the Congolese population had access.[381] The numbers are similar or worse in South Sudan, Somalia, Libera, Sierra Leone, Chad, Niger, Malawi, and the Central

African Republic, with only a few governments on the African continent able to provide electricity to more than 50% of their population. In countries like the Congo, electrification is expanding more slowly than population growth.[382]

Traditionally, citizens without electricity cut down trees for charcoal to help cook their meals, releasing significant amounts of carbon into the atmosphere.[383] Burning biofuels for cooking and heating is also a leading cause of indoor air pollution worldwide, leading to 1.6 million deaths per year, half of which are children under five.[384] But if bitcoin mining can be a bridge to help subsidize and encourage more hydro power to come online, it could be a worthy project for humanitarians to target to help stop deforestation, protect the local environment and empower the people. According to the International Food Policy Research Institute, the Congo "has the potential to become the breadbasket of the entire African continent."[385]

UN research states that getting electricity to those without it requires "increased private financing and adequate policy and fiscal incentives to spur faster development of new technologies."[386]

Bitcoin could very well be a mechanism to help align incentives and spark more electricity and agriculture for a part of the world that is underdeveloped and dependent on imports.

There are different models of how aid could work in this scenario. In a "less mature" model, a company like Gouspillou's BigBlock might be paid to handle everything and simply deliver a profit share to a local partner. In a "more mature" model, they could be contracted to just handle setup and training, and leave everything else behind for local authorities to run. In the latter model, one can begin to see how the inclusive economy could grow.

In this way, humanitarian aid could help strengthen local communities and bootstrap them so they can be in control of their own destiny, making them more productive and sovereign. There are already many such projects to give electricity to small communities away from population centers across Africa, Gouspillou said, and Bitcoin mining can make them much more profitable and effective. What if the Gates Foundation or the European Union, for instance, announced $100 million per year to finance bitcoin mining in Africa? With ongoing innovation in satellite internet connectivity, monetizing energy sources in remote regions becomes more compelling over time.

Gouspillou said the grid in his native France is still 70% nuclear, a legacy of Charles de Gaulle's vision for energy independence. But none of it is used for bitcoin mining, something Gouspillou called a big mistake. He estimated that if just 2% of the output of the nuclear system was directed toward bitcoin mining, it could be enough to overcome the state electric company's recent financial difficulties and put it back in the black. During the summers and at night, there is less demand on the grid, but today, that energy goes unused. Gouspillou said these times would be perfect occasions to flex in bitcoin mining. But the authorities, he said, are clueless, and he loses sleep thinking about the wasted opportunities.

To this end, Bitcoin could eventually play a significant role in helping to incentivize nuclear energy. Dozens of emerging market countries are exploring nuclear energy as a way to achieve energy independence. But according to the World Nuclear Association, the size of their grid systems is a major issue, as "many nuclear power plants are larger than the fossil fuel plants they supplement or replace."[387] But again, with Bitcoin, any excess energy can be directed to mining until the communities around the plant catch up. The idea of using Bitcoin to harness curtailed energy holds for developed countries, too, of course. Germany, for example, has famously created more wind power than it can use.[388]

A near-complete disregard for Bitcoin is chronic across the entire international development space, which has, until this point, not realized or ignored the currency's potential to reduce corruption and spark economic activity. Too many humanitarians have fallen victim to the mirage of "blockchain not Bitcoin" narratives, which have wasted hundreds of millions of dollars.

The French story unfolds to a much more depressing vision across the developing world, where many nations have abundant wind, solar, hydro, and even uranium resources, but lack the grid infrastructure and concentrated demand to take advantage. Gouspillou sees bitcoin mining, powered by humanitarians or investors, as the way to bootstrap this all into place.

Today, just 4% of the world's population has the exorbitant privilege of creating the global reserve currency (see Chapter III). But in a potential future where bitcoin is that reserve currency, mining from renewable sources could help empower any nation to directly earn the future base money of the world. And this could provide a massive incentive to continue expansion and innovation in renewable energy systems. "This," Gouspillou said, "is the beautiful dream."

Avoiding Pitfalls

If humanitarian organizations, foundations, and foreign offices could support Bitcoin mining operations at renewable energy sites, that could be a trigger for sustainable local economic activity.

Consider how in Norway, the Sovereign Wealth Fund, backed by oil, has financed some of the highest quality of life in the world. Could Sudan and Ethiopia, with massive wind and solar resources powering bitcoin mining and a growing electric grid, be Norways of the future?

A rosy outcome, of course, is far from guaranteed. The big obstacles of corrupt local authorities and exploitative foreign corporations remain.

One way to neutralize this threat is for international donors to position bitcoin mining projects as economic leverage opportunities, where they stipulate that part of the profits go toward microfinance or venture capital to form local businesses. If major foundations and governments can enforce these conditions in their deals setting up renewable mining infrastructure, they could have a lasting impact.

Even on the for-profit side, there is a possibility that foreign bitcoin miners can operate in a non-extractive way. They can be paid to set up operations and train local staff, leaving some or all of the ongoing profits in the hands of the region. The population could then absorb the wealth from renewables, instead of seeing it slip away to foreign lands, as it often does. In this way, investing in bitcoin payments and mining could be a compelling environmental, social, and corporate governance (ESG) narrative moving forward.

A major challenge for Bitcoin is how to avoid the fate of gold, which as a historical reserve currency was plundered by colonial powers in places like the Congo. Later, the United States custodied gold inside its borders through Executive Order 6102, and finally, after the Bretton Woods agreement, centralized much of the gold held by other governments. This helped President Nixon in 1971 to essentially move gold out of the monetary system and neutralize its restraining effects on war spending (see Chapter XII). So, what is to stop this kind of exploitation and capture from happening to bitcoin if it is being mined at renewable sites in developing countries?

Satoshi Nakamoto chose April 5 as their birthday, which was the day that Executive Order 6102 came into effect in 1933. They designed Bitcoin specifically to be resistant to this kind of capture. Because of its properties and the political incentives it creates, it will be difficult for one government to control all of the world's mining, and domestically, impossible for governments to effectively stop citizens from using it.

After all, Bitcoin is invisible, can teleport from one end of the Earth to the other in minutes, is programmable, easily divisible, and its spending power can be easily stored in a variety of ways and formats by individuals, making it highly confiscation resistant.

Gold and other mined commodities have none of these qualities and have helped, at times, to lead to extractive societies. Perhaps Bitcoin's open and permissionless attributes can help lead the world in a more inclusive direction.

A final obstacle is that a huge global aid industry now runs on propping up societies that cannot stand on their own. This may sound cynical, but will large foundations and government agencies actually want to reduce bureaucracy, corruption, and dependence through Bitcoin, if they themselves benefit from it?

***

For all of the hundreds of billions of dollars invested each year into international development to improve the lives of the most vulnerable, major obstacles remain.

Middleman corruption and forced dependency plague the humanitarian industry, and a lack of infrastructure prevents emerging markets from capitalizing on stranded renewable energy resources. For anyone interested in overcoming these challenges, Bitcoin is worth a long look as a humanitarian and environmental tool for change.

Whether as a corruption-resistant, peer-to-peer rail for transferring funds abroad, a spark for economic independence, or a subsidy for sovereign renewable electrification in developing nations, Bitcoin's future human impact outside of the traditional areas of finance and investing is just beginning to be understood.

Chapter XI

Bitcoin and the American Idea

In previous chapters, we have seen how individuals are using bitcoin as a "plan B" in places like Palestine, Togo, and Afghanistan. But what kind of impact might it have for Americans?

In seeking the answer, we need to go back to July 4, 1776, when the Founding Fathers declared independence from the British Empire:

> We ... the Representatives of the united States of America ... in the Name, and by Authority of the good People of these Colonies, solemnly publish and declare, That these United Colonies are, and of Right ought to be Free and Independent States; that they are Absolved from all Allegiance to the British Crown, and that all political connection between them and the State of Great Britain, is and ought to be totally dissolved; and that as Free and Independent States, they have full Power to levy War, conclude Peace, contract Alliances, establish Commerce, and to do all other Acts and Things which Independent States may of right do.

This was a bold and risky action. Never before had a colonial state defeated its overlord, especially one at the apex of its global power.

Against all odds, the Founding Fathers rallied a young nation and won freedom. The Fourth of July is still, nearly two-and-half centuries later, a cause for great pride across the United States. The idea of America, and the values on which it was founded, animate resistance struggles around the world. The principles of free speech, property rights, equality of opportunity, individual liberty, and checks and balances on government power are ones to aim for and live by.

But for some, the Fourth of July seems like a hollow festival. America the idea has grown distant from America the reality.

US history is in many respects shameful: We enslaved African Americans, pursued a genocidal conquest of Native Americans, interned Japanese Americans in prison camps, invaded Vietnam and Iraq and launched the "forever wars," backed coups against democratically elected leaders, pushed an ongoing War on Drugs and prison-industrial complex, and built a sophisticated surveillance state. These are just a few examples of how America has strayed from the breathtaking words of the Declaration of Independence.

At the base of the Statue of Liberty in New York Harbor rests a bronze plaque with the words of "The New Colossus," a sonnet by Jewish American poet Emma Lazarus.[389] The last few lines read:

> Keep, ancient lands, your storied pomp!" cries she
> With silent lips. "Give me your tired, your poor,
> Your huddled masses yearning to breathe free,
> The wretched refuse of your teeming shore.
> Send these, the homeless, tempest-tost to me,
> I lift my lamp beside the golden door!

As Allen Farrington has pointed out, the United States has, in many ways, lost this generous founding spirit.[390] Over time, that spirit has been sacrificed on the altar of the self-interested schemes of politicians and elites and on the pacts that our leaders made with dictators to secure US financial dominance. But could the Scarlet Letters on America's history be dimmed by a new act of rebellion — a declaration of monetary independence?

If the 1776 declaration was a document of political freedom, then in 2009 came a document of monetary freedom: Satoshi Nakamoto's "Bitcoin White Paper."

As noted by Joseph J. Ellis in *Founding Brothers*, a Pulitzer Prize winning–history of America's first leaders: "The creation of a separate American nation occurred suddenly rather than gradually, in revolutionary rather than evolutionary fashion, the decisive events that shaped the political ideas and institutions of the emerging state all taking place with dynamic intensity during the last quarter of the eighteenth century." Many of the lasting pillars of American society and governance were established in the span of just a few short years.

This is happening once again. Not with politics, but, this time, with money. As Ellis writes, the framework for America "was built in a sudden spasm of enforced inspiration and makeshift construction," as is happening now with Bitcoin.

The quest of the cypherpunks and Satoshi to establish digital cash beyond the control of the state was animated, not by fear of an imperial power, but by the nascent threat in the 1980s and 1990s of the electronic surveillance state and of the looming loss of our liberties as we entered the digital age (see Chapter II).

In 1961, President Dwight D. Eisenhower gave a powerful farewell speech.[391] He noted proudly how America was "the strongest, the most influential and most productive nation in the world," but he also warned how the military-industrial complex that had grown as a result of our wars abroad posed existential dangers. If one had told the Founding Fathers that, 150 years after their passing, the following words would be uttered by the leader of America to its people, it would have chilled them to the bone but probably not surprised them:

> This conjunction of an immense military establishment and a large arms industry is new in the American experience. The total influence — economic, political, even spiritual — is felt in every city, every state house, every office of the Federal government. We recognize the imperative need for this development. Yet we must not fail to comprehend its grave implications. Our toil, resources and livelihood are all involved; so is the very structure of our society. In the councils of government, we must guard against the acquisition of unwarranted influence, whether sought or unsought, by the military-industrial complex. The potential for the disastrous rise of misplaced power exists and will persist. We must never let the weight of this combination endanger our liberties or democratic processes. We should take nothing for granted.

Eisenhower also noted the technological revolution underway and warned against the rise of a "scientific-technological elite" uncaring to our founding freedoms.

The cypherpunks witnessed the realization of Eisenhower's dark vision, as by the 1980s, they felt the surveillance state creeping in and laying down roots for future expansion. They also recognized the limits of what could be achieved at the ballot box. There were diminishing returns to asking the government to protect our freedoms. Some liberties would have to be seized with open-source code.

Bitcoin is the instantiation of a revolutionary idea: a system that cannot discriminate; that does not wield violence; that does not have special rules for the rich; that does not require identification or a particular status or level of wealth or race or creed to use; and whose rules cannot be manipulated by governments. Satoshi arguably took the best ideas from Thomas Jefferson, John Adams, and their colleagues and gifted them to people around the world.

As the Declaration of Independence says, "When a long train of abuses and usurpations, pursuing invariably the same Object evinces a design to reduce [people] under absolute Despotism, it is their right, it is their duty, to throw off such Government, and to provide new Guards for their future security."

Our "new guard" is Bitcoin. Not just a founding document, but a network designed to fight the despotism of central banking and financial surveillance, a despotism set in motion hundreds of years ago.

A debate over the money system was at the heart of America's founding. One of Jefferson's biggest regrets was that, in securing the capital's shift south from Philadelphia to Washington, he compromised with Alexander Hamilton and agreed to assume individual state debts into a national debt, centralizing the American financial system. This centralizing momentum grew over the decades, finally manifesting in the Federal Reserve arrangement we have today, which gives unelected bureaucrats control of the monetary system.

Another item that gave the Founding Fathers pause was the weak performance of pre-revolutionary state paper currencies (which saw price inflations ranging from 800% to 2,300%) and the Continental dollar, which was printed into oblivion and lost 99.9% of its value during the Revolutionary War.[392] Maybe in that one case, some thought, it was worth it to debase a currency to win a war, but in the future, the same action of being able to debase the currency may launch many new, unnecessary wars. Those that followed this line of thinking would have neatly predicted America's current predicament — the "forever war" phenomenon, where the last three presidents have been at war every day of office, even though the domestic nation seems to be at peace.

What if our monetary future does not continue down this path of centralization and debasement but, rather, follows a new path of decentralization and growing value? Today's dollar hegemony was engineered by Richard Nixon and Henry Kissinger (see Chapter III). Tomorrow, the currency of America could be based on the twin ideals of the Founding Fathers and Satoshi Nakamoto.

Unlike America, which lost its first battle over centralization just a few years after its founding, Bitcoin won its first battle over centralization during the Blocksize War, where user control and personal freedom defeated business interests and the concentration of power.[393]

On July 4, 1821, Secretary of State John Quincy Adams warned of an America that would become a global imperium "in search of monsters to destroy." An America where the "fundamental maxims of her policy" have "insensibly changed from liberty to force," where we have become "the dictatress of the world."

Perhaps Bitcoin can help Americans reflect on our history and remember that our true glory, in Adams's words, is "not dominion, but liberty," and that our true march is "of the mind" and not the sword.

To help ponder this, I spoke to two people whose families and ancestries have borne the brunt of America's worst, who carry two strikingly different perspectives. They carry contrasting assessments of American history, and of our founding story, but own a similar optimism about the future of America, powered by Bitcoin.

Bitcoin and Black America

Isaiah Jackson is an entrepreneur and the author of *Bitcoin and Black America*, a searing critique of how the US financial system systematically discriminates against African Americans to this day.[394] The book is also a rallying cry for the Black community to explore using Bitcoin as a way out of a system that unfairly benefits elites.

Jackson writes how "before Bitcoin, no matter how much money you raised to support a liberation plan, civil rights movement or march, ultimately you had to use the banking system … you continued to feed a system that did not have our best interests at heart. All of those deposits would enrich banks who encouraged redlining, denied loans to qualified applicants, and, even beyond race, bankrupted the entire financial system in 2008 [and then] gave themselves bonuses to celebrate."

Bank after bank, Jackson points out, have been caught and fined for holding Blacks to different standards than whites. In one recent study, "Borrowers in upper-income black neighborhoods were twice as likely as homeowners in low-income white neighborhoods to refinance with a subprime loan." As a result of the legacy of slavery and practices like these, he writes that "Black households have the lowest median wealth among races in America."

His plan to change the fate of his community? To spread the word about "how Bitcoin could spark a revolution among regular, working class people." He says: "I specifically showed how we could gradually reject fiat currency, use Bitcoin, and start or own local economies … I propose that we build our foundation of social change and protest by steadily moving our funds out of the banking system."

Because of Bitcoin, forced dependency on a system that keeps Black people down is, he says, no longer the only option. He summarizes his mission simply: "Hopefully, during the period of the biggest transfer of wealth in human history, the black community won't be last to the party."

I reached out to Jackson (or Zay, as he's often known) to get his perspective on the Fourth of July as an American holiday, and his thoughts on the idea of America versus the history of America.

Jackson is half African American, and half Native American, with a family tree partly tracing back to slaves that were sold from Africa to Barbados and then onto South Carolina, and partly tracing back to Native Americans persecuted in Florida and Oklahoma.

He says that "growing up, in a black family, we're celebrating on July 4th, but it's not exactly a patriotic holiday. Hot dogs and cookouts and fireworks are fun, but for me, it's about being with family and enjoying the time off, not paying tribute to the founders."

Jackson says that July 4 really has become a "consumerist memorial" and not something that carries a deep meaning. He points to Juneteenth as something that resonates more, as it celebrates the emancipation of slaves and the liberation of humans.

Even on the idea of America, Jackson says that it was "*their* idea" of America. "Imagine," he says, "if they allowed black people or women to sit in on the creation of the Constitution. We wouldn't have had to wait around decades for the 13th or 19th Amendments."[395]

No, in practice, Jackson says, America is not the "land of the free."

"We're at a point in history," he says, "where we've gone away from that completely."

Jackson says that millions of Americans have been brainwashed by a broken public school system. He calls it the "Pocahontization of history," where many kids think that the relationship between the European settlers and the Native Americans was as depicted in the Disney movie, as opposed to the brutal conquest that actually happened.

"As a former public school teacher, and as someone whose mother and grandmother were public school teachers," he says, "let me just say: We didn't teach kids about the real history of America."

Jackson tells a story about his youth, when he was 14 years old and the US government invaded Iraq. He remembers watching the TV screen and seeing estimates that the military operation would cost more than a trillion dollars. (To date the United States has spent more than $6 trillion on the War on Terror).[396] He was stunned.

"A trillion dollars? I was sitting in a neighborhood filled with poor people. We had no infrastructure, terrible education, terrible healthcare. Even as a young kid," he says, "I knew we should have used that money domestically, instead of using it to destroy another country."

Jackson says he has one uncle who "doesn't believe anything in the media." Everyone, he says, thought this particular uncle was crazy for questioning the Iraq War, which was very popular at the time. His uncle told Jackson that the war would never end, and that even though they promised it would be short, that it would be long, and that the leaders of America want to be at war.

"I thought he was a crazy person, but he was right. That was 18 years ago," Jackson says, "and we're still fighting in Iraq today."

Jackson says he is privileged to live in America. "Here," he says, "we take indoor plumbing, air conditioning, having a robust transportation system, and even having a relatively stable currency for granted. Many people around the world lack these things." He stops short of saying he's proud to be American.

But, not wanting to depress, Jackson says despite the past he is hopeful for the future — because of Bitcoin.

Bitcoin, he says, is "more American than apple pie." It is "based on the initial ideals, where we started with a revolution, an overthrow of oppressors taking taxes without representation, challenging tyranny." He says Bitcoin "is doing the same thing, just in a global manner."

Could bitcoin give real freedom where a piece of paper failed?

"The reason why the revolutionary dream remains unfulfilled," he says, "is because the money is flawed. We have to fix the money."

While Jackson feels no deep connection with July 4, he does celebrate January 3, which is the birthday of the Bitcoin software. Jackson actually helped advocate for this date to be celebrated, to remind Bitcoin users to withdraw funds from exchanges into self-custody. In a meme popularized by Jackson, "No keys, no cheese."

Jackson tells stories of people in the Black community who have had their lives changed by Bitcoin. One of his favorites, he says, is a 15-year-old kid, who came to one of Jackson's presentations in 2016 with his mom. The mom thought Jackson's lecture on Bitcoin was interesting, but it was the son who called him every day for a full month after the class. The kid ended up buying bitcoin after working small jobs. By the time he was 17, he had made enough money through bitcoin to pay for college. Now he is 22 and runs his own web development company.

Another story Jackson tells is of his friend Justin, who went to jail for two years, but then when he got out, got into Bitcoin. He learned about dollar-cost averaging, mining, trading, and even started a food truck in Charlotte, selling food for bitcoin. Five years later, Justin has his own book, his own series on Clubhouse, and a program to help inmates earn bitcoin while they are in jail.

"People don't like to talk about the prison system," Jackson says. "I have a cousin and a friend who are both in jail. They are trapped, but they have cellphones, and they can hold bitcoin."

Justin has helped many prisoners find a future through Bitcoin. The prison guards do search the belongings of inmates, of course, but many are allowed to have cellphones, and the guards are not always combing through their phone apps.

"From the time we had slave patrols," Jackson says, "we've always had police that were there to keep the lower classes away from the higher classes. That ended up becoming racial. We do need our police, but for the black community, they have been the victim of the double standard of crack and cocaine laws, which put black men in prison for 40 years, while only giving 1 year for white men. There are millions of black people in American jails today for non-violent drug crimes. I'd like to see these people who are locked up supported by Bitcoiners."

Even if that does not happen, Jackson says, they are finding support in Bitcoin. "Every great leader in the black community knows we need allies," he says. "With Bitcoin, we have allies everywhere."

Jackson sees Bitcoin as remedying some of the worst aspects of jingoism and nationalism that have plagued America over the decades, whether it be the warfare state or the prison-industrial complex. In his mind, Bitcoin can help us achieve a greater connection with the world around us.

"Technically," Jackson says, pointing to his Native American descent, "my people were here first. Whatever this plot of land was, it wasn't called America. And it may not be America forever."

Bitcoin, he says, helped him change his perspective. "If you look at a map of the world," he says, "most of the lines were drawn by a group of colonizers a long time ago."

"These lines," he says, "have nothing to do with me or my generation. But I'm a citizen of the world now. The lines don't matter anymore."

From Baghdad to Bitcoin

"My first introduction to America," Faisal Saeed Al Mutar says, "was a tank in front of my house."

Al Mutar was born during the first Gulf War, and his first contact with the Americans was during the invasion of his country Iraq in 2003, when he was 12 years old.

He had grown up under the dictatorship of Saddam Hussein, in an education system whose goal was to "create as many ignorant people as possible," teaching only "how to be loyal to the president." He says you always had to worship, and you always had to say Saddam was right, no matter what.

To illustrate the climate of fear he grew up in, Al Mutar says, "Let's say that your father was against the president ... he'll ask the son to kill the father with a pistol, and ask the son to pay the price of the bullet that he killed his father with. That is the way that he could instill fear in the son and [force him to] show his loyalty to the president."[397]

Al Mutar could not access the internet or watch more than two state-controlled TV stations under Saddam. "It was hell," he says.[398]

But eventually, Al Mutar broke through the firewall. He called the open internet a "black market" for knowledge, which helped him develop a belief in using "reason, evidence, and scientific methods of inquiry — rather than faith and mysticism — in seeking solutions to human problems."[399]

The first foreign political text he came across was Thomas Paine's *Age of Reason*. Al Mutar actually found it, along with writings from Orwell, on a heavy metal message board. This was his rabbit hole for discovering freedom. He became more inspired, starting a blog where he explored secular ideas, and even distributed copies of the American Bill of Rights to classmates.

Al Mutar credits his father for instilling in him the values of critical thinking. He would tell Al Mutar that if he was going to form a belief, then he would have to build the supporting evidence for that belief. You cannot just blindly believe. From these words, Al Mutar said he followed "a life of learning and not hating."

When Saddam fell, he began to advocate for the separation of religion and state. "I advocated a lot for human rights, women's rights, LGBT rights," he said, "and that is not a friendly thing to do in the Middle East."

At the time, Al Mutar often thought: "Why did America invade us, and not us invade them?"

After all, he comes from Baghdad, which was once the capital of the Ababasid Caliphate in the Golden Age of Islam. At one point, long ago, his people invaded and controlled a huge percentage of the planet, from the Atlantic Ocean to India.

"What the hell happened?" asks Al Mutar. "How did we move from a superpower to a failed state? How did we move from occupiers to occupied?"

When the Arab empire reached its peak, Al Mutar says, it built its power on science and inquiry. Algebra, the clock, the camera, paper maps, and surgery all came to the world through Muslim culture during its Golden Age. That, Al

Mutar says, is when there was openness, inquiry, free thought, science, and reason, and the separation of powers. And then, there was a long decay into religious dogma.

Al Mutar says he saw some of these same Golden Age attributes in the texts of the Founding Fathers. And this, he says, is why the United States is still dominating the world today.

During the occupation, Al Mutar would go up to American soldiers and ask a lot of questions.

"They would be sitting in a humvee and holding M16s," he said, "but I was not afraid. I found the humanity in them. Some thought what they were doing was noble, others just wanted to pay bills. But after talking to so many of them, I didn't see them as monsters trying to kill Iraqis. It was war. In war, it's not good guys and bad guys, it's very gray about who is good and who is bad."

As he grew older, Al Mutar became a more outspoken atheist, founded the Global Secular Humanist Movement and became a target for Islamists over his writings and activities. "I survived three kidnappings," he says. A Shiite by birth, Al Mutar and his family got fake ID cards made with Sunni-sounding names to clear Al-Qaeda–held checkpoints in their neighborhood.[400]

Later, he said, his best friend was killed by radicals, possibly because they mistook him for Al Mutar. He ended up receiving death threats from Al-Qaeda and the Mahdi Army. His brother and cousin were killed in sectarian violence.[401]

In 2012, Al Mutar finally fled Iraq and was admitted into the United States as a refugee. Over the past decade, he has founded and worked at a variety of organizations to connect activists from closed societies with Americans who can help them, and also to make knowledge and information accessible to individuals in the Arab World, who are, according to Al Mutar, surrounded by propaganda and fake news.

Most recently, Al Mutar founded the nonprofit Ideas Beyond Borders along with the Singaporean journalist Melissa Chen. Together, they have employed more than 100 young individuals to translate works on liberty, human rights, philosophy, and science into Arabic, in total dozens of books and tens of thousands of Wikipedia pages. Al Mutar found inspiration for this work through the memory of the Bayt al-Hikma, or House of Wisdom, the storied Baghdad library that helped light up the Arab golden age.

Al Mutar tells the story of a famous bookshop that still operates in Jordan today, where *Mein Kampf*, the *Protocols of the Elders of Zion* and the *Communist Manifesto* are proudly displayed outside. Beyond the Quran, he said, these are the three most popular texts in the region. "This," he says, "is the stuff people have access to. Maybe people at the American University of Beirut would disagree, but for the average person in the Arab world, this is the text they can access. It creates a climate of hate."

Al Mutar says his goal is to "prevent refugee crises from happening in the first place, rather than dealing with refugees." He points to the fact that less than 1% of internet content is available in Arabic.[402] "Ideas and knowledge," he says, "will defeat ignorance and extremism more effectively than tanks and guns ever could."

Perhaps surprisingly, given his military introduction to America through an invasion of his homeland, Al Mutar has become a huge fan. He is immensely proud of becoming a US citizen on June 26, 2019.

"America," he says, "provided me and many others with a lot of opportunity and potential. I don't think another country could have made the best of me. I've lived in Europe and Asia. There were always restrictions, always obstacles. It's no surprise to me that immigrants can be so successful in America compared to other places."

"I could focus on the negatives," Al Mutar says, hinting at anti-Arab discrimination. "Yes, some people send me hate mail. But there are a lot of people who send me love mail. If you always think of yourself as a victim, you will only focus on the negative. I try not to do that."

"The immigrant experience in America today," he says, "is largely positive because of the opportunities that exist and the values that this country was founded on."

"Look at gay rights," Al Mutar says. "In the past 50 years, there's been a huge change of mindset, and a sweeping trend in favor of legalized gay marriage. Compare that to countries in Africa or Asia or the Muslim world. There are still places where they have the death penalty for being gay."

He argues that, despite all its flaws, the world is in a much better place because of American leadership. "The fact that you can not only protest but change policy is not available to the billions living under authoritarian regimes around the world," he says.

"People disagreed with Bush, so they voted for Obama," he said. "This option isn't available for those living under Xi Jinping or Vladimir Putin. Will the Russians who were against the war in Syria ever vote him out? No, they don't have that right. America is imperfect but the system allows for change which is different from the models of the other superpowers. We'd be living in a much worse world if the Soviets had won the Cold War," Al Mutar says.

Looking back at America's history, Al Mutar says that the evils that exist in the United States are not exceptionally American, that they, in fact, exist all over the world, and there is a case that can be made that America is one of the few nations that tried to move away from these evils.

"Yes, the Founding Fathers had slaves," Al Mutar said, "but they also enshrined the concept of individual freedom. America leans good, because of its founding principles. To me, these principles are like the scientific method. They help the nation self-correct over time."

"During their era," Al Mutar says, "the thoughts of the Founding Fathers were absolutely revolutionary. The concept of individual rights was revolutionary. The world had never seen anything like it."

"America," he says, "was founded in a way in which the government should fear its people, not where the people should fear its government. This is the opposite of the society where I grew up."

Recently, Al Mutar has grown an interest in how Bitcoin can play a role in helping to liberate people around the world. His organization handled the Arabic translation of *The Little Bitcoin Book*, and he has been exploring how to pay translators across the Arab world in bitcoin.[403]

"Bitcoin," he says, "is a tool that could spread American values more effectively than any war or intervention. I have seen how it can empower and connect people."

He says it has a similar combination of innovation, anti-censorship, and openness that made the American idea so great.

As the world continues to turn geopolitically, Al Mutar says we should consider how Bitcoin may benefit more open and free societies like America, that despite its flaws is based on enlightenment values, and how it may cause fatal issues for dictatorial regimes.

"Bitcoin expands free speech, property rights, individual sovereignty, open capital markets, and checks on government power. America was founded on these values, and can thrive with them. The Chinese Communist Party, Putin's dictatorship in Russia, or the Kingdom of Saudi Arabia?"

"Not so much," he says.

When asked who his favorite Founding Father was, he instantly says, "Thomas Jefferson." The first thing Al Mutar did when he got to America, he says, was go to Monticello. He finds Jefferson especially inspiring on the subject of freedom of religion and compares his push for separation of Church and State with Satoshi's push for separation of Money and State.

"Jefferson was not perfect," Al Mutar says, "but who is?" He says slavery and the depopulation of Native Americans are the "original sins" of the United States. "These stories need to be taught and remembered," he says, "but we cannot judge the values of those living three centuries ago with the values of those living today."

"In 100 years," he says, "we may look back at today and say that the t-shirts we are all wearing make us all immoral because they are made with slave labor. So, are we any more moral than the founding fathers? Consider that," he says, "in my part of the world, Mauritania didn't outlaw slavery until 1980, and today so much of the Gulf cities are built with slavery, including the infrastructure for the upcoming world cup. Some say that Martin Luther King Jr. was homophobic — is that what we should judge him on?"

"No," Al Mutar says. "We should acknowledge the evil and the good."

Saddles and Riders

In 1935, the African American poet Langston Hughes wrote "Let America Be America Again." Here are the final few lines:

> O, let America be America again — The land that never has been yet — And yet must be — the land where every man is free. The land that's mine — the poor man's, Indian's, Negro's, ME — Who made America, Whose sweat and blood, whose faith and pain, Whose hand at the foundry, whose plow in the rain, Must bring back our mighty dream again. Sure, call me any ugly name you choose — The steel of freedom does not stain. From those who live like leeches on the people's lives, We must take back our land again, America! O, yes, I say it plain, America never was America to me, And yet I swear this oath — America will be! Out of the rack and ruin of our gangster death, The rape and rot of graft, and stealth, and lies, We, the people, must redeem The land, the mines, the plants, the rivers. The mountains and the endless plain — All, all the stretch of these great green states — And make America again![404]

Hughes's words speak to the theme of this essay: There is a constant tension in American experience between the animating idea — so noble — and the reality — so flawed.

To celebrate the 50th anniversary of the Declaration of Independence in 1826, Thomas Jefferson wrote:

> All eyes are opened or opening to the rights of man. The general spread of the light of science has already laid open to every view the palpable truth, that the mass of mankind has not been born with saddles on their backs, nor a favored few, booted and

spurred, ready to ride them legitimately by the Grace of God. These are grounds of hope for others; for ourselves, let the annual return of this day forever refresh our recollection of these rights, and an unfinished devotion to them.

But today we still have saddles and riders.

Jefferson's own words reflect the ongoing imperfection of the American experiment, which has been lofty in ideals but darkly tarnished in execution. The lead author of "all men are created equal" — and even the hand behind the pen that inserted a harsh condemnation of slavery into the Declaration of Independence, which was later removed by others — enslaved more than 600 people in his lifetime and did not free any of them upon his death.[405]

The nebulous idea of America continues to defy simple black-and-white classification today. Even as Al Mutar is able to defend the greatness of America's vision and freedom, Jackson shows how the nation has a great rot inside and asks us to think about how its systems are fundamentally broken for so many citizens.

In an amazing coincidence, Thomas Jefferson and John Adams both passed away on July 4, 1826, exactly 50 years after the Declaration of Independence was signed. They could not possibly have predicted the struggles we face today, more than 200 years later, nor how the trade-offs they made to get America off the ground would evolve over time into civil wars, foreign occupations, and an increasingly centralized financial system.

What Jefferson, Adams, Al Mutar, and Jackson could all perhaps agree on is that, as we go deeper into the digital future, the original Declaration of Independence is not enough.

A new declaration is needed. One rooted in personal freedom, openness, prosperity, opportunity, property rights, and free expression; one opposed to slavery, discrimination, theft, double standards, confiscation, and censorship.

A declaration that could change America, just as its own people changed it from a place founded on slavery to a place where slavery was outlawed.

A declaration that can empower the Black community, just as it can help immigrants connect to their families back home in countries far away.

A declaration that could credibly claim a place next to the Statue of Liberty, alongside Emma Lazarus welcoming the huddled masses, yearning to breathe free.

In the end, Bitcoin may be that declaration, in the original American tradition of anti-authoritarianism and personal freedom, that helps finally rid us of our saddles and riders.

Chapter XII

The End of Super Imperialism

In the course of this book, we have examined Bitcoin's global adoption thus far, seeing its growth in emerging markets and authoritarian regimes, and learning from dissidents worldwide how it can be a tool to challenge power.

But will Bitcoin remain simply a tool for activists in their various fights for local struggles, or can it do something deeper and more profound, and transform the global monetary system?

To answer this question, we should review the history of our existing monetary system, and learn how the United States, acting as world hyperpower, defeated gold and made the dollar the center of the financial world.

One of the best possible guides for this journey is *Super Imperialism*, a radical critique of the dollar-dominated world economy, published by the financial historian and analyst Michael Hudson in 1972, one year after President Richard Nixon defaulted on the dollar and formally took the United States off of the gold standard for good.[406]

The book is overlooked by today's economic mainstream and puts forward a variety of provocative arguments that place it outside of the orthodoxy. However, for those seeking to understand how the dollar won the money wars of the past century, the book makes for essential reading.

Hudson's thesis comes from the left-leaning perspective — the title inspired by the German Marxist phrase "überimperialismus" — and yet thinkers of all political stripes, from progressives to libertarians, should find value in its approach and lessons.

In *Super Imperialism*, Hudson — who has updated the book twice over the past 50 years, with a third edition published in September 2021 — traces the evolution of the world financial system, where US debt displaced gold as the ultimate world reserve currency and premium collateral for financial markets.

How did the world shift from using asset money in the form of gold to balance international payments to using debt money in the form of American treasuries?

How did, as Hudson puts it, "America's ideal of implementing laissez-faire economic institutions, political democracy, and a dismantling of formal empires and colonial systems" turn into a system where the United States forced other nations to pay for its wars, defaulted on its debt, and exploited developing economies?

For those seeking to answer the question of how the dollar became so dominant — even as it was intentionally devalued over and over again in the decades after World War I — then *Super Imperialism* has a fascinating, and at times, deeply troubling answer.

Drawing on extensive historical source material, Hudson argues that the change from the gold standard to what he calls the "Treasury Bill Standard" happened over several decades, straddling the post–World War I era up through the 1970s.

In short, the United States was able to convince other nations to save in dollars instead of in gold by guaranteeing that the dollars could be redeemed for gold. But eventually, US officials rug-pulled the world, refusing to redeem billions of dollars that had been spent into the hands of foreign governments under the promise that they were as good as gold through fixed rate redemption.

This deceit allowed the US government to finance an ever-expanding military-industrial complex and inefficient welfare state without having to make the traditional trade-offs a country or empire would make if its deficit grew too large. Instead, since US policymakers figured out a way to bake American debt into the global monetary base, it never had to pay off its debt. Counterintuitively, Hudson says, America turned its Cold War debtor status into an "unprecedented element of strength rather than weakness."

As a result, the United States has been able to, in Hudson's words, pursue domestic expansion and foreign diplomacy with no balance of payment concerns: "Imposing austerity on debtor countries, America as the world's largest debtor economy acts uniquely without financial constraint."

A key narrative in Hudson's 380-page book is the story of how the US government systematically demonetized gold out of the international economic system. Curiously, he does not mention Executive Order 6102 — passed by President Roosevelt in 1933 to seize gold from the hands of the American public — but weaves a compelling narrative of how the US government pulled the world away from the gold standard, culminating in the Nixon Shock of 1971.

In Hudson's view, leaving the gold standard was all about America's desire to finance war abroad, particularly in Southeast Asia. He says the Vietnam War was "single-handedly" responsible for pushing the United States' balance of payments into the negative and drastically drawing down America's once staggering gold reserves.

Ultimately, Hudson's thesis argues that, unlike classic European imperialism — driven by private-sector profit motives — American super imperialism was driven by nation-state power motives. It was not steered by Wall Street, but by Washington. Bretton Woods institutions like the World Bank and International Monetary Fund (IMF) did not primarily help the developing world but rather harnessed its minerals and raw goods for America, forcing its leaders to buy US agricultural exports and preventing them from developing economic independence.

There are, of course, several criticisms of Hudson's narrative. It can be argued that dollar hegemony helped defeat the Soviet Union, pressuring its economy and paving the way for a more free world; usher in the age of technology, science, and information; push growth globally with surplus dollars; and isolate rogue regimes.[407] Perhaps most compellingly, history seems to suggest the world "wanted" dollar hegemony, if one considers the rise of the eurodollar system, where even America's enemies tried to accumulate dollars outside of the control of the Federal Reserve.[408]

Hudson was not without contemporary critics, either. A 1972 review in *The Journal of Economic History* argued that "it would require an exceptionally naive understanding of politics to accept the underlying assertion that the United States government has been clever, efficient, totally unscrupulous, and consistently successful in exploiting developed and developing nations."[409]

The reader can be the judge of that. But even with these criticisms in mind, Hudson's work is important to consider. The undeniable bottom line is that, by shifting the world economy from relying on gold to relying on American debt, the US government implemented a system where it could spend in a way no other country could, in a way where it never had to pay back its promises, and where other countries financed its warfare and welfare state.

"Never before," Hudson writes, "has a bankrupt nation dared insist that its bankruptcy become the foundation of world economic policy."

In 1972, the physicist and futurist Herman Kahn said that Hudson's work revealed how "the United States has run rings around Britain and every other empire-building nation in history. We've pulled off the greatest rip-off ever achieved."[410]

Governments always dreamed of transforming their debt into the most valuable asset on Earth. This essay explains how the United States succeeded in turning this dream into a reality, what the implications for the wider world were, how this era might be coming to a close, and why a Bitcoin standard might be next.

The Rise and Fall of America as a Creditor Nation

European powers, tempted by the ability to print paper money to finance war operations, broke off the gold standard entirely during World War I. The metal's restraint would have resulted in a much shorter conflict, but the warring factions decided instead to prolong the violence by debasing their currencies.

Between 1914 and 1918, German authorities suspended the convertibility of marks to gold and increased the money supply from 17.2 billion marks to 66.3 billion marks, while their British rivals increased their money supply from 1.1 billion pounds to 2.4 billion pounds.[411] They expanded the German monetary base by sixfold and the British monetary base by nearly fourfold.

While European powers went deeper and deeper into debt, America enriched itself by selling arms and other goods to the allies, all while avoiding conflict in its homeland. As Europe tore itself to shreds, American farms and industrial operations ran full steam. The world at large began to buy more from the United States than it sold back, creating a large American current account surplus.

Post-war, US officials broke with historical precedent and insisted that their European allies repay their war debts. Traditionally, this kind of support was considered a cost of war. At the same time, US officials put up tariff barriers that prevented the allies from earning dollars through more exports to America.

Hudson argues that the United States essentially starved Germany through protectionist policy as it was also unable to export goods to the US market to pay back its loans. Britain and France had to use whatever German reparations they did receive to pay back America.

The Federal Reserve, Hudson says, held down interest rates so as not to draw investment away from Britain, hoping in this way the English could pay back their war debt. But these low rates in turn helped spark a stock market bubble, discouraging capital outflows to Europe. Hudson argues this dynamic, especially after the Great Crash, created a global economic breakdown that helped trigger nationalism, isolationism, autarky, and depression, paving the way for World War II.

Hudson summarizes America's post–World War I global legacy as follows: the devastation of Germany, the collapse of the British Empire, and a stockpiling of gold. At home, President Roosevelt ended domestic convertibility of dollars for gold, made holding gold a felony, and devalued the dollar by 40%.[412] At the same time, the United States received most of Europe's "refugee gold" during the 1930s as the threat of renewed war with Germany led to capital flight from wealthy Europeans. Washington was accumulating gold in its own coffers, just as it was stripping the precious metal from the public.

As World War II neared, Germany halted reparation payments, drying up the allied cash flow. Britain was unable to pay its debts, something it wouldn't be able to fully do for another 80 years.[413] Capital flight to the "safe" United States accelerated, combining with Roosevelt's tariffs and export-boosting dollar devaluation to further enlarge America's balance-of-payments position and gold stock. America became the world's largest creditor nation.

This advantage grew even more dramatic when the allies spent the rest of their gold to fight the Nazis. By the end of the 1940s, the United States held more than 70% of non-Soviet, central bank–held gold, around 700 million ounces total.[414]

In 1922, European powers had gathered in Genoa to discuss the reconstruction of Central and Eastern Europe. One of the outcomes was an agreement to partially go back to the gold standard through a "gold exchange" system where central banks would hold currencies which could be exchanged for gold, instead of the metal itself, which was to be increasingly centralized in financial hubs like New York and London.

In the later stages of World War II in 1944, the United States advanced this concept even further at the Bretton Woods conference in New Hampshire. There, a proposal put forth by British delegate John Maynard Keynes suggesting the use of an internationally managed currency called the "bancor" was rejected. Instead, American diplomats — holding leverage over their British counterparts as a result of their gold advantage and the bailouts they had extended through Lend-Lease Act policies — created a new global trade system underpinned by dollars, which were promised to be backed by gold at the rate of $35 per ounce.[415] The World Bank, International Monetary Fund, and General Agreement on Tariffs and Trade were created as US-dominated institutions which would enforce the worldwide dollar system.

Moving forward, US foreign economic policy was very different from what it was after World War I, when Congress gave priority to domestic programs and America adopted a protectionist stance. US policymakers theorized that America would need to remain a "major exporter to maintain full employment during the transition back to peacetime life" after World War II.[416]

"Foreign markets," Hudson writes, "would have to replace the War Department as a source of demand for the products of American industry and agriculture."

This realization led the United States to determine it could not impose war debt on its allies like it did after World War I. A Cold War perspective began to take over: If the United States invested abroad, it could build up the allies and defeat the Soviets. The Treasury and the World Bank lent funds to Europe as part of the Marshall Plan so that it could rebuild and buy American goods.

Hudson distinguishes the new US imperial system from the old European imperial systems. He quotes Treasury Secretary Henry Morgenthau, who said Bretton Woods institutions "tried to get away from the concept of control of international finance by private financiers who were not accountable to the people," pulling power away from Wall Street to Washington. In dramatic contrast to "classic" imperialism, which was driven by corporate interests and straightforward military action, in the new "super imperialism" the US government would "exploit the world via the international monetary system itself." Hence why Hudson's original title for his book was *Monetary Imperialism.*

The other defining feature of super imperialism versus classic imperialism was that the former is based on a debtor position, while the latter was based on a creditor position. The American approach was to force foreign central banks to finance US growth, whereas the British or French approach was to extract raw materials from colonies, sell them back finished goods, and exploit low wage or even slave labor.

Classic imperialists, if they ran into enough debt, would have to impose domestic austerity or sell off their assets. Military adventurism had restraints. But Hudson argues that with super imperialism, America figured out not just how to avoid these limits but how to derive *positive benefits* from a massive balance-of-payments deficit. It forced foreign central banks to absorb the cost of US military spending and domestic social programs which defended Americans and boosted their standards of living.

Hudson points to the Korean War as the major event that shifted America's considerable post–World War II balance-of-payments surplus into a deficit. He writes that the fight on the Korean peninsula was "financed essentially by the Federal Reserve's monetizing the federal deficit, an effort that transferred the war's cost onto some future generation, or more accurately from future taxpayers to future bondholders."

The Failure of Bretton Woods

In the classic gold standard system of international trade, Hudson describes how things worked:

If trade and payments among countries were fairly evenly balanced, no gold actually changed hands: the currency claims going in one direction offset those going in the opposite direction. But when trade and payments were not exactly in balance, countries that bought or paid more than they sold or received found themselves with a balance-of-payments deficit, while nations that sold more than they bought enjoyed a surplus which they settled in gold ... If a country lost gold its monetary base would be contracted, interest rates would rise, and foreign short-term funds would be attracted to balance international trade movements. If gold outflows persisted, the higher interest rates would deter new domestic investment and incomes would fall, thereby reducing the demand for imports until balance was restored in the country's international payments.[417]

Gold helped nations account with each other in a neutral and straightforward way. However, just as European powers discarded the restraining element of gold during World War I, Hudson says, America did not like the restraint of gold either and instead "worked to 'demonetize' the metal, driving it out of the world financial system — a geopolitical version of Gresham's Law," where bad money drives out the good. By pushing a transformation of a world where the premium reserve was gold to a world where the premium reserve was American debt, the United States hacked the system to drive out the good money.

By 1957, US gold reserves still outnumbered dollar reserves of foreign central banks three to one. But in 1958, the system saw its first cracks, as the Federal Reserve had to sell off more than $2 billion worth of gold to keep the Bretton Woods system afloat.[418] The ability of the United States to hold the dollar at $35 per ounce of gold was being called into question. In one of his last acts in office, President Eisenhower banned Americans from owning gold anywhere in the world.[419] But following the presidential victory of John F. Kennedy — who was predicted to pursue inflationist monetary policies — gold surged anyway, breaking $40 per ounce. It was not easy to demonetize gold in a world of increasing paper currency.

American and European powers tried to band-aid the system by creating the London Gold Pool. Formed in 1961, the pool's mission was to fix the gold price. Whenever market demand pushed up the price, central banks coordinated to sell part of their reserves. The pool came under relentless pressure in the 1960s, both from the dollar depreciating against the rising currencies of Japan and Europe and from the enormous expenditures of Great Society programs and the US war in Vietnam.

Some economists saw the failure of the Bretton Woods system as inevitable. Robert Triffin predicted that the dollar could not act as the international reserve currency with a current account surplus. In what is known as the "Triffin dilemma," he theorized that countries worldwide would have a growing need for that "key currency," and liabilities would necessarily expand beyond what the key country could hold in reserves, creating a larger and larger debt position.[420] Eventually the debt position would grow so large so as to cause the currency to collapse, destroying the system.

By 1964, this dynamic began to visibly kick in, as American foreign debt finally exceeded the US Treasury's gold stock. Hudson says that American overseas military spending was "the entire balance-of-payments deficit as the private sector and non-military government transactions remained in balance."[421]

The London Gold Pool was held in place (buoyed by gold sales from the Soviet Union and South Africa) until 1968, when the arrangement collapsed and a new two-tiered system with a "government" price and a "market" price emerged.

That same year, President Lyndon B. Johnson shocked the American public when he announced he would not run for another term, possibly in part because of the stress of the unraveling monetary system. Richard Nixon won the presidency in 1968, and his administration did its part to convince other nations to stop converting dollars to gold.

By the end of that year, the United States had drawn down its gold from 700 million to 300 million ounces. A few months later, Congress removed the 25% gold-backing requirement for federal reserve notes, cutting one more link between the US money supply and gold. Fifty economists had signed a letter warning against such an action, saying it would "open the way to a practically unlimited expansion of Federal Reserve notes ... and a decline and even collapse in the value of our currency."[422]

In 1969, with the end of Bretton Woods palpably close, the IMF introduced Special Drawing Rights (SDRs) or "paper gold." These currency units were supposed to be equal to gold but not redeemable for the metal. The move was celebrated in newspapers worldwide as creating a new currency that would "fill monetary needs but exist only on books."[423] In Hudson's view, the IMF violated its founding charter by bailing out the United States with billions of SDRs.

He says the SDR strategy was "akin to a tax levied upon payments surplus nations by the United States ... it represented a transfer of goods and resources from civilian and government sectors of payments-surplus nations to payments deficit countries, a transfer for which no tangible quid pro quo was to be received by the nations who had refrained from embarking on the extravagance of war."

By 1971, short-term dollar liabilities to foreigners exceeded $50 billion, but gold holdings dipped below $10 billion. Mirroring the World War I behavior of Germany and Britain, the United States inflated its money supply to 18 times its gold reserves while it waged the Vietnam War.

The Death of the Gold Standard and the Rise of the Treasury Bill Standard

As it became clear that the US government could not possibly redeem extant dollars for gold, foreign countries found themselves in a trap. They could not sell off their US treasuries or refuse to accept dollars, as this would collapse the dollar's value in currency markets, advantaging US exports and harming their own industries. This is the key mechanism that made the Treasury Bill Standard work.

As foreign central banks received dollars from their exporters and commercial banks, Hudson says they had "little choice but to lend these dollars to the US government." They also gave seigniorage privilege to the United States as foreign nations "earned" a negative interest rate on American paper promises most years between the end of World War II and the fall of the Berlin Wall, in effect paying Washington to hold their money on a real basis.[424]

"Instead of US citizens and companies being taxed or US capital markets being obliged to finance the rising federal deficit," Hudson writes, "foreign economies were obliged to buy the new Treasury bonds ... America's Cold War spending thus became a tax on foreigners. It was their central banks who financed the costs of the war in Southeast Asia."

American officials, annoyed that the allies never paid them back for World War I, could now get their pound of flesh in another way.

French diplomat Jacques Rueff gave his take on the mechanism behind the Treasury Bill Standard in his book, *The Monetary Sin of the West*:

> Having learned the secret of having a "deficit without tears," it was only human for the US to use that knowledge, thereby putting its balance of payments in a permanent state of deficit. Inflation would develop in the surplus countries as they increased their own currencies on the basis of the increased dollar reserves held by their central banks. The convertibility of the reserve currency, the dollar, would eventually be abolished owing to the

gradual but unlimited accumulation of sight loans redeemable in US gold.[425]

The French government was vividly aware of this and persistently redeemed its dollars for gold during the Vietnam era, even sending a warship to Manhattan in August 1971 to collect what they were owed. A few days later, on August 15, 1971, President Nixon went on national television and formally announced the end of the dollar's international convertibility to gold.[426] The United States had defaulted on its debt, leaving tens of billions of dollars abroad, all of a sudden unbacked. By extension, every currency that was backed by dollars became pure fiat. Rueff was right, and the French were left with paper instead of precious metal.

Nixon could have simply raised the price of gold, instead of defaulting entirely, but governments do not like admitting to their citizenry that they have been debasing the public's money. It was much easier for his administration to break a promise to people thousands of miles away.

As Hudson writes, "More than $50 billion of short-term liabilities to foreigners owed by the US on public and private account could not be used as claims on America's gold stock." They could, of course, "be used to buy US exports, to pay obligations to US public and private creditors, or to invest in government corporate securities."

These liabilities were no longer liabilities of the US Treasury. American debt had been baked into the global monetary base.

"IOUs," Hudson says, became "IOU-nothings." The final piece of the strategy was to "roll the debt over" on an ongoing basis, ideally with interest rates below the rate of monetary inflation.

Americans could now obtain foreign goods, services, companies, and other assets in exchange for mere pieces of paper: "It became possible for a single nation to export its inflation by settling its payments deficit with paper instead of gold ... a rising world price level thus became in effect a derivative function of US monetary policy," Hudson writes.

If you owe $5,000 to the bank, it's your problem. If you owe $5 million, it's theirs. President Nixon's Treasury Secretary John Connolly riffed on that old adage, quipping at the time: "The dollar may be our currency, but now it's your problem."

Super Imperialism in Action: How the US Made the World Pay for the Vietnam War

As the US deficit increased, government spending accelerated, and Americans — in a phenomenon hidden from the average citizen — watched as other nations paid "the cost of this spending spree" as foreign central banks, not taxes, financed the debt.

The game that the Nixon administration was playing, Hudson writes, "was one of the most ambitious in the economic history of mankind … and was beyond the comprehension of the liberal senators of the United States … The simple device of not hindering the outflow of dollar assets had the effect of wiping out America's foreign debt while seeming to increase it. At the same time, the simple utilization of the printing press — that is, new credit creation — widened the opportunities for penetrating foreign markets by taking over foreign companies."

He continues:

> American consumers might choose to spend their incomes on foreign goods rather than to save. American business might choose to buy foreign companies or undertake new direct investment at home rather than buy government bonds, and the American government might finance a growing world military program, but this overseas consumption and spending would nonetheless be translated into savings and channeled back to the United States. Higher consumer expenditures on Volkswagens or on oil thus had the same effect as an increase in excise taxes on these products: they accrued to the U.S. Treasury in a kind of forced saving.

By repudiating gold convertibility of the dollar, Hudson argues that "America transformed a position of seeming weakness into one of unanticipated strength, that of a debtor over its creditors."

"What was so remarkable about dollar devaluation," he writes, "is that far from signaling the end of American domination of its allies, it became the deliberate object of US financial strategy, a means to enmesh foreign central banks further in the dollar-debt standard."

One vivid story about the power of the Treasury Bill Standard — and how it could force big geopolitical actors to do things against their will — is worth sharing. As Hudson tells it:

> German industry had hired millions of immigrants from Turkey, Greece, Italy, Yugoslavia and other Mediterranean

countries. By 1971 some 3 percent of the entire Greek population
was living in Germany producing cars and export goods ... when
Volkswagens and other goods were shipped to the United States
... companies could exchange their dollar receipts for deutsche
marks with the German central bank ... but Germany's central
bank could only hold these dollar claims in the form of US
Treasury bills and bonds... It lost the equivalent of one-third the
value of its dollar holdings during 1970–74 when the dollar fell by
some 52 percent against the deutsche mark, largely because the
domestic US inflation eroded 34 percent of the dollar's domestic
purchasing power.

In this way, Germany was forced to finance America's wars in Southeast
Asia and military support for Israel: Two things it strongly opposed.

Put another way by Hudson: "In the past, nations sought to run payments
surpluses in order to build up their gold reserves. But now all they were building
up was a line of credit to the US Government to finance its programs at home
and abroad, programs which these central banks had no voice in formulating,
and which were in some cases designed to secure foreign policy ends not
desired by their governments."

Hudson's thesis was that America had forced other countries to pay for its
wars regardless of whether they wanted to or not. Like a tribute system but
enforced without military occupation. "This was," he writes, "something never
before accomplished by any nation in history."

OPEC to the Rescue

Hudson wrote *Super Imperialism* in 1972, the year after the Nixon Shock.
The world wondered at the time: What will happen next? Who will continue to
buy all of this American debt? In his sequel, *Global Fracture*, published five
years later, Hudson got to answer the question.[427]

The Treasury Bill Standard was a brilliant strategy for the US government,
but it came under heavy pressure in the early 1970s.

Just two years after the Nixon Shock, in response to dollar devaluation and
rising American grain prices, Organization of the Petroleum Exporting
Countries (OPEC) nation-members led by Saudi Arabia quadrupled the dollar
price of oil past $10 per barrel. Before the creation of OPEC, "the problem of
the terms of trade shifting in favor of raw-materials exporters had been avoided
by foreign control over their economies, both by the international minerals
cartel and by colonial domination," Hudson writes.

But now that the oil states were sovereign, they controlled the massive inflow of savings accrued through the skyrocketing price of petroleum.

This resulted in a "redistribution of global wealth on a scale that hadn't been seen in living memory," as economist David Lubin puts it.

In 1974, the oil exporters had an account surplus of $70 billion, up from $7 billion the year before: an amount nearly 5% of US GDP. That year, the Saudi current account surplus was 51% of its GDP.[428]

The wealth of OPEC nations grew so fast that they could not spend it all on foreign goods and services.

"What are the Arabs going to do with it all?" asked The Economist in early 1974.

In Global Fracture, Hudson argues that it became essential for the United States "to convince OPEC governments to maintain petrodollars [meaning, a dollar earned by selling oil] in Treasury bills so as to absorb those which Europe and Japan were selling out of their international monetary reserves."

As detailed in Chapter III, Nixon's new Treasury Secretary William Simon traveled to Saudi Arabia as part of an effort to convince the House of Saud to price oil in dollars and "recycle" them into US government securities with their newfound wealth.

On June 8, 1974, the US and Saudi governments signed a military and economic pact. Secretary Simon asked the Saudis to buy up to $10 billion in treasuries. In return, the United States would guarantee security for the Gulf regimes and sell them massive amounts of weapons. The OPEC bond bonanza began.

"As long as OPEC could be persuaded to hold its petrodollars in Treasury bills rather than investing them in capital goods to modernize its economies or in ownership of foreign industry," Hudson says, "the level of world oil prices would not adversely affect the United States."

At the time, there was a public and much-discussed fear in America of Arab governments "taking over" US companies. As part of the new US–Saudi special relationship, American officials convinced the Saudis to reduce investments in the US private sector and simply buy more debt.

The Federal Reserve continued to inflate the money supply in 1974, contributing to the fastest domestic inflation since the Civil War. But the growing deficit was eaten up by the Saudis and other oil exporters, who would recycle tens of billions of dollars of petrodollar earnings into US treasuries over the following decade.

"Foreign governments," Hudson says, "financed the entire increase in publicly-held US federal debt" between the end of World War II and the 1990s and continued with the help of the petrodollar system to majorly support the debt all the way to the present day.

At the same time, the US government used the IMF to help "end the central role of gold that existed in the former world monetary system." Amid double-digit inflation, the institution sold off gold reserves in late 1974 to try and keep any possible upswing in gold down as a result of a new law in the United States, which finally made it legal again for Americans to own gold.

By 1975, other OPEC nations had followed Saudi Arabia's lead in supporting the Treasury Bill Standard. The British pound sterling was finally phased out as a key currency, leaving, as Hudson writes, "no single national currency to compete with the dollar."

The legacy of the petrodollar system would live on for decades, forcing other countries to procure dollars when they needed oil, causing America to defend its Saudi partners when threatened with aggression from Saddam Hussein or Iran, discouraging US officials from investigating Saudi Arabia's role in the 9/11 attacks, supporting the devastating Saudi war in Yemen, selling billions of dollars of weapons to the Saudis, and making Aramco the second-most valuable company in the world today.[429]

Exploitation of the Developing World

The Treasury Bill Standard carried massive costs. It was not free. However, these costs were not paid for by Washington but were often borne by citizens in Middle Eastern countries and in poorer nations across the developing world.

Even pre–Bretton Woods, gold reserves from regions like Latin America were sucked up by the United States. As Hudson describes, European nations would first export goods to Latin America. Europe would take the gold — settled as the balance of payments adjusted — and use it to buy goods from the United States. In this way, gold was "stripped" from the developing world, helping the US gold stock reach its peak of nearly $24.8 billion (or 700 million ounces) in 1949.[430]

Originally designed to help rebuild Europe and Japan, the World Bank and IMF became an "international welfare agency" for the world's poorest nations in the 1960s, per The Heritage Foundation.[431] But, according to Hudson, that was a cover for its true purpose: A tool through which the US government would enforce economic dependency from non-Communist nations worldwide.

The United States joined the World Bank and IMF only "on the condition that it was granted unique veto power ... this meant that no economic rules could be imposed that US diplomats judged did not serve American interests."

America began with 33% of the votes at the IMF and World Bank which — in a system that required an 80% majority vote for rulings — indeed gave it veto power. Britain initially had 25% of the votes, but given its subordinate role to the United States after the war, and its dependent position as a result of Lend-Lease policies, it would not object to Washington's desires.

A major goal of the United States post–World War II was to achieve full employment, and international economic policy was harnessed to help achieve that goal. The idea was to create foreign markets for American exports: Raw materials would be imported cheaply from the developing world, and farm goods and manufactured goods would be exported back to those same nations, bringing the dollars back.

Hudson says that US congressional hearings regarding Bretton Woods agreements revealed "a fear of Latin American and other countries underselling US farmers or displacing US agricultural exports, instead of the hope that these countries might indeed evolve towards agricultural self-sufficiency."

The Bretton Woods institutions were designed with these fears in mind: "The United States proved unwilling to lower its tariffs on commodities that foreigners could produce less expensively than American farmers and manufacturers," writes Hudson. "The International Trade Organization, which in principle was supposed to subject the US economy to the same free trade principles that it demanded from foreign governments, was scuttled."

In a meta-version of how the French exploit Communauté Financière Africaine (CFA) nations in Africa today, the United States employed many double standards, did not comply with the most-favored-nation rule, and set up a system that forced developing countries to "sell their raw materials to US-owned firms at prices substantially below those received by American producers for similar commodities."[432]

Hudson spends a significant percentage of *Super Imperialism* making the case that this policy helped destroy economic potential and capital stock of many developing countries. The United States, as he tells it, forced developing nations to export fruit, minerals, oil, sugar, and other raw goods instead of investing in domestic infrastructure and education — and forced them to buy American foodstuffs instead of growing their own.

Post-1971, why did the Bretton Woods institutions continue to exist? They were created to enforce a system that had expired. The answer, from Hudson's perspective, is that they were folded into this broader strategy, to get the (often dictatorial) leaders of developing economies to spend their earnings on food and weapons imports. This prevented internal development and internal revolution.

In this way, "super imperial" financial and agricultural policy could, in effect, accomplish what classic imperial military policy used to accomplish. Hudson even claims that *Super Imperialism*, his book, was used as a "training manual" in Washington in the 1970s by diplomats seeking to learn how to "exploit other countries via their central banks."

In Hudson's telling, US-directed aid was not used for altruism but for self-interest. From 1948 to 1969, American receipts from foreign aid approximated 2.1 times its investments.

"Not exactly an instrument of altruistic American generosity," he writes. From 1966 to 1970, the World Bank "took in more funds from 20 of its less developed countries than it disbursed."

In 1971, Hudson says, the US government stopped publishing data showing that foreign aid was generating a transfer of dollars from foreign countries to the United States. He says he got a response from the government at the time saying, "We used to publish that data, but some joker published a report showing that the US actually made money off the countries we were aiding."

Former grain-exporting regions of Latin America and Southeast Asia deteriorated to food-deficit status under "guidance" from the World Bank and IMF. Instead of developing, Hudson argues that these countries were retrogressing.

Normally, developing countries would want to keep their mineral resources. They act as savings accounts, but these countries couldn't build up capacity to use them, because they were focused on servicing debt to the United States and other advanced economies. The World Bank, Hudson argues, pushed them to "draw down" their natural resource savings to feed themselves, mirroring subsistence farming and leaving them in poverty. The final "logic" that World Bank leaders had in mind was that, in order to conform with the Treasury Bill Standard, "populations in these countries must decline in symmetry with the approaching exhaustion of their mineral deposits."

Hudson describes the full arc as such: Under super imperialism, world commerce has been directed not by the free market but by an "unprecedented intrusion of government planning, coordinated by the World Bank, IMF, and what has come to be called the Washington Consensus. Its objective is to supply the US with enough oil, copper, and other raw materials to produce a chronic over-supply sufficient to hold down their world price. The exception of this rule is for grain and other agricultural products exported by the United States, in which case relatively high world prices are desired. If foreign countries still are able to run payments surpluses under these conditions, as have the oil-exporting countries, their governments are to use the process to buy US arms or invest in long-term illiquid, preferably non-marketable US treasury obligations."

This, as Allen Farrington would say, is not capitalism.[433] Rather, it's a story of global central planning and central bank imperialism.

Most shockingly, the World Bank in the 1970s under Robert McNamara argued that population growth slowed down development and advocated for growth to be "curtailed to match the modest rate of gain in food output which existing institutional and political constraints would permit."

Nations would need to "follow Malthusians policies" to get more aid. McNamara argued that "the population be fitted to existing food resources, not that food resources be expanded to the needs of existing or growing populations."

To stay in line with World Bank loans, the Indian government forcibly sterilized millions of people.[434]

As Hudson concludes, the World Bank focused the developing world "on service requirements rather than on the domestic needs and aspirations of their peoples. The result was a series of warped patterns of growth in country after country. Economic expansion was encouraged only in areas that generated the means of foreign debt service, so as to be in a position to borrow enough to finance more growth in areas that might generate yet further means of foreign debt service, and so on ad infinitum.

"On an international scale, Joe Hill's 'We go to work to get the cash to buy the food to get the strength to go to work to get the cash to buy the food to get the strength to go to work to get the cash to buy the food ...' became reality.[435] The World Bank was pauperizing the countries that it had been designed in theory to assist."

Financial Implications of the Treasury Bill Standard

By the 1980s, the United States had achieved, as Hudson writes, "what no earlier imperial system had put in place: a flexible form of global exploitation that controlled debtor countries by imposing the Washington Consensus via the IMF and World Bank, while the Treasury Bill Standard obliged the payments-surplus nations of Europe and East Asia to extend forced loans to the US government."

But threats still remained, including Japan. Hudson explains how, in 1985 at the Louvre Accords, the US government and IMF convinced the Japanese to increase their purchasing of American debt and revalue the yen upward so that their cars and electronics became more expensive. This is how, he says, they disarmed the Japanese economic threat. The country "essentially went broke."[436]

On the geopolitical level, super imperialism not only helped the United States defeat its Soviet rival — which could only exploit the economically weak Comecon countries — but also kept any potential allies from getting too strong.[437] On the financial level, the shift from the restraint of gold to the continuous expansion of American debt as the global monetary base had a staggering impact on the world.

Despite the fact that, today, the United States has a much larger labor force and much higher productivity than it did in the 1970s, prices have not fallen and real wages have not increased. The "FIRE" sector (finance, insurance, and real estate) has, Hudson says, "appropriated almost all of the economic gains."[438] Industrial capitalism, he says, has evolved into finance capitalism.

For decades, Japan, Germany, the United Kingdom, and others were "powerless to use their economic strength for anything more than to become the major buyers of Treasury bonds to finance the US federal budget deficit ... [these] foreign central banks enabled America to cut its own tax rates (at least for the wealthy), freeing savings to be invested in the stock market and property boom," according to Hudson.

The past 50 years witnessed an explosion of financialization. Floating currency markets sparked a proliferation of derivatives used to hedge risk. Corporations all of a sudden had to invest resources in foreign exchange futures. In the oil and gold markets, there are hundreds or thousands of paper claims for each unit of raw material. It is not clear if this is a direct result of leaving the gold standard, but it's certainly a prominent feature of the post-gold era.

Hudson argues that US policy pushes foreign economies to "supply the consumer goods and investment goods that the domestic US economy no longer is supplying as it post-industrializes and becomes a bubble economy, while buying American farm surpluses and other surplus output. In the financial sphere, the role of foreign economies is to sustain America's stock market and real estate bubble, producing capital gains and asset-price inflation even as the US industrial economy is being hollowed out."

Over time, equities and real estate boomed as "American banks and other investors moved out of government bonds and into higher-yielding corporate bonds and mortgage loans." Even though wages remained stagnant, prices of investments kept going up — and up, and up — in a velocity previously unseen in history.

As financial analyst Lyn Alden has pointed out, the post-1971, fiat-based financial system has contributed to structural trade deficits for the United States.[439] Instead of drawing down gold reserves to maintain the system like it did during the Bretton Woods framework, America has drawn down and "sold off" its industrial base, where more and more of its stuff is made elsewhere, and more and more of its equity markets and real estate markets are owned by foreigners. The United States, she argues, has extended its global power by sacrificing some of its domestic economic health. This sacrifice has mainly benefited US elites at the cost of blue-collar and middle-income workers. Dollar hegemony, then, might be good for American elites and diplomats and the wider empire but not for the everyday citizen.

Data from the work of political economists Shimshon Bichler and Jonathan Nitzan highlights this transformation and shines a light on how wealth is moving to the haves from the have-nots: In the early 1950s, a typical dominant capital firm commanded a profit stream 5,000 times the income of an average worker; in the late 1990s, it was 25,000 times greater.[440] In the early 1950s, the net profit of a Fortune 500 firm was 500 times the average; in the late 1990s, it was 7,000 times greater. Trends have accelerated since then: Over the past 15 years, the eight largest companies in the world grew from an average market capitalization of $263 billion to $1.68 trillion.[441]

Inflation, Bichler and Nitzan argue, became a "permanent feature" of the 20th century. Prices rose 50-times from 1900 to 2000 in the United Kingdom and United States, and much more aggressively in developing countries. They use a staggering chart that shows consumer prices in the United Kingdom from 1271 to 2007 to make the point.[442] The visual is depicted in a logarithmic scale and shows steady prices all the way through the middle of the 16th century, when Europeans began exploring the Americas and expanding their gold supply. Prices remain relatively steady again though the beginning of the 20th century. But then, at the time of World War I, they shoot up dramatically, cooling off a bit during the Great Depression, only to go hyperbolic since the 1960s and 1970s as the gold standard fell apart and as the world shifted onto the Treasury Bill Standard.

Bichler and Nitzan disagree with those who say inflation has a "neutral" effect on society, arguing that inflation, especially stagflation, redistributes income from workers to capitalists, and from small businesses to large businesses.[443] When inflation rises significantly, they argue that capitalists tend to gain, and workers tend to lose. This is typified by the staggering increase in net worth of America's richest people during the otherwise very difficult last 18 months.[444] The economy continues to expand, but for most people, growth has ended.

Bichler and Nitzan's meta-point is that economic power tends to centralize, and when it cannot anymore through amalgamation (merger and acquisition activity), it turns to currency debasement. As Rueff said in 1972, "Given the option, money managers in a democracy will always choose inflation; only a gold standard deprives them of the option."

As the Federal Reserve continues to push interest rates down, Hudson notes that prices rise for real estate, bonds, and stocks, which are "worth whatever a bank will lend." Writing more recently in the wake of the Global Financial Crisis, he said, "For the first time in history, people were persuaded that the way to get rich was by running into debt, not by staying out of it. New borrowing against one's home became almost the only way to maintain living standards in the face of this economic squeeze."

This analysis of individual actors neatly mirrors the global transformation of the world reserve currency over the past century: from a mechanism of saving and capital accumulation to a mechanism of one country taking over the world through its growing deficit.

Hudson pauses to reflect on the grotesque irony of pension funds trying to make money by speculating. "The end game of finance capitalism," he says, "will not be a pretty sight."

Counter-Theories and Criticisms

There is surely a case to be made for how the world benefited from the dollar system. This is, after all, the orthodox reading of history. With the dollar as the world reserve currency, everything as we know it grew from the rubble of World War II.

One of the strongest counter-theories relates to the USSR, where it seems clear that the Treasury Bill Standard — and the unique ability for the United States to print money that could purchase oil — helped America defeat the Soviet Union in the Cold War.

To get an idea of what the implications are for liberal democracy's victory over totalitarian communism, take a look at a satellite image of the Korean peninsula at night.[445] Compare the vibrant light of industry in the south with the total darkness of the north.

So, perhaps the Treasury Bill Standard deserves credit for this global victory. After the fall of the Berlin Wall, however, the United States did not hold another Bretton Woods to decentralize the power of holding the world's reserve currency. If the argument is that we needed the Treasury Bill Standard to defeat the Soviets, then the failure to reform after their downfall is puzzling.

A second powerful counter-theory is that the world shifted from gold to US debt simply because gold could not do the job. Analysts like Jeff Snider assert that demand for US debt is not necessarily part of some scheme but rather as a result of the world's thirst for pristine collateral.[446]

In the late 1950s, as the United States enjoyed its last years with a current account surplus, something else major happened: the creation of the eurodollar. Originally borne out of an interest from the Soviets and their proxies to have dollar accounts that the American government could not confiscate, the idea was that banks in London and elsewhere would open dollar-denominated accounts to store earned US dollars beyond the purview of the Federal Reserve.

Sitting in banks like Moscow Narodny in London or Banque Commerciale pour L'Europe du Nord in Paris, these new "eurodollars" became a global market for collateralized borrowing, and the best collateral one could have in the system was US treasuries.

Eventually, and largely due to the changes in the monetary system post-1971, the eurodollar system exploded in size. It was unburdened by Regulation Q, which set a limit on interest rates on bank deposits in the US. Eurodollar banks, free from this restriction, could charge higher rates.[447] The market grew from $160 billion in 1973 to $600 billion in 1980 — a time when the inflation-adjusted federal funds rate was negative.[448] Today, there are many more eurodollars than there are actual dollars.

To revisit the Triffin dilemma, the demand for "reserve" dollars worldwide would inevitably lead to a draining of US domestic reserves and, subsequently, confidence in the system breaking down.

How can a stockpile of gold back an ever-growing global reserve currency? Snider argues that the Bretton Woods system could never fulfill the role of a global reserve currency. But a dollar unbacked by gold could. And, the argument goes, we see the market's desire for this most strongly in the growth of the eurodollar.

If even America's enemies wanted dollars, then how can we say that the system only came into dominance through US design? Perhaps the design was simply so brilliant that it co-opted even America's most hated rivals. And finally, in a world where gold had not been demonetized, would it have remained the pristine collateral for this system? We'll never know.

A final major challenge to Hudson's work is found in the discourse arguing that the World Bank has helped increase living standards in the developing world. It is hard not to argue that most are better off in 2021 than in 1945. And cases like South Korea are provided to show how World Bank funding in the 1970s and 1980s were crucial for the country's success.[449]

But how much of this relates to technology deflation and a general rise in productivity, as opposed to American aid and support? And how does this rise compare differentially to the rise in the West over the same period? Data suggests that, under World Bank guidance between 1970 and 2000, poorer countries grew more slowly than rich ones.[450]

One thing is clear: Bretton Woods institutions have not helped everyone equally. A 1996 report covering the World Bank's first 50 years of operations found that "of the 66 less developed countries receiving money from the World Bank for more than 25 years, 37 are no better off today than they were before they received such loans."[451] And of these 37, most "are poorer today than they were before receiving aid from the Bank."

In the end, one can argue that the Treasury Bill Standard helped defeat Communism; that it's what the global market wanted; and that it helped the developing world. But what cannot be argued is that the world left the era of asset money for debt money, and that as the ruler of this new system, the US government gained special advantages over every other country, including the ability to dominate the world by forcing other countries to finance its operations.

The End of an Era?

In philosopher of the Enlightenment Immanuel Kant's landmark 1795 essay, "Toward Perpetual Peace," he argues for six primary principles, one of which is that "no national debt shall be contracted in connection with the external affairs of the state":

> A credit system, if used by the powers as an instrument of aggression against one another, shows the power of money in its most dangerous form. For while the debts thereby incurred are always secure against present demands (because not all the creditors will demand payment at the same time), these debts go on growing indefinitely. This ingenious system, invented by a commercial people in the present century, provides a military fund which may exceed the resources of all the other states put together. It can only be exhausted by an eventual tax-deficit, which may be postponed for a considerable time by the commercial stimulus which industry and trade receive through the credit system. This ease in making war, coupled with the warlike inclination of those

in power (which seems to be an integral feature of human nature),
is thus a great obstacle in the way of perpetual peace.[452]

Kant seemingly predicted dollar hegemony. With his thesis in mind, would a true gold standard have deterred the war in Vietnam? If anything, it seems certain that such a standard would have made the war at least much shorter. The same, obviously, can be said for World War I, the Napoleonic Wars, and other conflicts where the belligerents left the gold standard to fight.

"The unique ability of the US government," Hudson says, "to borrow from foreign central banks rather than from its own citizens is one of the economic miracles of modern times."

But "miracle" is in the eye of the beholder. Was it a miracle for the Vietnamese, the Iraqis, or the Afghans?

Nearly 50 years ago, Hudson writes that "the only way for America to remain a democracy is to forgo its foreign policy. Either its world strategy must become inward-looking or its political structure must become more centralized. Indeed since the start of the Vietnam War, the growth of foreign policy considerations has visibly worked to disenfranchise the American electorate by reducing the role of congress in national decision making."

This trend obviously has become much more magnified in recent history. In the past few years, America has been at war in arguably as many as seven countries (Afghanistan, Iraq, Syria, Yemen, Somalia, Libya, and Niger), yet the average American knows little to nothing about these wars. In 2021, the United States spent more on its military than the next 10 countries combined.[453] Citizens have more or less been removed from the decision-making process, and one of the key reasons — perhaps *the* key reason — why these wars are able to be financed is through the Treasury Bill Standard.

How much longer can this system last?

In 1977, Hudson revisited the question on everyone's mind in the early 1970s: "Will OPEC supplant Europe and Japan as America's major creditors, using oil earnings to buy US Treasury securities and thereby fund US federal budget deficits? Or will Eastern Hemisphere countries subject the United States to a gold-based system of international finance in which renewed US payments deficit will connote a loss of its international financial leverage?"[454]

We, of course, know the answer: OPEC did indeed fund the US budget for the next decade. Eastern hemisphere countries then failed to subject the United States to a gold-based system, in which payments deficit marked loss of leverage. In fact, the Japanese and Chinese, in turn, kept buying American debt once the oil countries ran out of money in the 1980s.

The system, however, is once again showing cracks.

As of 2013, foreign central banks have been dishoarding their US treasuries. As of today, the Federal Reserve is the majority purchaser of American debt. The world is witnessing a slow decline of the dollar as the dominant reserve currency, both in terms of percentage of foreign exchange reserves and in terms of percentage of trade.[455] These still significantly outpace America's actual contribution to global GDP — a legacy of the Treasury Bill Standard, for sure — but they are declining over time.

De-dollarization toward a multi-polar world is gradually occurring. As Hudson says, "Today we are winding down the whole free lunch system of issuing dollars that will not be repaid."

Bitcoin Versus Super Imperialism

Writing in the late 1970s, Hudson predicts that "without a Eurocurrency, there is no alternative to the dollar, and without gold (or some other form of asset money yet to be accepted), there is no alternative to national currencies and debt-money serving international functions for which they have shown themselves to be ill-suited."[456]

Thirty years later, in 2002, he writes that "today it would be necessary for Europe and Asia to design an artificial, politically created alternative to the dollar as an international store of value. This promises to be the crux of international political tensions for the next generation."

It's a prescient comment, though it wasn't Europe or Asia that designed an alternative to the dollar, but Satoshi Nakamoto. A new kind of asset money, bitcoin has a chance to unseat the super-imperial dollar structure to become the next world reserve currency.

As Hudson writes, "One way to discourage governments from running payments deficit is to oblige them to finance these deficits with some kind of asset they would prefer to keep, yet can afford to part with when necessary. To date, no one has come up with a better solution than that which history has institutionalized over a period of about two thousand years: gold."

In January 2009, Satoshi Nakamoto came up with a better solution. There are many differences between gold and bitcoin. Most importantly, for the purposes of this discussion, is the fact that bitcoin is easily self-custodied and thus confiscation-resistant.

Gold was looted by colonial powers worldwide for hundreds of years, and, as discussed in this essay, was centralized mainly into the coffers of the US government after World War I. Then, through shifting global monetary policy of the 1930s, 1940s, 1950s, 1960s, and 1970s, gold was demonetized, first domestically in the United States and then internationally. By the 1980s, the US government had "killed" gold as a money through centralization and through control of the derivatives markets. It was able to prevent self-custody and manipulate the price down.

Bitcoin, however, is notably easy to self-custody. Any of the billions of people on Earth with a smartphone can, in minutes, download a free and open-source bitcoin wallet, receive any amount of bitcoin, and back up the passphrase offline. This makes it much more likely that users will actually control their bitcoin, as opposed to gold investors, who often entered through a paper market or a claim, and not actual bars of gold. Verifying an inbound gold payment is impossible to do without melting the delivery bar down and assaying it. Rather than go through the trouble, people deferred to third parties. In Bitcoin, verifying payments is trivial.

In addition, gold historically failed as a daily medium of exchange. Over time, markets preferred paper promises to pay gold — it was just easier, and so gold fell out of circulation, where it was more easily centralized and confiscated. Bitcoin is built differently and could very well be a daily medium of exchange.

In fact, as we see more and more people demand to be paid in bitcoin, we get a glimpse of a future where Thiers' law (found in dollarizing countries, where good money drives out the bad) is in full effect, where merchants would prefer bitcoin to fiat money. In that world, confiscation of bitcoin would be impossible. It may also prove hard to manipulate the spot price of bitcoin through derivatives. As BitMEX founder Arthur Hayes writes:

> Bitcoin is not owned or stored by central, commercial, or bullion banks. It exists purely as electronic data, and, as such, naked shorts in the spot market will do nothing but ensure a messy destruction of the shorts' capital as the price rises. The vast majority of people who own commodity forms of money are central banks who it is believed would rather not have a public scorecard of their profligacy. They can distort these markets because they control the supply. Because bitcoin grew from the grassroots, those who believe in Lord Satoshi are the largest holders outside of centralised exchanges.

> The path of bitcoin distribution is completely different to how all other monetary assets grew. Derivatives, like ETFs and futures, do not alter the ownership structure of the market to such a degree that it suppresses the price. You cannot create more bitcoin by

digging deeper in the ground, by the stroke of a central banker's keyboard, or by disingenuous accounting tricks. Therefore, even if the only ETF issued was a short bitcoin futures ETF, it would not be able to assert any real downward pressure for a long period of time because the institutions guaranteeing the soundness of the ETF would not be able to procure or obscure the supply at any price thanks to the diamond hands of the faithful.[457]

If governments cannot kill bitcoin, and it continues its rise, then it stands a good chance to eventually be the next reserve currency.[458] Will we have a world with bitcoin-backed fiat currencies similar to the gold standard? Or will people actually use native bitcoin itself — through the Lightning Network and smart contracts — to do all commerce and finance? Neither future is clear.

But the possibility inspires. A world where governments are constrained from undemocratic forever wars because restraint has once again been imposed on them through a neutral global balance-of-payments system is a world worth looking forward to. Kant's writings inspired democratic peace theory, and they may also inspire a future Bitcoin peace theory.[459]

Under a Bitcoin standard, citizens of democratic countries would more likely choose investing in domestic infrastructure as opposed to military adventurism. Foreigners would no longer be as easily forced to pay for any empire's wars. There would be consequences even for the most powerful nation if it defaults on its debt.

Developing countries could harness their natural resources and borrow money from markets to finance bitcoin mining operations and become energy sovereign, instead of borrowing money from the World Bank to fall deeper into servitude and the geopolitical equivalent of subsistence farming.

Finally, the massive inequalities of the past 50 years might also be slowed, as the ability of dominant capital to enrich itself in downturns through rent-seeking and easy monetary policy could be checked.

In the end, if such a course for humanity is set, and Bitcoin does eventually win, it may not be clear what happened:

Did Bitcoin defeat super imperialism?

Or did super imperialism defeat itself?

Endnotes

[1] Julia La Roche, "Charlie Munger: 'Of Course, I Hate the Bitcoin Success'," Yahoo! Finance, May 1, 2021, https://finance.yahoo.com/news/buffett-and-munger-on-bitcoin-213317653.html.

[2] Theron Mohamed, "Warren Buffett Blasted Bitcoin as a Worthless Delusion and 'Rat Poison Squared.' Here Are His 16 Best Quotes About Crypto," *Business Insider*, January 16, 2021, https://markets.businessinsider.com/news/currencies/warren-buffett-best-quotes-bitcoin-cryptocurrencies-investing-rat-poison-squared-2021-1.

[3] Evelyn Cheng, "Bill Gates: I Would Short Bitcoin If I Could," *CNBC Buffett Watch*, May 7, 2018, https://www.cnbc.com/2018/05/07/bill-gates-i-would-short-bitcoin-if-i-could.html.

[4] J. G. Collins, "Bill Maher Just Made Bitcoin Decidedly 'Uncool'," *Seeking Alpha*, May 4, 2021, https://seekingalpha.com/article/4424132-bill-maher-just-made-bitcoin-decidedly-uncool.

[5] Hiroko Tabuchi, "In Coinbase's Rise, a Reminder: Cryptocurrencies Use Lots of Energy," *New York Times*, April 14, 2021, https://www.nytimes.com/2021/04/14/climate/coinbase-cryptocurrency-energy.html.

[6] Martin Wolf, "The Libertarian Fantasies of Cryptocurrencies," *Financial Times*, February 12, 2019, https://medium.com/financial-times/the-libertarian-fantasies-of-cryptocurrencies-f514cc16bcd1.

[7] Shawn Tully, "Famed Economist Jeffrey Sachs Rails Against Bitcoin: Highly Polluting and 'Almost Like Counterfeiting'," *Fortune*, March 16, 2021, https://fortune.com/2021/03/16/bitcoin-jeffrey-sachs-critiques-btc/; Reuters Staff, "ECB's Lagarde Calls for Regulating Bitcoin's 'Funny Business'," *Reuters*, January 13, 2021, https://www.reuters.com/article/us-crypto-currency-ecb/ecbs-lagarde-calls-for-regulating-bitcoins-funny-business-idUSKBN29I1B1.

[8] "Rentier States," *Suburban Emergency Management Project*, June 23, 2005, https://web.archive.org/web/20120209131411/http:/www.semp.us/publications/biot_reader.php?BiotID=227.

[9] Olanrewaju Rufai, "Once Poor, Always Poor?" *Stears Business*, August 23, 2018, https://www.stearsng.com/article/once-poor-always-poor.

[10] Matt Stoller, "The Cantillon Effect: Why Wall Street Gets a Bailout and You Don't," *BIG*, April 9, 2020, https://mattstoller.substack.com/p/the-cantillon-effect-why-wall-street.

[11] Peter Chawaga, "Nigerian Aid Group Finds Sovereign Lifeline in Bitcoin," *Bitcoin Magazine*, October 21, 2020, https://bitcoinmagazine.com/culture/nigerian-protest-group-finds-sovereign-lifeline-in-bitcoin.

[12] Ahyke Otutubuike, "Bitcoin Will Persist in Nigeria, But the Ban Changes Things," *Bitcoin Magazine*, February 17, 2021, https://bitcoinmagazine.com/business/bitcoin-will-persist-in-nigeria-but-the-ban-changes-things.

[13] "What Is Fistula?" *Fistula Foundation*, https://fistulafoundation.org/what-is-fistula/.

[14] Jamal Mahjoub, "My Father Died Before He Could See al-Bashir Fall," *New York Times*, April 12, 2019, https://www.nytimes.com/2019/04/12/opinion/my-father-died-before-he-could-see-bashir-fall.html.

[15] "A Closer Look: Sudan the Peoples of Darfur," *Cultural Survival*, September 2004, https://www.culturalsurvival.org/publications/cultural-survival-quarterly/closer-look-sudan-peoples-darfur.

[16] Afua Hirsch, "WikiLeaks Cables: Sudanese President 'Stashed $9bn in UK Banks'," *The Guardian*, December 17, 2010, https://www.theguardian.com/world/2010/dec/17/wikileaks-sudanese-president-cash-london.

[17] Andreas M. Antonopoulos, *The Internet of Money* (CreateSpace Independent Publishing Platform, 2016).

[18] "Becoming Uncle Jim," *Diverter*, March 14, 2021, https://diverter.hostyourown.tools/becoming-uncle-jim/.

[19] "Money Laundering," *United Nations: Office on Drugs and Crime*, https://www.unodc.org/unodc/en/money-laundering/overview.html.

[20] Bitcoin Collective et al., *The Little Book of Bitcoin* (North Dakota: Whispering Candle Books, 2019).

[21] Neal Stephenson, *Snow Crash* (New York: Random House, 2000); Neal Stephenson, *Cryptonomicon* (New York: Avon Books, 2002).

[22] Satoshi Nakamoto, "Bitcoin: A Peer-to-Peer Electronic Cash System," October 31, 2008, https://bitcoin.org/bitcoin.pdf.

[23] Xische and Co, "Birth of Bitcoin," February 12, 2018, https://medium.com/xische-reports/birth-of-bitcoin-9fb451e00886.

[24] Cryddit, "Bitcoin Source from November 2008," *BitcoinTalk*, December 23, 2013, https://bitcointalk.org/index.php?topic=382374.msg4108706#msg4108706.

[25] David Burnham, *The Rise of the Computer State* (New York: Random House, 1983).

[26] Jim Epstein, "Before the Web: The 1980s Dream of a Free and Borderless Virtual World," *Reason*, October 7, 2020, https://reason.com/video/2020/10/07/before-the-web-the-1980s-dream-of-a-free-and-borderless-virtual-world/.

[27] Whitfield Diffie and Martin E. Hellman, "New Directions in Cryptography," *IEEE Transactions on Information* Theory 22, no. 6 (November 1976).

[28] "Cypherpunks Mailing List Archive," 1992–1999, https://mailing-list-archive.cryptoanarchy.wiki/.

[29] Eric Hughes, "A Cypherpunk's Manifesto," March 9, 1993, https://nakamotoinstitute.org/static/docs/cypherpunk-manifesto.txt.

[30] "History," OpenPGP, August 15, 2016, https://www.openpgp.org/about/history/.

[31] Steven Levy, "Cypher Wars: Pretty Good Privacy Gets Pretty Legal," *Wired*, November 1, 1994, https://www.wired.com/1994/11/cypher-wars/.

[32] "Crypto Wars, Phil Zimmermann and PGP," *Crypto Anarchy Wiki*, https://cryptoanarchy.wiki/events/90s-crypto-wars.

[33] "History," OpenPGP.

[34] Steven Levy, "E-Money (That's What I Want)," *Wired*, December 1, 1994, https://www.wired.com/1994/12/emoney/.

[35] David Chaum, "Security Without Identification: Transaction Systems to Make Big Brother Obsolete," *Communications of the ACM* 28, no. 10 (October 1985), https://www.cs.ru.nl/~jhh/pub/secsem/chaum1985bigbrother.pdf.

[36] Chaum, "E-Money."

[37] David Chaum, "Achieving Electronic Privacy," *Scientific American*, August 1992, https://groups.csail.mit.edu/mac/classes/6.805/articles/money/chaum-electronic-privacy.html.

[38] Aaron van Wirdum, "The Genesis Files: Hashcash or How Adam Back Designed Bitcoin's Motor Block," *Bitcoin Magazine*, June 4, 2018, https://bitcoinmagazine.com/technical/genesis-files-hashcash-or-how-adam-back-designed-bitcoins-motor-block; Adam Back, "ANNOUNCE: Hash cash postage implementation," https://cypherpunks.venona.com/date/1997/03/msg00774.html.

[39] Jim Epstein, "Bitcoin and the End of History," *Reason*, October 28, 2020, https://reason.com/video/2020/10/28/bitcoin-and-the-end-of-history/.

[40] Wei Dai, "B-Money," http://www.weidai.com/bmoney.txt/.

[41] Wei Dai, "Law vs. Technology," https://keybase.pub/doubleyousee23/Cypherpunk/Law.vs.Technology.Wei.Dai.txt.

[42] Nick Szabo, "Bit Gold," *Satoshi Nakamoto Institute*, December 29, 2005, https://nakamotoinstitute.org/bit-gold/.

[43] Aaron van Wirdum, "The Genesis Files: With Bit Gold, Szabo Was Inches Away from Inventing Bitcoin," *Bitcoin Magazine*, July 12, 2018, https://bitcoinmagazine.com/culture/genesis-files-bit-gold-szabo-was-inches-away-inventing-bitcoin.

[44] "RPOW: Reusable Proofs of Work," *Satoshi Nakamoto Institute*, 2004, https://nakamotoinstitute.org/finney/rpow/.

[45] Nakamoto, "Bitcoin: Peer-to-Peer Electronic."

[46] Van Wirdum, "The Genesis Files: Hashcash."

[47] Hal Finney (@halfin), "Running bitcoin," *Twitter*, January 10, 2009, 10:33 p.m., https://twitter.com/halfin/status/1110302988.

[48] Satoshi Nakamoto, "P2P Foundation: Bitcoin open source implementation of P2P currency," *Satoshi Nakamoto Institute*, February 11, 2009, https://satoshi.nakamotoinstitute.org/postsP2P/p2pfoundation/1/.

[49] Francis Elliott, "Chancellor Alistair Darling on brink of second bailout for banks," *The Times*, January 3, 2009, https://www.thetimes.co.uk/article/chancellor-alistair-darling-on-brink-of-second-bailout-for-banks-n9l382mn62h.

[50] Nakamoto, "P2P Foundation."

[51] Pete Rizzo, "The Last Days of Satoshi," *Bitcoin Magazine*, April 26, 2021, https://bitcoinmagazine.com/technical/what-happened-when-bitcoin-creator-satoshi-nakamoto-disappeared.

[52] Satoshi Nakamoto, reply to "Bitcoin open source implementation of P2P currency," P2P Foundation, February 15, 2009, https://bitcoinmagazine.com/technical/what-happened-when-bitcoin-creator-satoshi-nakamoto-disappeared.

[53] "Clark Moody Bitcoin Dashboard," https://bitcoin.clarkmoody.com/dashboard/.

[54] Tomas Sander and Amnon Ta-Shma, "Auditable, Anonymous Electronic Cash," 1999, https://www.cs.tau.ac.il/~amnon/Papers/ST.crypto99.pdf.

[55] Ian Miers, Christina Garman, Matthew Green, and Aviel D. Rubin, "Zerocoin: Anonymous Distributed E-Cash from Bitcoin," *IEEE Symposium on Security and Privacy*, May 19–22, 2013, https://ieeexplore.ieee.org/document/6547123.

[56] "What Is Taproot and How Does It Benefit Bitcoin?" *River Financial*, https://river.com/learn/what-is-taproot/.

[57] Jonathan Bier, "The Blocksize War" (Self-published, 2021).

[58] Satoshi Nakamoto, "Bitcoin P2P e-Cash Paper," *Satoshi Nakamoto Institute*, November 6, 2008, https://satoshi.nakamotoinstitute.org/emails/cryptography/4/.

[59] John D'Antona Jr., "88% of All 2019 Forex Transactions Are in US Dollars," *Traders Magazine*, January 24, 2020, https://www.tradersmagazine.com/am/88-of-all-2019-forex-transactions-are-in-us-dollars/; "Currency Composition of Official Foreign Exchange Reserves (COFER)," *International Monetary Fund*, https://data.imf.org/?sk=E6A5F467-C14B-4AA8-9F6D-5A09EC4E62A4; "Global Financial Stability Report: Lower for Longer," *International Monetary Fund*, October 2019, https://www.imf.org/en/Publications/GFSR/Issues/2019/10/01/global-financial-stability-report-october-2019.

[60] Lee E. Ohanian, "The Macroeconomic Effects of War Finance in the United States: World War II and the Korean War," *The American Economic Review* 87, no. 1 (March 1997), https://www.jstor.org/stable/2950852.

[61] John L. Hess, "The Monetary Sin of the West," *New York Times*, March 26, 1972, https://www.nytimes.com/1972/03/26/archives/the-monetary-sin-of-the-west-by-jacques-rueff-translated-from-the.html; Ben S. Bernanke, "The Dollar's International Role: An 'Exorbitant Privilege'?" *Brookings*, January 7, 2016, https://www.brookings.edu/blog/ben-bernanke/2016/01/07/the-dollars-international-role-an-exorbitant-privilege-2/.

[62] Adam Tooze, "The Rise and Fall and Rise (and Fall) of the U.S. Financial Empire," *Foreign Policy*, January 15, 2021, https://foreignpolicy.com/2021/01/15/rise-fall-united-states-financial-empire-dollar-global-currency/.

[63] Michael J. Graetz and Olivia Briffault, "A 'Barbarous Relic': The French, Gold, and the Demise of Bretton Woods," *Columbia Law School*, 2016, https://scholarship.law.columbia.edu/cgi/viewcontent.cgi?article=3545&context=faculty_scholarship.

[64] "Speech by Richard Nixon," August 15, 1971, https://www.cvce.eu/content/publication/1999/1/1/168eed17-f28b-487b-9cd2-6d668e42e63a/publishable_en.pdf.

[65] "49 Years Ago: President Nixon to "Suspend Temporarily" the Gold Standard," *GoldSeek.com*, August 16, 2020, https://goldseek.com/article/49-years-ago-president-nixon-suspend-temporarily-gold-standard.

[66] "Transcript of a Recording of a Meeting Between the President and H. R. Haldeman in the Oval Office on June 23, 1972, from 10:04 to 11:39 AM," *Nixon Library*, https://www.nixonlibrary.gov/sites/default/files/forresearchers/find/tapes/watergate/wspf/741-002.pdf.

[67] Andrea Wong, "The Untold Story Behind Saudi Arabia's 41-Year U.S. Debt Secret," *Bloomberg*, May 30, 2016, https://www.bloomberg.com/news/features/2016-05-30/the-untold-story-behind-saudi-arabia-s-41-year-u-s-debt-secret.

[68] Duccio Basosi, "Oil, Dollars, and US Power in the 1970s: Re-Viewing the Connections," *Journal of Energy History*, no. 3 (June 2, 2020), https://www.energyhistory.eu/en/special-issue/oil-dollars-and-us-power-1970s-re-viewing-connections.

[69] "Declassified/Released US Department of State EO Systematic Review," NARA, June 30, 2005, https://aad.archives.gov/aad/createpdf?rid=270129&dt=2474&dl=1345.

[70] Wong, "The Untold Story."

[71] "OPEC Share of World Crude Oil Reserves, 2018," in *OPEC Annual Statistical Bulletin, 2019*, https://aad.archives.gov/aad/createpdf?rid=270129&dt=2474&dl=1345.

[72] Basosi, "Oil, Dollars, and US Power."

[73] "Crude Oil Prices - 70 Year Historical Chart," *Macrotrends*, https://www.macrotrends.net/1369/crude-oil-price-history-chart.

[74] David E. Spiro, *The Hidden Hand of American Hegemony: Petrodollar Recycling and International Markets* (Cornell University Press, 1999), http://www.jstor.org/stable/10.7591/j.ctvv414gb.

[75] Basosi, "Oil, Dollars, and US Power."

[76] Edward J. Frydl, "The Eurodollar Conundrum," *FRBNY Quarterly Review* (Spring 1982).

[77] Nathaniel Whittemore, "ENCORE: Luke Gromen on the History and (Declining) Future of the Global Dollar System," *CoinDesk*, September 14, 2021, https://www.coindesk.com/markets/2020/11/27/encore-luke-gromen-on-the-history-and-declining-future-of-the-global-dollar-system/.

[78] "Why IMF Loans Always Get Repaid," *NPR*, February 3, 2012, https://www.npr.org/2012/02/03/146327391/why-imf-loans-always-get-repaid; Yakov Feygin and Dominik Leusder, "The Class Politics of the Dollar System," *Phenomenal World*, May 1, 2020, https://www.phenomenalworld.org/analysis/the-class-politics-of-the-dollar-system/.

[79] Dean Baker, "Debunking the Dumping-the-Dollar Conspiracy," *Foreign Policy*, October 7, 2009, https://foreignpolicy.com/2009/10/07/debunking-the-dumping-the-dollar-conspiracy/.

[80] Baker, "Debunking the Dumping-the-Dollar Conspiracy."

[81] Charles Recknagel, "Iraq: Baghdad Moves to Euro," *Radio Free Europe/Radio Liberty*, November 1, 2000, https://www.rferl.org/a/1095057.html.

[82] Faisal Islam, "Iraq Nets Handsome Profit by Dumping Dollar for Euro," *The Guardian*, February 16, 2003, https://www.theguardian.com/business/2003/feb/16/iraq.theeuro.

[83] Ed Vulliamy, "Scramble to Carve Up Iraqi Oil Reserves Lies Behind US Diplomacy," *The Guardian*, October 6, 2002, https://www.theguardian.com/world/2002/oct/06/russia.oil.

[84] Carola Hoyos and Kevin Morrison, "Iraq Returns to International Oil Market," *The Dossier*, June 5, 2003, https://www.thedossier.info/articles/ft_iraq-returns-to-international-oil-market.pdf.

[85] C. Fred Bergsten, "The Euro Versus the Dollar: Will There Be a Struggle for Dominance?" Presented at the Annual Meeting of the American Economic

Association, January 4, 2002,
https://www.piie.com/publications/papers/bergsten0102-1.pdf.

[86] Ezra Klein, "What the Iraq Disaster Can Teach Us About Trump," *Vox*, September 2, 2020, https://www.vox.com/2020/9/2/21417224/why-did-america-invade-iraq-the-ezra-klein-show-to-start-a-war-bush-trump-administration.

[87] Ron Suskind, "Chapter 4: Base Elements," in *The Price of Loyalty* (New York: Free Press, 2004), http://www.nlpwessex.org/docs/suskind.htm.

[88] Frank Newport, "Seventy-Two Percent of Americans Support War Against Iraq," *Gallup*, March 24, 2003, https://news.gallup.com/poll/8038/seventytwo-percent-americans-support-war-against-iraq.aspx.

[89] "Full Text of Dick Cheney's Speech," *The Guardian*, August 27, 2002, https://www.theguardian.com/world/2002/aug/27/usa.iraq.

[90] History.com Editors, "Iran-Iraq War," *History*.com, July 13, 2021, https://www.history.com/topics/middle-east/iran-iraq-war.

[91] JoAnne Allen, "Greenspan Clarifies Iraq War and Oil Link," *Reuters*, September 17, 2007, https://www.reuters.com/article/uk-greenspan/greenspan-clarifies-iraq-war-and-oil-link-idUKN1728646120070917.

[92] Nico Pitney, "Abizaid: 'Of Course It's About Oil, We Can't Really Deny That'," *HuffPost*, May 25, 2011, https://www.huffpost.com/entry/abizaid-of-course-its-abo_n_68568.

[93] Antonia Juhasz, "Why the War in Iraq Was Fought for Big Oil," *CNN*, April 15, 2013, https://www.cnn.com/2013/03/19/opinion/iraq-war-oil-juhasz.

[94] "U.S. Crude Oil Imports by Country of Origin," *Energy Information Administration*, Monthly Energy Review May 2020, Tables 3.3c and 3.3d., https://afdc.energy.gov/data/10621.

[95] Howard Fineman, "Living Politics: In Round 2, It's the Dollar Vs. Euro," *Newsweek*, April 22, 2003, https://www.newsweek.com/living-politics-round-2-its-dollar-vs-euro-134363.

[96] Yusho Cho and Takeshi Kumon, "China, Russia and EU Edge Away from Petrodollar," *Nikkei Asia*, January 7, 2019, https://asia.nikkei.com/Economy/China-Russia-and-EU-edge-away-from-petrodollar.

[97] Lita Epstein, Charles Jaco, and Julianne C. Iwersen-Niemann, *The Complete Idiot's Guide to the Politics of Oil* (Indianapolis: Alpha Books, 2003), p. 188.

[98] Mark Mazzetti, "Saudi Arabia Warns of Economic Fallout if Congress Passes 9/11 Bill," *New York Times*, April 16, 2016, https://www.nytimes.com/2016/04/16/world/middleeast/saudi-arabia-warns-ofeconomic-fallout-if-congress-passes-9-11-bill.html.

99 Tim Golden and Sebastian Rotella, "The Saudi Connection: Inside the 9/11 Case that Divided the FBI," *New York Times*, January 23, 2020, https://www.nytimes.com/2020/01/23/magazine/9-11-saudi-arabia-fbi.html.

100 Christina Wilkie, "Trump Says King of Saudi Arabia Offered His 'Sincere Condolences' in Wake of Pensacola Shooting," *CNBC*, December 6, 2019, https://www.cnbc.com/2019/12/06/trump-saudi-king-offered-condolences-in-wake-of-pensacola-shooting.html.

101 David E. Sanger, "Biden Won't Penalize Saudi Crown Prince Over Khashoggi's Killing, Fearing Relations Breach," *New York Times*, February 26, 2021, https://www.nytimes.com/2021/02/26/us/politics/biden-mbs-khashoggi.html.

102 Simon Tilford and Hans Kundnani, "It Is Time to Abandon Dollar Hegemony," *Foreign Affairs*, July 28, 2020, https://www.foreignaffairs.com/articles/americas/2020-07-28/it-time-abandon-dollar-hegemony.

103 Feygin and Leusder, "The Class Politics of the Dollar System."

104 Lyn Alden, "The Fraying of the US Global Currency Reserve System," *Investment Strategy*, December 2, 2020, https://www.lynalden.com/fraying-petrodollar-system/.

105 Christopher Witko, "How Wall Street Became a Big Chunk of the U.S. Economy — and When the Democrats Signed On," *Washington Post*, March 29, 2016, https://www.washingtonpost.com/news/monkey-cage/wp/2016/03/29/how-wall-street-became-a-big-chunk-of-the-u-s-economy-and-when-the-democrats-signed-on/.

106 Mike Dolan, "Does a Greener World Need Less Greenbacks?" *Reuters*, February 10, 2021, https://www.reuters.com/article/us-global-petrodollars-column-idUSKBN2AA0NC.

107 Ken Silverstein, "Are Fossil Fuel Interests Bankrolling The Anti-Nuclear Energy Movement?" *Forbes*, July 13, 2016, https://www.forbes.com/sites/kensilverstein/2016/07/13/are-fossil-fuel-interests-bankrolling-the-anti-nuclear-energy-movement/?sh=5d959c8e7453.

108 Susan Su, "Think BTC Is a Dirty Business? Consider the Carbon Cost of a Dollar," *Medium*, February 22, 2021, https://susanfsu.medium.com/think-btc-is-a-dirty-business-consider-the-carbon-cost-of-a-dollar-c38122fb55c5.

109 Whittemore, "Luke Gromen on the History."

110 Office of Management and Budget, The White House, "United States Gross Federal Debt to GDP," *Trading Economics*, 2020, https://tradingeconomics.com/united-states/government-debt-to-gdp.

111 "America's Aggressive Use of Sanctions Endangers the Dollar's Reign," *The Economist*, January 18, 2020, https://www.economist.com/briefing/2020/01/18/americas-aggressive-use-of-sanctions-endangers-the-dollars-reign.

[112] Reuters Staff, "Chinese Banks Urged to Switch Away from SWIFT as U.S. Sanctions Loom," *Reuters*, July 29, 2020, https://www.reuters.com/article/us-china-banks-usa-sanctions/chinese-banks-urged-to-switch-away-from-swift-as-u-s-sanctions-loom-idUSKCN24U0SN; Rodrigo Campos and David Lawder, "Venezuela Leadership Issue Still Blocking IMF, World Bank Aid," *Reuters*, April 11, 2019, https://www.reuters.com/article/us-imf-worldbank-venezuela/venezuela-leadership-issue-still-blocking-imf-world-bank-aid-idUSKCN1RN1TH; Ian Talley and Benoit Faucon, "U.S. to Block Iran's Request to IMF for $5 Billion Loan to Fight Coronavirus," *Wall Street Journal*, April 7, 2020, https://www.wsj.com/articles/u-s-to-block-irans-request-to-imf-for-5-billion-loan-to-fight-coronavirus-11586301732.

[113] Katrina Manson, "Biden Shows He Will Wield US Financial System as Foreign Policy Weapon," *Financial Times*, April 17, 2021, https://www.ft.com/content/cf8e8a79-63b6-48b4-98c1-30904897c80e.

[114] Anders Aslund and Steven Fisher, "New Challenges and Dwindling Returns for Russia's National Champions, Gazprom and Rosneft," *Atlantic Council*, June 5, 2020, https://www.atlanticcouncil.org/in-depth-research-reports/report/new-challenges-and-dwindling-returns-for-russias-national-champions-gazprom-and-rosneft/.

[115] Natasha Bertrand, "Biden Looks to Appoint Special Envoy to Kill Russia-Germany Energy Pipeline," *Politico*, April 7, 2021, https://www.politico.com/news/2021/04/07/biden-envoy-nord-stream-2-479706.

[116] Alden, "Fraying of US Global Currency."

[117] Reuters Staff, "EU's Junker Wants Bigger Global Role for Euro," *Reuters*, September 12, 2018, https://www.reuters.com/article/us-eu-juncker-euro/eus-juncker-wants-bigger-global-role-for-euro-idUSKCN1LS0BK.

[118] Kaelyn Forde, "What Are SDRs and Why Are They a Hot Topic at the IMF Meeting?" *Al Jazeera*, April 6, 2021, https://www.aljazeera.com/economy/2021/4/6/what-is-an-sdr.

[119] Hess, "Monetary Sin."

[120] Yves Smith, "Changes in Super Imperialism," mronline.com, February 9, 2021, https://mronline.org/2021/02/09/michael-hudson-changes-in-super-imperialism/.

[121] Steffen Murau, Joe Rini, and Armin Haas, "The evolution of the Offshore US-Dollar System: Past, Present and Four Possible Futures," *Journal of Institutional Economics* 16, no. 6 (May 6, 2020), https://www.cambridge.org/core/journals/journal-of-institutional-economics/article/evolution-of-the-offshore-usdollar-system-past-present-and-four-possible-futures/B36ED9082CECE54F3F5B8E8F40D15148.

[122] Jae Chia, "S'pore Sovereign Wealth Fund Temasek Holdings Said to Be Buying Bitcoin Since 2018," *MSN News*, March 26, 2021, https://www.msn.com/en-sg/news/singapore/spore-sovereign-wealth-fund-temasek-holdings-said-to-be-buying-bitcoin-since-2018/ar-BB1eZqbo.

[123] "Bitcoin Is Key to an Abundant, Clean Energy Future," *Bitcoin Clean Energy Initiative Memorandum*, April 2021, https://assets.ctfassets.net/2d5q1td6cyxq/5mRjc9X5LTXFFihIlTt7QK/e7bcba47217b 60423a01a357e036105e/BCEI_White_Paper.pdf; Douglas Broom, "5 Charts Show the Rapid Fall in Costs of Renewable Energy," *Energy Post*, November 16, 2020, https://energypost.eu/5-charts-show-the-rapid-fall-in-costs-of-renewable-energy/.

[124] Virgil, *The Aeneid*, ed. Rhonda L. Kelley, trans. John Dryden, http://faculty.sgc.edu/rkelley/The%20Aeneid.pdf.

[125] Romain Dillet, "Crypto Company Anchorage Raises $80 Million After Getting Federal Banking Charter," *TechCrunch*, February 25, 2021, https://techcrunch.com/2021/02/25/crypto-company-anchorage-raises-80-million-after-getting-federal-banking-charter/.

[126] John Authers, "Bitcoin Is Displacing Gold as an Inflation Hedge," *Bloomberg*, April 9, 2021, https://www.bloomberg.com/opinion/articles/2021-04-09/bitcoin-is-displacing-gold-as-an-inflation-hedge.

[127] "Bitcoin Treasuries," *Buy Bitcoin Worldwide*, 2021.

[128] Stephen Alpher, "New York Life CEO Ted Mathas Warms to Bitcoin – Joins NYDIG," *Seeking Alpha*, March 10, 2021, https://seekingalpha.com/news/3671187-new-york-life-ceo-ted-mathas-warms-to-bitcoin-joins-nydig.

[129] Croesus BTC, "Am I Too Late for Bitcoin?" *Swan Bitcoin*, January 18, 2021, https://www.swanbitcoin.com/am-i-too-late-for-bitcoin/.

[130] Anna Baydakova, "Bitcoin Dissidents: Those Who Need It Most," *CoinDesk*, December 8, 2020, https://www.coindesk.com/markets/2020/12/08/bitcoin-dissidents-those-who-need-it-most/.

[131] "Current Membership of the Human Rights Council for the 15th Cycle, 1 January-21 December 2022" *United Nations Human Rights Council*, 2020, https://www.ohchr.org/EN/HRBodies/HRC/Pages/CurrentMembers.aspx; "FATF Members and Observers," *FATF*, 2021, https://www.fatf-gafi.org/about/membersandobservers/; Stephen Wade, "Rights groups target sponsors in protest over 2022 Beijing Olympics," *CBC*, February 25, 2021, https://www.cbc.ca/sports/olympics/olympics-beijing-2022-boycott-sponsors-1.5928953; Andrew Ross Sorkin et al., "Wall Street Returns to Riyadh," *New York Times*, January 25, 2021, https://www.nytimes.com/2021/01/25/business/dealbook/wall-street-saudi-arabia.html.

[132] Bier, "Blocksize War."

[133] "Our Top Charities," *GiveWell*, November 2021, https://www.givewell.org/charities/top-charities.

[134] Jimmy Song, "The Future of Bitcoin Privacy: Cross-Input Signature Aggregation," *Bitcoin Tech Talk*, November 30, 2020, https://jimmysong.substack.com/p/the-future-of-bitcoin-privacy-cross.

[135] Real Vision Finance, "The SPAC Apex, Market Memes, and the Biggest Opportunities in Tech (w/Josh Wolfe and Michael Green," *YouTube*, March 16, 2021, https://www.youtube.com/watch?v=8NGo5i6jbk0&ab_channel=RealVisionFinance.

[136] "Remittances to El Salvador Rebound After Early Pandemic Drop," *AP News*, January 18, 2021, https://apnews.com/article/san-salvador-coronavirus-pandemic-el-salvador-1623416c0ddc7aa238911f8a422b6c8b; "Remittances in Central America: The Role of Cabei," *Central American Bank for Economic Integration*, 2021, https://www.bcie.org/fileadmin/user_upload/Remittances_in_Central_America_the_R ole_of_CABEI.pdf.

[137] Aaron van Wirdum (@AaronvanW), "Just walked into a McDonald's in San Salvador to see if I could pay for my breakfast with bitcoin, tbh fully expecting to be told no. But low and behold, they printed a ticket with QR that took me to a webpage with Lightning invoice, and now I'm enjoying my desayuno traditional!" Twitter, September 7, 2021, 9:41 a.m., https://twitter.com/AaronvanW/status/1435236902274220040?s=20.

[138] Aaron van Wirdum, "Chivo Demonstration with Thanks Mat Ahlborg (@esiattorney)," *YouTube*, September 10, 2021, https://www.youtube.com/watch?v=G-Q-CFirTLU.

[139] José Miguel Vivanco, "Bukele ha puesto a El Salvador al borde del abismo autoritario. Hay que detenerlo," *New York Times Espanol*, September 8, 2021, https://www.nytimes.com/es/2021/09/08/espanol/opinion/bukele-reforma-judicial.html.

[140] Izalco, "Indígenas de El Salvador recuerdan la matanza de 1932 y claman por justicia," *Agencia EFE*, January 22, 2018, https://www.efe.com/efe/america/sociedad/indigenas-de-el-salvador-recuerdan-la-matanza-1932-y-claman-por-justicia/20000013-3500389.

[141] Choetsow Tenzin, "A Caffeinated Crisis: An Unfiltered Look at the Struggles of the Coffee Industry in El Salvador," *Harvard International Review*, January 15, 2020, https://hir.harvard.edu/a-caffeinated-crisis-an-unfiltered-look-at-the-struggles-of-the-coffee-industry-in-el-salvador/.

[142] H. Paull, "Salvadoran Coffee: 10 Reasons Why the Industry Is in Decline – and How to Stop It?" *Perfect Daily Grind*, June 8, 2016, https://perfectdailygrind.com/2016/06/salvadoran-coffee-10-reasons-why-the-industry-is-in-decline-and-how-to-stop-it/.

[143] Sarah Gammage, "El Salvador: Despite End to Civil War, Emigration Continues," *Migration Policy Institute*, July 26, 2007, https://www.migrationpolicy.org/article/el-salvador-despite-end-civil-war-emigration-continues.

[144] History.com Editors, "United States Calls Situation in El Salvador a Communist Plot," *History.com*, February 19, 1981, https://www.history.com/this-day-in-history/united-states-calls-situation-in-el-salvador-a-communist-plot.

[145] Raymond Bonner, "Time for a US Apology to El Salvador," *The Nation*, April 15, 2016, https://www.thenation.com/article/archive/time-for-a-us-apology-to-el-salvador/.

[146] Bonner, "Time for a US Apology."

[147] Matt Fratus, "A Brief History of the CIA in El Salvador During the 1980s," *Coffee or Die*, July 1, 2020, https://coffeeordie.com/cia-el-salvador/.

[148] Raymond Bonner, "America's Role in El Salvador's Deterioration," *The Atlantic*, January 20, 2018, https://www.theatlantic.com/international/archive/2018/01/trump-and-el-salvador/550955/.

[149] Jeremy Scahill, "U.S. Support for Military Dictatorship in El Salvador," *The Intercept*, April 27, 2021, https://theintercept.com/empire-politician/biden-el-salvador-reagan-military-junta/.

[150] Bonner, "Time for a US Apology."

[151] Bonner, "America's Role."

[152] Marcia Towers and Silvia Borzutzky, "The Socioeconomic Implications of Dollarization in El Salvador," *Latin American Politics and Society* 46, no. 3 (Autumn 2004), https://www.jstor.org/stable/4141619.

[153] Grammage, "El Salvador: Despite End to Civil War."

[154] "From Madness to Hope: The 12-Year War in El Salvador," United States Institute of Peace, January 26, 2001, https://www.usip.org/sites/default/files/file/ElSalvador-Report.pdf.

[155] Bonner, "Time for a US Apology."; Bonner, "America's Role."

[156] Peter Canby, "Is El Salvador's President Trying to Shut Down a Hearing on the Infamous El Mozote Massacre?" *The New Yorker*, September 10, 2021, https://www.newyorker.com/news/daily-comment/is-el-salvadors-president-trying-to-shut-down-a-hearing-on-the-infamous-el-mozote-massacre; Mark Danner, "The Truth of El Mozote," *The New Yorker*, December 6, 1993, http://www.markdanner.com/articles/the-truth-of-el-mozote.

[157] Raymond Bonner, "Massacre of Hundreds Reported in Salvador Village," *New York Times*, January 27, 1982, https://www.nytimes.com/1982/01/27/world/massacre-of-hundreds-reported-in-salvador-village.html.

[158] Bernard Weinraub, "Reagan Certifies Salvador for Aid," *New York Times*, July 28, 1982, https://www.nytimes.com/1982/07/28/world/reagan-certifies-salvador-for-aid.html.

[159] "Salvadorans TPS to Expire," *Migration News* 2, no. 1 (January 1995), https://migration.ucdavis.edu/mn/more.php?id=512.

[160] Julian Borger, "Fleeing a Hell the US Helped Create: Why Central Americans Journey North," *The Guardian*, December 19, 2018,

https://www.theguardian.com/us-news/2018/dec/19/central-america-migrants-us-foreign-policy.

[161] David Luhnow, "Latin America Is the Murder Capital of the World," *Wall Street Journal*, September 20, 2018, https://www.wsj.com/articles/400-murders-a-day-the-crisis-of-latin-america-1537455390.

[162] Jonathan Watts, "One Murder Every Hour: How El Salvador Became the Homicide Capital of the World," *The Guardian*, August 22, 2015, https://www.wsj.com/articles/400-murders-a-day-the-crisis-of-latin-america-1537455390.

[163] Watts, "One Murder Every Hour."

[164] "Central America After Hurricane Mitch," *Consultative Group for the Reconstruction and Transformation of Central America*, October 26, 2005, https://web.archive.org/web/20051026083640/http:/www.iadb.org/regions/re2/consultative_group/backgrounder4.htm; USAID, "El Salvador: Earthquakes Final Fact Sheet, Fiscal Year (FY) 2001," *US Agency for International Development*, September 7, 2001, https://reliefweb.int/report/el-salvador/el-salvador-earthquakes-final-fact-sheet-fiscal-year-fy-2001.

[165] Towers and Borzutzky, "Socioeconomic Implications."

[166] Grammage, "El Salvador: Despite End to Civil War."

[167] Towers and Borzutzky, "Socioeconomic Implications."

[168] "Agrosocioeconomic Data," *Food and Agriculture Organization of the United Nations*, November 2001, https://www.fao.org/3/Y2784E/y2784e03.htm.

[169] Towers and Borzutzky, "Socioeconomic Implications."

[170] Marla Dickerson, "In El Salvador, the Dollar Is No Panacea," *Los Angeles Times*, August 4, 2007, https://www.latimes.com/archives/la-xpm-2007-aug-04-fi-dollarize4-story.html.

[171] Alex Gladstein, "Fighting Monetary Colonialism with Open-Source Code," *Bitcoin Magazine*, September 21, 2021, https://bitcoinmagazine.com/culture/bitcoin-a-currency-of-decolonization.

[172] Dickerson, "In El Salvador."

[173] "Bitcoin World #2 - Bitcoin Youth Programme in El Salvador with Michael Peterson," *What Bitcoin Did*, December 24, 2019, https://www.whatbitcoindid.com/podcast/bitcoin-youth-programme-in-el-salvador-with-michael-peterson.

[174] Tatiana Koffman, "This El Salvador Village Adopts Bitcoin as Money," *Forbes*, July 14, 2020, https://www.forbes.com/sites/tatianakoffman/2020/07/14/this-el-salvador-village-adopts-bitcoin-as-money/?sh=38769bc12044.

[175] The Economist Staff, "El Salvador's Bitcoin Bro President Is Beloved and Dangeros," *The Economist*, September 9, 2021, https://www.economist.com/the-americas/2021/09/09/el-salvadors-bitcoin-bro-president-is-beloved-and-dangerous.

[176] Canby, "Is El Salvador's President."

[177] Enrique Miranda, "Autoritarismo pleno en reforma de Ulloa: se abre paso a partido único," *ElSalvadore.com*, August 21, 2021, https://www.elsalvador.com/noticias/nacional/reformas-a-la-constitucion-felix-ulloa/871231/2021/.

[178] The Economist Staff, "El Salvador's Bitcoin Bro."

[179] Vivanco, "Bukele ha puesto."

[180] Nelson Renteria, "El Salvador Ends Anti-Corruption Accord with OAS, Dismaying U.S.," *Reuters*, June 4, 2021, https://www.reuters.com/world/americas/salvadoran-attorney-general-ends-anti-corruption-accord-with-oas-2021-06-04/.

[181] "On the Expulsion of Daniel Lizárraga," *El Faro*, July 8, 2021, https://elfaro.net/en/202107/columns/25598/On-the-Expulsion-of-Daniel-Liz%C3%A1rraga.htm.

[182] Carlos Dada (@CarlosDada), "Bitcoin has been impossed on an impoverished population by an opaque, authoritarian and corrupt government," Twitter, September 8, 2021, 6:05 p.m., https://twitter.com/CarlosDada/status/1435726017205874691?s=20.

[183] Canby, "Is El Salvador's President."

[184] Ned Pride, "Salvadoran Re-Election Ruling Undermines Democracy," *U.S. Department of State*, September 5, 2021, https://www.state.gov/salvadoran-re-election-ruling-undermines-democracy/.

[185] The Economist Staff, "El Salvador's Bitcoin Bro."

[186] Fabienne Lang, "El Salvador Plans on Harnessing Volcanic Energy to Mine Bitcoin," *Interesting Engineering*, June 14, 2021, https://interestingengineering.com/el-salvador-to-harness-volcanic-energy-for-bitcoin.

[187] Jessica Guzmán, "Población rechaza adopción del Bitcoin," *ElSalvadore.com*, September 2, 2021, https://www.elsalvador.com/noticias/negocios/poblacion-rechaza-adopcion-bitcoin-encuesta-uca/875175/2021/.

[188] Simon Kemp, "Digital 2021: El Salvador," *DataReportal*, February 11, 2021, https://datareportal.com/reports/digital-2021-el-salvador.

[189] Alex Gladstein (@gladstein), "Flawless experience using @MuunWallet here in El Zonte to buy all sorts of things with Bitcoin. If you visit, make sure to stop by for a coffee with Karla, an excellent barista. You can tip her instantly from anywhere in the world with Lightning here: https://strike.me/karla," Twitter, September 2, 2021, 5:48 p.m., https://twitter.com/gladstein/status/1433547324991623169?s=20.

[190] Fanny Pigeaud and Ndongo Samba Sylla, *Africa's Lost Colonial Currency* (London: Pluto Press, 2021).

[191] "Metropole," *Wikipedia*, https://en.wikipedia.org/wiki/Metropole.

[192] René Coty, "Constitution de la République et de la Communauté, 4 octobre 1958," https://www.senat.fr/evenement/revision/texte_originel.html#XII.

[193] Ndongo Samba Sylla, "The Franc Zone, a Tool of French Neocolonialism in Africa," *Jacobin Magazine*, January 6, 2020, https://www.jacobinmag.com/2020/01/franc-zone-french-neocolonialism-africa.

[194] Kimberly Amadeo, "Real GDO Per Capita, How to Calculate It, and Date Since 1947," *The Balance*, September 17, 2020, https://www.thebalance.com/real-gdp-per-capita-how-to-calculate-data-since-1946-3306028; "Ivory Coast GDP per Capita," *Trading Economics*, https://tradingeconomics.com/ivory-coast/gdp-per-capita.

[195] Allen Farrington, "The Capital Strip Mine," *Medium*, January 16, 2021, https://allenfarrington.medium.com/the-capital-strip-mine-ec627e9fe40a.

[196] "'We Must Unite Now or Perish' – President Kwame Nkrumah," *New African*, May 3, 2014, https://newafricanmagazine.com/3721/.

[197] Leon Dash, "Guinea's Longtime President, Ahmed Sekou Toure, Dies," *Washington Post*, March 28, 1984, https://www.washingtonpost.com/archive/local/1984/03/28/guineas-longtime-president-ahmed-sekou-toure-dies/18f31685-878c-4759-8028-3bef7fbc568b/?utm_term=.2035e3d7b762.

[198] Maurice Robert, "'Ministre' de l'Afrique," *Politique étrangère*, no. 1 (2005): pp. 200–203.

[199] Albert Savana, "The Malian Franc: From the Jump to the Ups and Downs," *Kapital Afrik*, September 28, 2020, https://www.kapitalafrik.com/2020/09/28/the-malian-franc-from-the-jump-to-the-ups-and-downs/.

[200] Pigeaud and Sylla, *Africa's Lost Colonial*.

[201] Melissa Mahtani, "Faure Must Go: How One Togolese Woman Is Risking Her Life to End the 50-Year Gnassingbé Dynasty," *CNN*, June 13, 2018, https://www.cnn.com/2018/06/13/africa/farida-nabourema-togo-activist/index.html.

[202] "ECOWAS: West African bloc aims to launch single currency in 2027," *DW*, https://www.dw.com/en/ecowas-west-african-bloc-aims-to-launch-single-currency-in-2027/a-57970299,

[203] Angelique Chrisafis, "Macron Launches Drive to Boost French Language Around World," *The Guardian*, March 20, 2018, https://www.theguardian.com/world/2018/mar/20/macron-launches-drive-to-boost-french-language-around-world; Lydia Smith, "Emmanuel Macron Vows to Make French the World's First Language," *Independent*, November 30, 2017, https://www.independent.co.uk/news/world/europe/emmanuel-macron-french-language-france-president-world-first-africa-burkina-faso-a8084586.html.

[204] "Why the Future of French Is African," *BBC News*, April 8, 2019, https://www.bbc.com/news/world-africa-47790128.

[205] Sandrine Blanchard, Eric Topona, and Fréjus Quenum, "Why France Is Backing Chad's New Leader, Mahamat Idriss Deby," *DW*, https://www.dw.com/en/why-france-is-backing-chads-new-leader-mahamat-idriss-deby/a-57316728.

[206] "In Tribute to Friend Deby, Macron Says France Will Not Tolerate Threats to Chad," *Reuters*, April 23, 2021, https://www.reuters.com/world/africa/french-president-macron-says-he-will-not-let-anybody-threaten-chad-2021-04-23/.

[207] Shweta Desai, "France Calls Mali Coup 'Unacceptable,' Threatens Sanctions," *Anadolu Agency*, May 25, 2021, https://www.aa.com.tr/en/europe/france-calls-mali-coup-unacceptable-threatens-sanctions/2254140.

[208] Nakamoto, "Bitcoin: Peer-to-Peer Electronic."

[209] "Personal Remittances, Received (% of GDP), Sub-Saharan Africa," *World Bank*, https://data.worldbank.org/indicator/BX.TRF.PWKR.DT.GD.ZS?locations=ZG.

[210] "Remittance Prices Worldwide Quarterly, Issue 37" *World Bank*, March 2021, https://remittanceprices.worldbank.org/sites/default/files/rpw_main_report_and_annex_q121_final.pdf.

[211] Michael J. Saylor, The Mobile Wave: How Mobile Intelligence Will Change Everything (New York City: Vanguard Press, 2012).

[212] "El Salvador: Country Commercial Guide," November 4, 2021, https://www.trade.gov/country-commercial-guides/el-salvador-market-overview.

[213] "Our Mission, Journalism, and Editorial Independence," *Radio Free Europe/Radio Liberty*, https://pressroom.rferl.org/about-us.

[214] Sylla, "Franc Zone."

[215] Joseph Tchundjang Pouémi, Monnaie, Servitude et Liberté: La Répression Monétaire de l'Afrique (Paris: Éditions J.A, 1980).

[216] Larry White, "Defending Dollarization in Ecuador," *Alt-M*, December 4, 2014, https://www.alt-m.org/2014/12/04/defending-dollarization-in-ecuador/.

[217] Rodrigo Campos, "World Bank Rejects EL Salvador Request for Help on Bitcoin Implementation," *Reuters*, June 16, 2021, https://www.reuters.com/business/el-salvador-keep-dollar-legal-tender-seeks-world-bank-help-with-bitcoin-2021-06-16/.

[218] "Thousands Descend on Miami to Glorify Bitcoin," *New York Times*, June 5, 2021, https://www.nytimes.com/2021/06/05/technology/miami-worship-bitcoin.html.

[219] "Gaza Bombing Map Explorer," Earth Engine Apps, June 4, 2021, https://coscher510.users.earthengine.app/view/gazabombing.

[220] Steven Erlanger, "Victory Ends 40 Years of Political Domination by Arafat's Party," *New York Times*, January 26, 2006,

https://www.nytimes.com/2006/01/26/international/middleeast/victory-ends-40-years-of-political-domination-by.html.

[221] "What Is Hamas? Who Supports Hamas? What You Need to Know," *DW*, https://www.dw.com/en/who-is-hamas/a-57537872.

[222] "Gaza Rapid Damage and Needs Assessment," *World Bank*, June 2021, https://unsco.unmissions.org/sites/default/files/gaza_rapid_damage_and_needs_assessment_july_2021_1.pdf.

[223] "Gaza in 2020: A Liveable Place?" *United Nations Relief and Works Agency*, August 28, 2012, https://www.unrwa.org/newsroom/press-releases/gaza-2020-liveable-place.

[224] "Gaza Rapid Damage," *World Bank*.

[225] "West Bank and Gaze," *International Monetary Fund*, August 31, 2017, https://www.imf.org/-/media/Files/Publications/CR/2017/091117WBG.ashx [download].

[226] "Fertility Rate, Total (Births per Woman): West Bank and Gaze," *World Bank*, https://data.worldbank.org/indicator/SP.DYN.TFRT.IN?locations=PS.

[227] "The Economic Costs of the Israeli Occupation for the Palestinian People," *United Nations Conference on Trade and Development*, September 2020, https://unctad.org/system/files/official-document/gdsapp2020d1_en.pdf.

[228] Alaa Tartir, Tariq Dana, and Timothy Seidel, *Political Economy of Palestine: Critical, Interdisciplinary, and Decolonial Perspectives* (London: Palgrave Macmillan, 2021).

[229] Ari Rabinovitch and Nidal Al-mughrabi, "Gas to Gaza? The Pipeline That Might Provide a Lifeline," *Reuters*, February 23, 2021, https://www.reuters.com/business/energy/gas-gaza-pipeline-that-might-provide-lifeline-2021-02-23/.

[230] Tartir, Dana, and Seidel, *Political Economy of Palestine*.

[231] "Israeli Occupation Cost Gaza $16.7 Billion in Past Decade: UNCTAD Estimates," *UNCTAD*, November 25, 2020, https://unctad.org/news/israeli-occupation-cost-gaza-167-billion-past-decade-unctad-estimates.

[232] Sara Roy, "The Gaze Strip: A Case of Economic De-Development," *Journal of Palestine Studies* 17, no. 1 (Autumn 1987), https://www.jstor.org/stable/2536651.

[233] Tartir, Dana, and Seidel, *Political Economy of Palestine*.

[234] "Blinken Pledges $75m in US Assistance to Palestinians," *Al Jazeera*, May 25, 2021, https://www.aljazeera.com/news/2021/5/25/netanyahu-vows-very-powerful-response-if-ceasefire-broken.

[235] Fares Akram and Joseph Krauss, "Palestinians See Victory in Gaza Truce as Israel Warns Hamas," *AP News*, May 21, 2021, https://apnews.com/article/africa-middle-

east-israel-palestinian-conflict-health-coronavirus-pandemic-41d515a273b54187d429887a3ae9d9e8.

[236] Tartir, Dana, and Seidel, *Political Economy of Palestine.*

[237] Omar Shakir, "A Threshold Crossed," *Human Rights Watch*, April 27, 2021, https://www.hrw.org/report/2021/04/27/threshold-crossed/israeli-authorities-and-crimes-apartheid-and-persecution.

[238] Tartir, Dana, and Seidel, *Political Economy of Palestine.*

[239] Tartir, Dana, and Seidel, *Political Economy of Palestine.*

[240] Shir Hever, The *Political Economy of Israel's Occupation: Repression Beyond Exploitation* (London: Pluto Press, 2010).

[241] Tartir, Dana, and Seidel, *Political Economy of Palestine.*

[242] Tartir, Dana, and Seidel, *Political Economy of Palestine.*

[243] Hever, *Political Economy of Israel's Occupation.*

[244] Steven A. Barnett, "4. Monetary Policy in the West Bank and Gaza Strip in the Absence of a Domestic Currency," In *The Economy of West Bank and Gaza* (USA: International Monetary Fund, 1998), https://doi.org/10.5089/9781557757258.071.ch004.

[245] The New Arab Staff, "Tel Aviv Seeking Revival of Oslo Era Palestine-Israel Economic Cooperation Board," *The New Arab*, July 6, 2021, https://english.alaraby.co.uk/news/palestine-israel-economic-cooperation-board-be-revived.

[246] "Palestinian Captive Market," *Who Profits*, https://www.whoprofits.org/involvement/palestinian-captive-market/.

[247] "Area C and the Future of the Palestinian Economy," *World Bank*, https://openknowledge.worldbank.org/bitstream/handle/10986/18930/893700PUB097 8100Box385270B00PUBLIC0.pdf.

[248] Tartir, Dana, and Seidel, *Political Economy of Palestine.*

[249] "$48 Billion Is the Estimated Revenue Loss by Palestine from 2000-2017 Due to Occupation," *UNCTAD*, December 2, 2019, https://unctad.org/news/48-billion-estimated-revenue-loss-palestine-2000-2017-due-occupation.

[250] Hever, *Political Economy of Israel's Occupation.*

[251] Hever, *Political Economy of Israel's Occupation.*

[252] Tzipi Hotovely, "Where Does All That Aid for Palestinians Go?" *Wall Street Journal*, January 24, 2016, https://www.wsj.com/articles/where-does-all-that-aid-for-palestinians-go-1453669813.

[253] Nikki Tillekens, "71% of Aid to the Palestinians Ends Up in the Israeli Economy," *Mronline*, September 30, 2010, https://mronline.org/2010/09/30/71-of-aid-to-the-palestinians-ends-up-in-the-israeli-economy/.

[254] "U.S. Foreign Aid to Israel: Total Aid (1949-Present)," Jewish Virtual Library, 2021, https://www.jewishvirtuallibrary.org/total-u-s-foreign-aid-to-israel-1949-present; "Israel Trade Balance, Exports and Imports by Country 2019," *WITS*, 2019, https://wits.worldbank.org/CountryProfile/en/Country/ISR/Year/LTST/TradeFlow/EXPIMP/Partner/by-country.

[255] Hever, *Political Economy of Israel's Occupation*.

[256] Tartir, Dana, and Seidel, *Political Economy of Palestine*.

[257] Matt Rees, "Where's Arafat's Money?" *TIME*, November 14, 2004, http://content.time.com/time/magazine/article/0,9171,782141,00.html; Tricia McDermott, "Arafat's Billions," *CBS News*, November 7, 2003, https://www.cbsnews.com/news/arafats-billions/; Jon Henley, "Why Was €1m a Month Sent to Arafat's Wife?" *The Guardian*, February 12, 2004, https://www.theguardian.com/world/2004/feb/12/france.israel.

[258] Yoni Ben Menachem, "The Businesses of Mahmoud Abbas and His Sons," *Jerusalem Center for Public Affairs*, September 14, 2016, https://jcpa.org/article/the-businesses-of-mahmoud-abbas-and-his-sons/.

[259] Ziva Dahl, "Palestinian Kleptocracy: West Accepts Corruption, People Suffer the Consequences," *The Hill*, November 15, 2016, https://thehill.com/blogs/congress-blog/foreign-policy/306179-palestinian-kleptocracy-west-accepts-corruption-people.

[260] Menachem, "Businesses of Mahmoud Abbas."

[261] Dahl, "Palestinian Kleptocracy."

[262] Yara Hawari, "Money Can't 'Fix' Palestine's Occupied Economy," *Al Jazeera*, January 27, 2020, https://www.aljazeera.com/opinions/2020/1/27/money-cant-fix-palestines-occupied-economy.

[263] Tartir, Dana, and Seidel, *Political Economy of Palestine*.

[264] Tartir, Dana, and Seidel, *Political Economy of Palestine*.

[265] Hawari, "Money Can't 'Fix'."

[266] Tartir, Dana, and Seidel, *Political Economy of Palestine*.

[267] Tartir, Dana, and Seidel, *Political Economy of Palestine*.

[268] Tartir, Dana, and Seidel, *Political Economy of Palestine*.

[269] Tartir, Dana, and Seidel, *Political Economy of Palestine*.

[270] "The Separation Barrier," *B'Tselem*, November 11, 2017, https://www.btselem.org/separation_barrier.

[271] "A Regime of Jewish Supremacy from the Jordan River to the Mediterranean Sea: This Is Apartheid," *B'Tselem*, January 12, 2021, https://www.btselem.org/publications/fulltext/202101_this_is_apartheid.

[272] "Area C and the Future," *World Bank*.

[273] "Israeli Solar Fields in the West Bank," *Who Profits*, January 2017, https://www.whoprofits.org/infographics/israeli-solar-fields-in-the-west-bank/; "The Occupation of Water," *Amnesty International*, November 29, 2017, https://www.amnesty.org/en/latest/campaigns/2017/11/the-occupation-of-water/.

[274] "COVID-19 Devastates Palestine's Shattered Economy," *UNCTAD*, September 8, 2020, https://unctad.org/fr/node/27712.

[275] "Area C and the Future," *World Bank*.

[276] "Regime of Jewish Supremacy," *B'Tselem*.

[277] "A Private Israeli Firm Has Helped Governments Hack Journalists and Human Rights Advocates," *Washington Post*, July 15, 2021, https://www.washingtonpost.com/nation/2021/07/15/private-israeli-firm-has-helped-governments-hack-journalists-human-rights-advocates/; Oded Yaron, "Cellebrite Used to 'Violate Human Rights,' Stop Their IPO, Rights Groups Urge," *Haaretz*, July 13, 2021, https://www.haaretz.com/israel-news/tech-news/.premium-cellebrite-used-to-violate-human-rights-stop-their-ipo-rights-groups-urge-1.9995469; Grace Woodruff, "What We Know About the Secretive Company Behind the Pegasus Spy Software," *Future Tense*, July 20, 2021, https://slate.com/technology/2021/07/nso-group-pegasus-spyware.html.

[278] "Regime of Jewish Supremacy," *B'Tselem*.

[279] "Loss of Land Map," *Palestine Portal*, January 2017, https://www.palestineportal.org/wp-content/uploads/2017/01/LossOfLandMapCard.png.

[280] Greg Myre and Larry Kaplow, "7 Things To Know About Israeli Settlements," *NPR*, December 29, 2016, https://www.npr.org/sections/parallels/2016/12/29/507377617/seven-things-to-know-about-israeli-settlements; Joseph Krauss, "Israeli Settler Population Surged During Trump Era," *AP News*, January 27, 2021, https://apnews.com/article/race-and-ethnicity-israel-coronavirus-pandemic-west-bank-jerusalem-c43de2ad0da01ef3d9b174691290338d.

[281] Shalini Nagarajan, "Israel Is Seizing Cryptocurrency Wallets from the Palestinian Militant Group Hamas, Which Has Been Using Them to Raise Funds from Donors Worldwide," *Insider*, July 10, 2021, https://www.businessinsider.com/israel-hamas-crypto-wallet-seizure-order-palestinian-militant-gaza-strip-2021-7.

[282] "Top Fiat Currencies by Market Capitalization," *Fiat Market Cap*, https://fiatmarketcap.com/.

[283] Tartir, Dana, and Seidel, *Political Economy of Palestine*.

[284] TOI Staff, "Defense Ministry Starts Seizing Bitcoin Being Used by Hamas," *Times of Israel*, July 9, 2021, https://www.timesofisrael.com/defense-ministry-starts-seizing-bitcoin-being-used-by-hamas/.

[285] "Buy Bitcoin Instantly in Palestine," *Paxful*, https://paxful.com/buy/bitcoin/palestine.

[286] "Population of Palestine," *Fanack*, August 10, 2020, https://fanack.com/palestine/population-of-palestine/; Kemp, "Digital 2021: Palestine."

[287] Inigo Alexander, "El Salvador: A Pro-Israel President of Palestinian Descent Deepens Divide Among Diaspora," *Middle East Eye*, June 16, 2021, https://www.middleeasteye.net/news/israel-palestine-el-salvador-gaza-solidarity-president-diaspora-divide.

[288] Alexander, "El Salvador: Pro-Israel President."

[289] Jonathan Lis, "Israel, Palestinian Authority to Form Joint Committee for Economic Ventures," *Haaretz*, July 6, 2021, https://www.haaretz.com/israel-news/.premium-israel-palestinian-authority-to-form-joint-committee-for-economic-ventures-1.9972291.

[290] Lis, "Israel, Palestinian Authority."

[291] Manus Cranny and Gwen Ackerman, "Palestinian Monetary Authority Eyes Digital Currency Launch," *Bloomberg*, June 24, 2021, https://www.bloomberg.com/news/articles/2021-06-24/palestinian-monetary-authority-mulls-digital-currency-launch.

[292] Boaz Sobrado, "A Day Using Money in Cuba," *Boaz Sobrado*, May 22, 2020, http://boazsobrado.com/blog/2020/05/22/a-day-using-money-in-cuba/.

[293] "Uprising on Havana's Malecón 20 Years Ago Set Off Exodus," *Miami Herald*, August 4, 2014, https://www.miamiherald.com/news/local/community/miami-dade/article1978451.html.

[294] Associated Press, "Protesters Battle Police in Havana; Castro Warns U.S.," *New York Times*, August 6, 2021, https://www.nytimes.com/1994/08/06/world/protesters-battle-police-in-havana-castro-warns-us.html.

[295] Steve Holland, "White House May Ease Ban on Remittances as Part of Cuba Review," *Reuters*, July 14, 2021, https://www.reuters.com/world/americas/white-house-may-ease-ban-remittances-part-cuba-review-sources-2021-07-14/.

[296] Anthony DePalma, *The Cubans: Ordinary Lives in Extraordinary Times* (New York City: Viking, 2020).

[297] Jorge I. Dominguez, "What You Might Not Know About the Cuban Economy," *Harvard Business Review*, August 17, 2015, https://hbr.org/2015/08/what-you-might-not-know-about-the-cuban-economy.

[298] DePalma, *The Cubans*.

[299] Sobrado, "Day Using Money in Cuba."

[300] "The Sounds That Haunted U.S. Diplomats in Cuba? Lovelorn Crickets, Scientists Say," *New York Times*, January 4, 2019, https://www.nytimes.com/2019/01/04/science/sonic-attack-cuba-crickets.html.

[301] Sobrado, "Day Using Money in Cuba."

[302] Sobrado, "Day Using Money in Cuba."

[303] "Cuban Revolution," *Encyclopedia Britannica*, July 19, 2021, https://www.britannica.com/event/Cuban-Revolution/.

[304] "The Republic of Cuba," *Encyclopedia Britannica*, April 29, 2021, https://www.britannica.com/place/Cuba/The-Republic-of-Cuba.

[305] Armando Valladares, *Against All Hope: A Memoir of Life in Castro's Gulag* (New York City: Encounter Books, 2001).

[306] DePalma, *The Cubans*.

[307] John Lee Anderson, *Che Guevara: A Revolutionary Life* (New York City: Grove Press, 2010).

[308] "National Evolution and Soviet Influence," *Encyclopedia Britannica*, April 29, 2021, https://www.britannica.com/place/Cuba/National-evolution-and-Soviet-influence.

[309] History.com Editors, "Fidel Castro Announces Mariel Boatlift, Allowing Cubans to Emigrate to U.S.," *History.com*, April 20, 1980, https://www.history.com/this-day-in-history/castro-announces-mariel-boatlift.

[310] DePalma, *The Cubans*; Sobrado, "Day Using Money in Cuba."

[311] DePalma, *The Cubans*.

[312] Sarah Marsh, "An Island Without Fish? Cuba Aims to Tackle Problem with Law Overhaul," *Reuters*, August 27, 2019, https://www.reuters.com/article/us-cuba-fishing-idUSKCN1VH15Y.

[313] Marsh, "Island Without Fish?"

[314] "Cuban Peso," *OANDA*, https://www1.oanda.com/currency/iso-currency-codes/CUP.

[315] Sobrado, "Day Using Money in Cuba."

[316] DePalma, *The Cubans*.

[317] Marc Frank, "Cuba Still Battling Cholera a Year After First Cases Reported," *Reuters*, August 22, 201.3, https://www.reuters.com/article/us-cuba-cholera-idUSBRE97L0YJ20130822.

[318] Adrian Florido, "End Of 'Wet-Foot, Dry-Foot' Means Cubans Can Join Ranks Of 'Undocumented'," *NPR*, January 15, 2017, https://www.npr.org/sections/codeswitch/2017/01/15/509895837/end-of-wet-foot-dry-foot-means-cubans-can-join-ranks-of-the-undocumented?t=1628632303402.

[319] "Cuba," *Freedom House*, 2021, https://freedomhouse.org/country/cuba.

[320] "Freedom in the World 2021: Cuba," *Freedom House*, https://freedomhouse.org/country/cuba/freedom-world/2021.

[321] "Cuban-Exile Community Worries and Mobilizes to Support Loved Ones on the Island," *Washington Post*, August 8, 2021, https://www.washingtonpost.com/national/cuban-exile-community-worries-and-mobilizes-to-support-loved-ones-on-the-island/2021/08/08/c3f6e54a-f6c7-11eb-9738-8395ec2a44e7_story.html.

[322] "The Movimiento San Isidro Challenges Cuba's Regime," *The Economist*, December 3, 2020, https://www.economist.com/the-americas/2020/12/03/the-movimiento-san-isidro-challenges-cubas-regime.

[323] "'A Powder Keg About to Explode': Long Marginalized Afro Cubans at Forefront of Island's Unrest," *Washington Post*, July 19, 2021, https://www.washingtonpost.com/world/2021/07/19/cuba-protests-afro-cubans/.

[324] Maurice Vicent, "Cuba and the US Return to the Era of Confrontation," *El Pais*, May 31, 2021, https://english.elpais.com/usa/2021-05-31/cuba-and-the-us-return-to-the-era-of-confrontation.html.

[325] "A Death and Desperation in Sanctions-Hit Cuba," *The Guardian*, July 18, 2021, https://www.theguardian.com/world/2021/jul/18/a-death-and-desperation-in-sanctions-hit-cuba.

[326] DePalma, *The Cubans*.

[327] Ciara Nugent, "How Doctors Became Cuba's Biggest Export," *TIME*, November 30, 2018, https://time.com/5467742/cuba-doctors-export-brazil/.

[328] "Cuba to Withdraw Doctors from Brazil After Bolsonaro Snub," *Reuters*, November 14, 2018, https://www.reuters.com/article/us-brazil-cuba-doctors-idUSKCN1NJ2B6.

[329] Associated Press, "Because of Trump Sanctions, Western Union Remittances Come to an End in Cuba," *NBC News*, November 24, 2020, https://www.nbcnews.com/news/latino/because-trump-sanctions-western-union-remittances-come-end-cuba-n1248790.

[330] Sarah Marsh, "The Facebook Group that Staged First in Cuba's Wave of Protests," *Reuters*, August 9, 2021, https://www.reuters.com/world/americas/facebook-group-that-staged-first-cubas-wave-protests-2021-08-09/.

[331] Antonio Garcia Martinez, "Inside Cuba's D.I.Y. Internet Revolution," *Wired*, July 26, 2017, https://www.wired.com/2017/07/inside-cubas-diy-internet-revolution/.

[332] Kevin Litpak and Paul LeBlanc, "Biden Orders Review of Remittances to Cuba," *CNN*, July 20, 2021, https://edition.cnn.com/2021/07/19/politics/cuba-remittances-biden/index.html.

[333] Jose Marti, "Rights are to be taken, not requested; seized, not begged for," *AZ Quotes*, https://www.azquotes.com/quote/879358.

[334] Sheryl Sandberg, "The 2013 TIME 100: Roya Mahboob," *TIME*, April 18, 2013, https://time100.time.com/2013/04/18/time-100/slide/roya-mahboob/.

[335] u/moejoe13, "Whats an average salary in Kabul," Reddit, September 1, 2020, 1:33 a.m., https://www.reddit.com/r/Afghan/comments/ikeloo/whats_an_average_salary_in_kabul/.

[336] Chainalysis Team, "The 2021 Global Crypto Adoption Index: Worldwide Adoption Jumps Over 880% With P2P Platforms Driving Cryptocurrency Usage in Emerging Markets," *Chainalysis*, October 14, 2021, https://blog.chainalysis.com/reports/2021-global-crypto-adoption-index/.

[337] "Afghanistan Faces an Economic Crisis, as well as a Humanitarian One," *Financial Times*, August 24, 2021, https://www.ft.com/content/6395d167-3175-4332-8329-ae1478c616ca; "Nearly 20 Years of War, 10 Days to Fall: Afghanistan, by the Numbers," *Washington Post*, August 20, 2021, https://www.washingtonpost.com/world/2021/08/20/afghanistan-war-key-numbers/.

[338] Tate Ryan-Mosley, Charlotte Jee, and Eileen Guo, "Afghanistan Had a Plan to Free Itself from Cash. Now It Risks Running Out," *Technology Review*, August 20, 2021, https://www.technologyreview.com/2021/08/20/1032344/afghanistan-cash-crisis-digital-money/.

[339] "Afghanistan Faces an Economic Crisis," *Financial Times*.

[340] Anwar Iqbal, "WV Follows IMF, US in Stopping Aid to Afghanistan," *Dawn*, August 26, 2021, https://www.dawn.com/news/1642683/wb-follows-imf-us-in-stopping-aid-to-afghanistan.

[341] Tom Arnold, "Western Union Suspends Services in Afghanistan," *Reuters*, August 19, 2021, https://www.reuters.com/business/western-union-suspends-services-afghanistan-2021-08-19/; Cyrus Farivar and Jacob Ward, "Afghanistan Braces for Even Greater Financial Disaster," *NBC News*, August 18, 2021, https://www.nbcnews.com/business/business-news/afghanistan-braces-even-greater-financial-disaster-n1277032; Clarissa-Jan Lim, "Organizers of a GoFundMe to Help Queer and Trans Afghans Say the Platform Won't Allow Them to Access the Money," *BuzzFeed News*, August 18, 2021, https://www.buzzfeednews.com/article/clarissajanlim/gofundme-fundraiser-afghanistan-queer-trans.

[342] Arnold, "Western Union Suspends."

[343] Ryan-Mosley, Jee, and Guo, "Afghanistan Had a Plan."

[344] Ryan-Mosley, Jee, and Guo, "Afghanistan Had a Plan."

[345] "Afghanistan Faces an Economic Crisis," *Financial Times*.

[346] "Afghanistan Faces an Economic Crisis," *Financial Times*.

[347] "Why Afghanistan's Economic Distress May Be Taliban's Biggest," *Times of India*, August 23, 2021, https://timesofindia.indiatimes.com/business/international-business/why-afghanistans-economic-distress-may-be-talibans-biggest-challenge/articleshow/85514068.cms.

[348] Tom Arnold and Krisztian Sandor, "Crisis Pushes Afghanistan's Economy Closer to the Brink," *Reuters*, August 20, 2021, https://www.reuters.com/world/asia-pacific/crisis-pushes-afghanistans-economy-closer-brink-2021-08-20/.

[349] "Afghanistan Faces an Economic Crisis," *Financial Times*.

[350] Saad Hasan, "How an Australian Held Hostage by the Taliban Converted to Islam," *TRTWorld*, January 28, 2021, https://www.trtworld.com/magazine/how-an-australian-held-hostage-by-the-taliban-converted-to-islam-43681.

[351] Allen Farrington, "Bitcoin Is Halal," *Medium*, February 20, 2021, https://allenfarrington.medium.com/bitcoin-is-halal-4a8f0560c3d0.

[352] Katanga Johnson and Anthony Esposito, "Afghan All-Girl Robotics Team Members, Journalists Land in Mexico," *Reuters*, August 25, 2021, https://www.reuters.com/world/afghan-all-girl-robotics-team-members-land-mexico-2021-08-25/.

[353] Kemp, "Digital 2021: Afghanistan"; Mir Haidar Shah Omid, "Ministry Confirms 90% of Afghans Live Below Poverty Line," *ToOLOnews Reporter*, July 20, 2020, https://tolonews.com/business/ministry-confirms-90-afghans-live-below-poverty-line.

[354] Atefa Alizada and Amie Ferris-Rotman, "The U.S. Is Leaving Afghanistan, the Taliban Is Growing in Power, and Education for Girls and Women Is Already at Risk," *TIME*, July 7, 2021, https://time.com/6078072/afghanistan-withdrawal-taliban-girls-education/.

[355] Mychael Schnell, "Afghan Ambassador Says Ghani Stole Millions, Calls for Arrest," *The Hill*, August 18, 2021, https://thehill.com/policy/international/568433-afghan-ambassador-says-ghani-stole-millions-calls-for-arrest.

[356] "Costs of War: Afghan Civilians," *Watson Institute International and Public Affairs*, April 2021, https://watson.brown.edu/costsofwar/costs/human/civilians/afghan.

[357] "Nearly 20 Years of War," *Washington Post*; Ellen Knickmeyer, "Costs of the Afghanistan War, in Lives and Dollars," *AP News*, August 17, 2021, https://apnews.com/article/middle-east-business-afghanistan-43d8f53b35e80ec18c130cd683e1a38f.

[358] Knickmeyer, "Costs of the Afghanistan War."

359 Adam Andrzejewski, "Staggering Costs – U.S. Military Equipment Left Behind In Afghanistan," *Forbes*, August 23, 2021, https://www.forbes.com/sites/adamandrzejewski/2021/08/23/staggering-costs--us-military-equipment-left-behind-in-afghanistan/?sh=13c8c05741db.

360 C. Christine Fair, "Pakistan and the United States Have Betrayed the Afghan People," *Foreign Policy*, August 16, 2021, https://foreignpolicy.com/2021/08/16/pakistan-united-states-afghanistan-taliban/.

361 Roxana Tiron and Paul Murphy, "Biden's Afghan Exit Alarms Contractors Who Outnumber U.S. Troops," *Bloomberg Law*, April 23, 2021, https://news.bloomberglaw.com/federal-contracting/bidens-afghan-exit-alarms-contractors-who-outnumber-u-s-troops.

362 Seth J. Frantzman, "The Afghan Gov't Overthrown by Taliban Never Existed," *Jerusalem Post*, August 19, 2021, https://www.jpost.com/middle-east/the-afghan-govt-overthrown-by-taliban-never-existed-source-677178.

363 Philip Gourevitch, "Alms Dealers," *The New Yorker*, October 4, 2010, https://www.newyorker.com/magazine/2010/10/11/alms-dealers.

364 Wolfgang Fengler and Homi Kharas, *Delivering Aid Differently* (Washington, DC: Brookings Institution Press, 2010).

365 Fengler and Kharas, *Delivering Aid Differently*.

366 George Ingram, "What Every American Should Know About US Foreign Aid," *Brookings*, October 15, 2019, https://www.brookings.edu/policy2020/votervital/what-every-american-should-know-about-us-foreign-aid/.

367 Sean Ross, "What Are the Different Types of Foreign Aid?" *Investopedia*, August 16, 2021, https://www.investopedia.com/articles/investing/082616/what-are-different-types-foreign-aid.asp.

368 M. G. Guibria, "Foreign Aid and Corruption: Anti-Corruption Strategies Need Greater Alignment with the Objective of Aid Effectiveness," *Georgetown Journal of International Affairs*, December 28, 2017, https://www.georgetownjournalofinternationalaffairs.org/online-edition/2017/12/22/foreign-aid-and-corruption-anti-corruption-strategies-need-greater-alignment-with-the-objective-of-aid-effectiveness.

369 Ollie A. Williams, "Corrupt Elites Siphon Aid Money Intended for World's Poorest," *Forbes*, February 20, 2020, https://www.forbes.com/sites/oliverwilliams1/2020/02/20/corrupt-elites-siphen-aid-money-intended-for-worlds-poorest/?sh=502e79c15658; Fengler and Kharas, *Delivering Aid Differently*.

370 Williams, "Corrupt Elites Siphon Aid."

371 "Secretary-General's Closing Remarks at High-Level Panel on Accountability, Transparency and Sustainable Development," *United Nations*, July 9, 2012,

https://www.un.org/sg/en/content/sg/statement/2012-07-09/secretary-generals-closing-remarks-high-level-panel-accountability.

[372] Simon Parrish, Marc J. Cohen, and Tigist Mekuria, "Tracing US Development Flows," *Oxfam*, January 2018, https://oxfamilibrary.openrepository.com/bitstream/handle/10546/620404/rr-tracing-us-development-aid-ghana-050118-en.pdf;jsessionid=6E51B8527EFBAAF992FFD86CF5A20768?sequence=1.

[373] "How Can We Help the World's Poor?" *New York Times*, November 22, 2009, https://www.nytimes.com/2009/11/22/books/review/Kristof-t.html.

[374] Guibria, "Foreign Aid and Corruption."

[375] Daniel Maxwell et al., "Preventing Corruption in Humanitarian Assistance," *Feinstein International Center*, July 2018, https://www.calpnetwork.org/wp-content/uploads/2020/01/ti_final-research-report_humanitarian_assistance_july-2008.pdf.

[376] Colin Harper, "Strikes Launches Bitcoin Lightning Payment App in El Salvador; Full EU Support is Next," *Yahoo!Finance*, March 31, 2021, https://finance.yahoo.com/news/strike-launches-bitcoin-lightning-payment-170053650.html.

[377] Daron Acemoglu and James A. Robinson, *Why Nations Fail: The Origins of Power, Prosperity, and Poverty* (Redfern, NSW: Currency Press, 2013).

[378] "The Power Plants That May Save a Park, and Aid a Country," *New York Times*, August 30, 2017, https://www.nytimes.com/2017/08/30/business/congo-power-plants-poaching.html.

[379] BigBlock DC Bitcoin (@BigBlock_DC), "Visit of one mining container, in the jungle." Twitter, January 16, 2021, 6:31 a.m., https://twitter.com/BigBlock_DC/status/1350405207302287363?s=20.

[380] "Power Plants," *New York Times*.

[381] "Access to Electricity," *IEA*, 2019, https://www.iea.org/reports/sdg7-data-and-projections/access-to-electricity.

[382] Kasha Patel, "Plugging-In Sub-Saharan Africa," *Earth Observatory*, 2018, https://earthobservatory.nasa.gov/images/148069/plugging-in-sub-saharan-africa.

[383] Nathanial Gronewold, "One-Quarter of World's Population Lacks Electricity," *Scientific America*, November 24, 2009, https://www.scientificamerican.com/article/electricity-gap-developing-countries-energy-wood-charcoal/.

[384] "Indoor Air Pollution and Household Energy," *WHO: Health and Environment Linkages Initiative*, https://www.who.int/heli/risks/indoorair/indoorair/en/.

[385] "Power Plants," *New York Times*.

[386] "More people have access to electricity than ever before, but world is falling short of sustainable energy goals," World Health Organization, May 21, 2019, https://www.who.int/news/item/21-05-2019-more-people-have-access-to-electricity-than-ever-before-but-world-is-falling-short-of-sustainable-energy-goals.

[387] "Emerging Nuclear Energy Countries," *World Nuclear Association*, September 2021, https://www.world-nuclear.org/information-library/country-profiles/others/emerging-nuclear-energy-countries.aspx.

[388] Paul Hockenos, "Is Germany Making Too Much Renewable Energy?" *Foreign Policy*, February 10, 2021, https://foreignpolicy.com/2021/02/10/is-germany-making-too-much-renewable-energy/.

[389] Emma Lazarus, "The New Colossus," *National Park Service*, November 2, 1883, https://www.nps.gov/stli/learn/historyculture/colossus.htm.

[390] *Bitcoin Magazine*, "Bitcoin Is American – Allen Farrington – Bitcoin 2021 Clips," *YouTube*, June 29, 2021, https://www.youtube.com/watch?v=OvI0ZyG0Su8.

[391] "Transcript of President Dwight D. Eisenhower's Farewell Address (1961)," *OurDocuments.gov*, https://www.ourdocuments.gov/doc.php?flash=false&doc=90&page=transcript.

[392] "Not Worth a Continental," *WTF1971*, June 12, 2020, https://wtf1971.com/2020/06/12/3-not-worth-a-continental/.

[393] Bier, "Blocksize War."

[394] Isaiah Jackson, *Bitcoin and Black America* (Self-published, 2019).

[395] "Abolition of Slavery," Constitution Center, Amendment XIII and XIX, https://constitutioncenter.org/interactive-constitution/amendment/amendment-xiii.

[396] Paulina Cachero, "US taxpayers have reportedly paid an average of $8,000 each and over $2 trillion total for the Iraq war alone," *Insider*, February 6, 2020, https://www.businessinsider.com/us-taxpayers-spent-8000-each-2-trillion-iraq-war-study-2020-2.

[397] https://web.archive.org/web/20160114054928/http://eggvan.com/faisal-al-mutar-the-rationalist-from-an-irrational-world-pt-1/.

[398] https://web.archive.org/web/20160114054928/http://eggvan.com/faisal-al-mutar-the-rationalist-from-an-irrational-world-pt-1/.

[399] Ken Chitwood, "Iraqi Refugee Works to Make Life Safer for Secular Humanists," *Washington Post*, December 3, 2013, https://www.washingtonpost.com/national/on-faith/iraqi-refugee-works-to-make-life-safer-for-secular-humanists-_-resend/2013/12/03/d1778876-5c4e-11e3-8d24-31c016b976b2_story.html.

[400] Riley Robinson, "This Man Brings Hope to Arab Youth, One Wikipedia Page at a Time," *Christian Science Monitor*, February 5, 2020, https://www.csmonitor.com/World/Making-a-difference/2020/0205/This-man-brings-hope-to-Arab-youth-one-Wikipedia-page-at-a-time.

[401] Robinson, "This Man Brings Hope"; Chitwood, "Iraqi Refugee Works."

[402] Robinson, "This Man Brings Hope."

[403] https://drive.google.com/file/d/1-XdTQEd1nrs11Yiu5OEBAkU-9sBeyQKS/view.

[404] Langston Highes, "Let America Be America Again," *Poetry Foundation*, 1995, https://www.poetryfoundation.org/poems/147907/let-america-be-america-again.

[405] https://americainclass.org/sources/makingrevolution/rebellion/text6/jeffersondraftdeci ndep.pdf.

[406] Michael Hudson, *Super Imperialism: The Economic Strategy of American Empire* (Islet Publishing, 2021).

[407] Marc Trachtenberg, "Assessing Soviet Economic Performance During the Cold War: A Failure of Intelligence?" *Texas National Security Review* 1, no. 2 (February 2018), https://doi.org/10.15781/T2QV3CM4W.

[408] Adam Smith (George J.W. Goodman), "When Currencies Began to Float," 1981, https://www.pbs.org/wgbh/commandingheights/shared/minitext/ess_currenciesfloat.ht ml.

[409] Hudson, Super Imperialism.

[410] Hudson, Super Imperialism.

[411] T. Balderston, "War Finance and Inflation in Britain and Germany, 1914-1918," *Economic History Review* 42, no. 2 (May 1989), https://www.jstor.org/stable/2596203.

[412] "Gold Reserve Act (1934)," *The Living New Deal*, November 18, 2016, https://livingnewdeal.org/glossary/gold-reserve-act-1934/.

[413] "Government to Pay Off WWI Debt," *BBC News*, December 3, 2014, https://www.bbc.com/news/business-30306579.

[414] Ferdinand Lips, *Gold Wars: The Battle Against Sound Money as Seen from a Swiss Perspective* (New York: FAME, 2002).

[415] "Lend-Lease," *Wikipedia*, https://en.wikipedia.org/wiki/Lend-Lease.

[416] Hudson, Super Imperialism.

[417] Michael Hudson, *Global Fracture: The New International Economic Order* (New York: Harper and Row, 2003).

[418] Lips, *Gold Wars*.

[419] Richard E. Mooney, "U.S. Bars Citizens from Possession of Gold Overseas," *New York Times*, January 15, 1961, https://www.nytimes.com/1961/01/15/archives/us-bars-citizens-from-possession-of-gold-overseas-eisenhower-orders.html.

[420] "Trifflin Dilemma," *Wikipedia*, https://en.wikipedia.org/wiki/Triffin_dilemma.

[421] Hudson, *Global Fracture*.

[422] "Gold Cover," *Committee on Banking and Currency*, January 30, 1968, https://www.google.com/books/edition/Gold_Cover/wBY3AQAAIAAJ?gbpv=1.

[423] Edwin L. Dale Jr., "I.M.F. Nations Vote for 'Paper Gold' as a World Money," *New York Times*, October 4, 1969, https://www.nytimes.com/1969/10/04/archives/imf-nations-vote-for-paper-gold-as-a-world-money-special-drawing.html.

[424] "Historical Returns on Stocks, Bonds and Bills: 1928-2020," *Historical Returns for the US*, January 2021, https://pages.stern.nyu.edu/~adamodar/New_Home_Page/datafile/histretSP.html.

[425] Hess, "Monetary Sin."

[426] Brian Domitrovic, "August 15, 1971: A Date Which Has Lived in Infamy," August 14, 2011, https://www.forbes.com/sites/briandomitrovic/2011/08/14/august-15-1971-a-date-which-has-lived-in-infamy/?sh=5bcdb8ad581a.

[427] Hudson, *Global Fracture*.

[428] David Lubin, *Dance of the Trillions: Developing Countries and Global Finance* (Washington, DC: Brookings, 2018).

[429] "Biden Administration Approves $650m Weapon Sale to Saudi Arabia," *Al Jazeera*, November 4, 2021, https://www.aljazeera.com/news/2021/11/4/biden-administration-approves-650m-weapon-sale-to-saudi-arabia.

[430] "The United States Balance of Payments—Perspectives and Policies," *Joint Economic Committee*, November 12, 1963, https://www.jec.senate.gov/reports/88th%20Congress/The%20United%20States%20Balance%20of%20Payments%20-%20Perspectives%20and%20Policies%20(247).pdf.

[431] Bryan Johnson, "The World Bank and Economic Growth: 50 Years of Failure," *Heritage Foundation*, May 16, 1996, https://www.heritage.org/trade/report/the-world-bank-and-economic-growth-50-years-failure.

[432] Gladstein, "Fighting Monetary Colonialism"; Will Kenton, "Most-Favored-Nation Clause," *Investopedia*, June 28, 2021, https://www.investopedia.com/terms/m/mostfavorednation.asp; Hudson, *Super Imperialism*.

[433] Farrington, "This is Not Capitalism."

[434] Soutik Biswas, "India's Dark History of Sterilisation," *BBC News*, November 14, 2014, https://www.bbc.com/news/world-asia-india-30040790.

[435] Jeff Smith, "The Big Noise: The Free Speech Fight of 1912, Part One," *San Diego Reader*, May 3, 2012, https://www.sandiegoreader.com/news/2012/may/23/unforgettable/.

[436] Michael Hudson, "We Make the Rules," *MichaelHudson.com*, October 20, 2021, https://michael-hudson.com/2021/10/we-make-the-rules/.

[437] "Comecon," *Wikipedia*, https://en.wikipedia.org/wiki/Comecon.

[438] Hudson, *Super Imperialism*.

[439] Alden, "Fraying of US Global Currency."

[440] "Bichler and Nitzan Archive," https://bnarchives.yorku.ca/.

[441] Martin Armstrong, "The Age of the Tech Giants," *statista*, November 4, 2021, https://www.statista.com/chart/22677/the-age-of-the-tech-giants/.

[442] Jonathan Nitzan and Shimshon Bichler, *Capital as Power* (Abingdon, Oxon: Routledge, 2009).

[443] Nitzan and Bichler, *Capital as Power*.

[444] Chuck Collins, "U.S. Billionaires Got 62 percent Richer During Pandemic. They're Now Up $1.8 Trillion." *Institute for Policy* Studies, August 24, 2021, https://ips-dc.org/u-s-billionaires-62-percent-richer-during-pandemic/.

[445] "Korean Peninsula at night from space.jpg," *Wikipedia Image*, https://commons.wikimedia.org/wiki/File:Korean_Peninsula_at_night_from_space.jpg.

[446] "Eurodollar University," https://alhambrapartners.com/tag/eurodollar-university/.

[447] Will Kenton, "Regulation Q," *Investopedia*, December 28, 2020, https://www.investopedia.com/terms/r/regulationq.asp.

[448] Lubin, *Dance of the Trillions*.

[449] Devesh Kapur, John P. Lewis, and Richard Webb, "The World Bank: Its First Half Century," *Brookings Institution*, 1997, https://documents1.worldbank.org/curated/en/405561468331913038/text/578750PUB0v20W10Box353775B01PUBLIC1.txt.

[450] Charles R. Hulten and Anders Isaksson, "Why Development Levels Differ," *National Bureau of Economic Research*, October 2007, https://www.nber.org/system/files/working_papers/w13469/w13469.pdf.

[451] Johnson, "World Bank and Economic Growth."

[452] Immanuel Kant, "Toward Perpetual Peace," in *Kant: Political Writings* (Cambridge University Press, 1991).

[453] Avery Koop, "U.S. Military Spending vs Other Top Countries," *Visual Capitalist*, July 30, 2021, https://www.visualcapitalist.com/u-s-military-spending-vs-other-top-countries/.

[454] Hudson, *Global Fracture*.

[455] Serkan Arslanalp and Chima Simpson-Bell, "US Dollar Share of Global Foreign Exchange Reserves Drops to 25-Year Low," *IMFBlog*, May 5, 2021, https://blogs.imf.org/2021/05/05/us-dollar-share-of-global-foreign-exchange-reserves-drops-to-25-year-low/.

[456] Hudson, *Global Fracture*.

[457] Arthur Hays, "Thanks for Nothing," *BitMEX*, October 28, 2021, https://blog.bitmex.com/thanks-for-nothing/.

[458] Alex Gladstein, "Can Governments Stop Bitcoin?" *Quillette*, February 21, 2021, https://quillette.com/2021/02/21/can-governments-stop-bitcoin/.

[459] "Democratic Peace Theory," *Wikipedia*, https://en.wikipedia.org/wiki/Democratic_peace_theory.

About the Author

Alex Gladstein is the chief strategy officer at the Human Rights Foundation. He has also served as vice president of strategy for the Oslo Freedom Forum since its inception in 2009. In his work, Alex has connected hundreds of dissidents and civil society groups with business leaders, technologists, journalists, philanthropists, policymakers, and artists to promote free and open societies.

Alex's writing and views on human rights and technology have appeared in media outlets across the world including *The Atlantic*, BBC, CNN, *The Guardian*, *Foreign Policy*, *The New York Times*, NPR, *TIME*, *The Washington Post*, *WIRED*, and *The Wall Street Journal*. He has spoken at universities ranging from MIT to Stanford, briefed the European Parliament and US State Department, and serves as faculty at Singularity University and as an advisor to Blockchain Capital, a leading venture firm in the fintech industry.

He frequently speaks and writes about why Bitcoin matters for freedom, co-authored *The Little Bitcoin Book* in 2019, and writes essays for *Bitcoin Magazine.*

Printed in Great Britain
by Amazon